Indigenous Religion *and* Cultural Per
in the New Maya World

Indigenous Religion *and* Cultural Performance *in the* New Maya World

GARRETT W. COOK *and* THOMAS A. OFFIT

WITH A CONTRIBUTION FROM RHONDA TAUBE

UNIVERSITY OF NEW MEXICO PRESS

ALBUQUERQUE

18   17   16   15   14   13   1   2   3   4   5   6

Library of Congress Cataloging-in-Publication Data

Cook, Garrett W., 1947–
Indigenous religion and cultural performance in the new Maya world / Garrett W.
Cook and Thomas A. Offit; with a contribution from Rhonda Taube.
p. cm.
Includes bibliographical references and index.
ISBN 978-0-8263-5318-4 (cloth : alk. paper) — ISBN 978-0-8263-5319-1 (electronic)
1. Mayas—Guatemala—Momostenango—Religion. 2. Mayas—Guatemala—
Momostenango—Rites and ceremonies. 3. Mayas—Guatemala—Momostenango—
Social life and customs. 4. Festivals—Guatemala—Momostenango.
5. Shamanism—Guatemala—Momostenango. 6. Cofradías (Latin America)—
Guatemala—Momostenango. 7. Momostenango (Guatemala)—Religious life and
customs. 8. Momostenango (Guatemala)—Social life and customs. I. Offit, Thomas
A., 1968– II. Taube, Rhonda. III. Title.
F1465.1.M66C66 2013
299.7'842—dc23
2012042170

BOOK DESIGN AND COMPOSITION: Catherine Leonardo
Composed in 10.25/13.5 Minion Pro Regular
Display type is Adobe Garamond Pro and Helvetica Neue LT Std

Contents

Illustrations

Acknowledgments

The authors thank the Baylor University Research Committee for funding in 2005 and 2006 and the Foundation for the Advancement of Mesoamerican Studies, Inc., for funding in 2007. This support as well as five years of Baylor University field schools made the study of the cult of Santiago in contemporary Momostenango possible. We are eternally grateful to the fifty Baylor students who accompanied us to Momostenango during these years and to their parents for trusting us to introduce their children to anthropology and the Maya people at a time of increasing and often well-publicized criminal violence in Guatemala and of occasional volcanic eruptions and hurricanes during the field season.

Among the many Momostecans who facilitated our research on indigenous religion in important ways we wish to acknowledge and thank Francisco LajPop, Pedro Torres, Pedro Martinez, Obispo Baten, Venancio Baten, Marcelino Baten, Mauricio Torres, and Selvín Poroj, his wife, Alejandrina Póncio Ralak, and his mother, Leonora Espinoza. Not all of the members of the dance troupe of the Monkeys, Deer, Tiger, and Lions were active participants in interviewing, but all accepted our participation over several years at performances, practice sessions, and ceremonies. We especially thank the veteran dancers Tyson, Shuro, and Sapo for reserving judgment during the initial season and allowing us to participate and for inviting us to the practice pole session in 2008.

Many other Momostecans offered friendship and various forms of logistical support and mentoring to us and our students during the five seasons of fieldwork that supported the writing of this book. Among the most important of these we acknowledge Emiliano Herrera, without whose advice and logistical support year after year none of this would have been possible. We also counted on the advice and help of Fermín Rojas, his sister Odelia, and her son Marvin and daughter Paola. This family of tailors, bakers, and teachers has always made us feel at home in their home. Julián Chanchavac, his wife, and his wonderful students at the Colégio Mesoamericano are dedicated to developing models for local development that seek to build on rather than replace Maya tradition and community, and they have educated our students and us in fundamental ways about the potential for a positive but distinctively Mayan future in Momostenango. Cooperation with the *colégio* would not have been possible without the support of principal Júlio Zárate.

Anthropologists Maury Hucheson and Marvin Cohodas were often present in Momostenango during the festival, and though they lamentably were unable to participate in the collaborative project that led to this book we were always grateful for their company and for their sharing with us of their fascinating work on other regional dances. Their good-natured companionship and thoughtful comments made during many conversations undoubtedly shaped our broader understandings of indigenous religion and expressive culture in the Guatemalan highlands.

Finally, none of our research and writing would have been possible without the unwavering support of our wives, Oriel Jane Offit and Lori Cook, and our children, Benson, Anya, and Bobby Offit and Ezra and Amy Cook.

Introduction

Understanding Maya Religion in the New Millennium

ecently two books (Molesky-Poz 2006; Hart 2008), authored by non-anthropologists with intimate knowledge of Maya religion, have depicted an ongoing tradition of Maya religious thought and practice, a Maya spirituality, which is portrayed in both books as an indigenous religious system with roots in the preconquest Maya culture. At the same time, other research reported in recent years (Mackenzie 1999, 2005; Deuss 2007) clearly indicates that there are two somewhat different, and potentially conflicting, takes on Maya religious tradition within the indigenous communities of highland Guatemala today. One is embodied in perpetuation of the syncretized local community religions known as Costumbre, the practice of which, in its many local manifestations, has been documented by anthropologists over the past seventy-five years. Another, Maya Spirituality proper, derives initially from efforts at systematization and communication of a standardized Maya religion by indigenous religious entrepreneurs (Mackenzie 2005:452–81) and is based primarily on use of the K'iche' divining calendar and on reading and application of the *Popol Wuj*, the surviving sixteenth-century charter myth for the K'iche' polity centered on K'umark'a'j (Utatlan).

Maya Spirituality is a religious movement situated culturally and politically within the broader patterns of Guatemalan indigenous cultural activism. Informed by a historical understanding of the evangelization of the Maya, it seeks to eliminate Christian influence from Maya religious practice and to return to a pure Maya religion. Thus it has been characterized by Mackenzie, utilizing terminology developed by Stewart and Shaw (1994) from the analysis of similar nativistic religious movements within the postcolonial world, as an antisyncretic movement that is in some respects opposed to the syncretized Costumbre tradition from which it emerged. We see these currently as reform and orthodox sects, respectively, within indigenous Maya religion.

The writing of this book reflects an effort on the part of three ethnographers working in Santiago Momostenango, and focusing there on the expressive culture performed in the annual festival, to account for how these two traditions are interacting within a single local community and how community members' agendas for adapting Maya religiosity to a very new and continually changing, transnationalized political economy are perpetuating and changing Maya religious tradition. To place this effort within the context of an academic tradition in Maya-focused ethnographic work, we seek to continue the investigation of the deep generative principles expressed in local Maya cultures (Gossen 1986), an idea recently reformulated as the schemas that define a characteristically Maya cultural logic (Fischer 2001) resulting in the perpetuation of a Maya way of life and a distinctive Maya worldview, even in the face of sometimes radical societal and economic change and pressures to assimilate to national and transnational cultures.

Our central focus, though, is on efforts by traditionalists to perpetuate the Costumbre tradition, which allows us to investigate how the production of Maya religious expressive culture is adapting to a rapidly changing and transnationalized festival. Clearly Maya Spirituality has emerged from Costumbre, and specifically from K'iche'an variants of Costumbre, and so is one such mode of adaptation. For now, though, it is best understood as a cotradition with local variants of Costumbre proper and in some respects, in its antisyncretism, as a competing, alternative sect, a different tradition, though one with a shared ancestry and some common interests, for example, in the protection of sacred sites. Our approach to the traditionalist religion develops case studies related to a traditional sacred dance and to the sponsorship and production of the *cofradía* ceremonies within Santiago's festival that illustrate the dynamics of this latest effort at the "reconstitution" of Maya culture (following usage in Farris 1984), an effort that can finally be observed and documented while it is occurring rather than reconstructed by looking at snapshots of several ethnographic presents arranged like beads on a string and then trying to interpolate process. This on-the-ground investigation of unfolding adaptive strategies also facilitates the documentation of individual agency in a way that has been largely missing from previous studies of Maya religious change and reconstitution processes. Finally, Fischer's (2001) analysis of the effects of his imputed cultural logic on the production of identity and on new models for economic production did not explore the implications of Maya cultural logic for the production of religious culture, an area of investigation that is clearly related to but analytically distinct from the construction of identity. Thus we hope to fill in a gap in the description and analysis of Maya culture that is noticeable in the recent focus on Maya identity and on the pan-Maya movement and its reflection in Maya Spirituality. What agendas and strategies are currently manifested in the actions of local traditionalists to perpetuate a local Maya religious tradition? What are the consequences of the implementation of these strategies for the tradition itself, for example, in the revision of its institutional arrangements or in the transformation of its ritual symbols? And what are the consequences for the menu of religious choices within the increasingly pluralistic local culture? Finally, what does the research indicate about the current relationships and the prospects for conflict and cooperation between the practitioners of Costumbre and their cultural activist neighbors in the production of religious performances within a local village's annual festival and, by extrapolation, in the broader culture?

THE FIELDWORK AND ITS SETTING
IN THE NEW MAYA WORLD

The fieldwork between 2005 and 2011 that is the basis for most of the ethnographic material in this book began with a desire on the part of the senior author to update *Renewing the Maya World* (Cook 2000) in order to document and interpret the recent history of the traditional Maya religion called Costumbre and especially its cult of the patron saint, which he had studied in 1975–1976, and to consider its prospects. Detailed discussion of the fieldwork agenda and of strategies relevant to the several components of this project is provided at the outset of each of the ethnographic chapters. However, an impressionistic portrait of the setting of the fieldwork is provided here to set the stage for a discussion of the conceptual framework employed in conducting cultural investigations and analysis in an emergent and shifting local manifestation of a rapidly changing and as yet poorly understood new Maya world.[1]

Costumbristas are still active in Momostenango, and though changed in significant ways the cult of the saints is still viable and still pursues traditional goals of reconstructing and renewing a world inherited from the ancestors. Yet some things are very different, and the Maya world has been redesigned so thoroughly that it is a Rip Van Winkle experience to visit it after a prolonged absence, to discover that the Momostenango of thirty years ago, even the Momostenango that Cook visited several times in the early nineties without observing major changes, is gone and exists only in the dream time of memory. The closed corporate community, construct or reality, is no longer closed nor corporate and is perhaps no longer a community.

While *Renewing the Maya World* (Cook 2000) began with a slow bus ride into town from the high bunchgrass plateau to the south and situated Momostenango in the headwaters of the Usumacinta River and its classic period sites, focusing on a Maya world and largely ignoring Guatemala, this book would begin with a dauntingly fast ride from a gritty commercial zone near the central bus depot in Guatemala City to Momostenango in a pickup truck owned by a successful indigenous Momostecan entrepreneur who started life as the son of a *milpero* in an *aldea*, and used to walk into the market barefoot from his father's house at two in the morning with fifty pounds of tomatoes on his back, and now owns several buildings and businesses and six vehicles. In this book Momostenango has three banks, where there were none in 1976, two ATMs that work quite well, and a couple of Western Union offices that do not. A major construction boom in the urbanized center was mostly financed by remittances and, perhaps in a contemporary expression of the institutionalized envy that still bubbles below the surface, some also claim by drug money. On the edge of town a modern and very comfortable hotel, constructed up to normal international standards and managed up to urban Guatemalan standards, opened in 2008.

Though the resident population is about twice the size it was in the 1970s, most of the able-bodied young men are away for months and years at a time seeking gainful employment (for Momostecan migrants working in Guatemala City, see Offit 2011, 2008). Everyone has relatives working in the United States. The women and children were barefoot in the 1970s but they wear shoes today, and most of the young women in town have a pair of high-heeled sandals. While the blanket market on Sundays used to extend around three sides of the park and sometimes also out into the plaza, there are now only six merchants and their wares are displayed along only part of the southern side of the park. Lots of ancient, massive foot treadle looms stand idle under corrugated metal roofs in household compounds in Barrio St. Isabel, and in some aldeas milpa land is resting for a lack of manpower to keep it in production. Milpas in some aldeas have been abandoned and little adobe houses are boarded up, as the owners have moved to town or Guatemala City, often leaving their parents and their children behind while they pursue employment.

Maya day-keepers still make offerings of copal and candles at hilltop shrines, but they interrupt their invocations to answer cell phones, and the invocations may have been learned from teachers in classes in Quetzaltenango and often come directly from the *Popol Wuj*, which had been lost to the Maya and was not known or used in the oral tradition of indigenous religionists in 1976. Two Maya ritualists today may be performing ceremonies at adjoining fires on the same altar, with one burning candles and the other not because candles were introduced by the Spanish conquerors and so do not belong in real Maya religion. The twenty-one cofradías have been whittled down to eight. The hilltop ancestral altars where the shaman-priest, the mother-father (*chuchkajaw*) of a local lineage segment, made offerings for his agnatic kin have been abandoned, sometimes along with many of the nearby houses, though in many cases the altars were abandoned a generation ago as local families converted to Catholic Action and later to Pentecostalism. Evangelical churches are everywhere today, as opposed to the single New Jerusalem congregation in 1976.

Between about 1980 and 1990 the people of Momostenango adjusted as best they could to Guatemala's civil war (see Carmack 1992; Menchú 1983). Momostecans were spared the large-scale local violence that characterized this decade in Quiché (Falla 1993), the Ixil triangle (Stoll 1993), or the Kanjobal region (Montejo 1987). The relative lack of local military intervention and the absence of massacres or population displacement resulted from the lack of effective guerilla organizing within Momostenango, and Carmack (1995) relates the relative safety of Momostenango to decades of strong support there for right-wing political parties and the military. The most obvious lasting effect of this terrible decade on Momostecan indigenous religion, the subject of this work, is that cofradía service was replaced by civil patrolling and never recovered after the war.

THE FIELDWORK AND ITS SETTING
IN THE ACADEMIC WORLD

Herein, then, is an assessment of the current situation of the publicly and privately performed indigenous cult of the patron saint in Momostenango, a unique place but also emblematic of, and in many respects typical of, what is happening in the K'iche' towns and in post-peasant highland Maya villages generally. Fundamental shifts are still occurring in Momostenango, and they require fundamental shifts in ethnographic perspectives from those that were accepted practice thirty years ago if viable understandings of indigenous religion are to be realized. Thus an assessment of some of the recent arguments and tentative new perspectives that structure the work of contemporary Maya ethnographers is undertaken here in search of an appropriate and useful way to think about the new Maya world as a subset of the new and transforming world of global indigenous/traditional peoples and societies.

While the current work is not explicitly organized as a dialogue or a conversation, it follows several years of conversations while doing fieldwork between a natural history–oriented, and it might be fair to say stubbornly and self-righteously traditional, social anthropologist with a structuralist bent who came of age in the anthropology of the early 1970s and an economic anthropologist who is twenty years younger, with a strong grounding in critical theory tinged with postmodernism and postcolonial thinking who was trained in the 1990s and early twenty-first century. Here, then, are some important conceptual issues that shape our vision of the field setting and that have been tentatively resolved in this collaborative attempt to make sense of the situation of the K'iche' Maya cult of the patron saint in the new millennium.

It is our endeavor to investigate within a specific, defined social formation with a documented history (Santiago Momostenango, a post-peasant Maya village) and within religious life there how the dialectic between the individual and culture (between agency and structure) is being enacted and how the transnational economic and social infrastructure and the related media-generated transnational/global-modern/postmodern symbolic system interacts with local tradition, in this case as local agents struggle within a fast-changing and therefore liminal context to produce religious expressive culture for local consumption. To what extent is the cult of the patron saint in Momostenango today the embodiment of Maya tradition, what Nancy Farris (1984) called reconstituted Indian culture, and to what extent is it, like ethnicity and identity, a construction utilizing selected symbols to tell a new story?

Though we accept the need to update ethnography via multisited research (Marcus 1995) in a world of interconnections and flow of people and capital, we believe that our findings thoroughly revalidate ethnography located in "the village," not as a closed universe unto itself but as the most important single and spatially definable nexus for understanding both the perpetuation and the construction of culture within the complex webs of relationships in the contemporary multisited world of Maya social life. We seek therefore to use a local ethnography to better understand the post-peasant society and to rethink the village as a place where there is a dynamic and constructive encounter between locale-based traditional community and the postcommunities that it has given rise to in its encounter with the forces described above.[2] Thus a specific village is the setting, and named actors in that place illustrate an ongoing historical transformation as tradition, custom, and preexisting knowledge on one side and a new economic order and new, imported institutional arrangements on the other side both stimulate and constrain the actions of individuals caught in the middle, who are involved in redesigning key religious institutions that will meet their goals and function effectively in the new world. Here, within the production of a village festival, traditionalism (i.e., Costumbre, a syncretized world order with locally rooted symbolism), concretized as ritual (*costumbre*) expressing the motivating ideology for some actors, confronts an indigenous constructivism (i.e., cultural activism, antisyncretic religion with more universal symbolism) that is intentionally changing culture, though at least in part guided by an indigenous cultural logic. Meanwhile everyone is forced to adjust to a privatized, neoliberal order and the failure of the traditional economy of subsistence farming and production for regional markets to provide a livelihood adequate for raising a family or supporting great public blowouts, especially in light of expectations of enhanced levels of consumption. In this endeavor we seek to provide an understanding of symbolic production and cultural performance/spectacle production that is missing from the current analysis of how Maya cultural logic has more concretely affected economic production and identity construction in highland Guatemala (Fischer 2001).

While some influential ethnographers of the Maya have shifted from village-based studies of Maya culture to the study of Maya identity, the endeavor here is to revalidate not just the local but also the study of village culture, though that culture must be understood as complex, pluralistic, and hybridized and as involving both tradition and innovation as factions with different agendas negotiate with each other and together negotiate new terrain. The village, then, is here construed simultaneously as an ongoing local community in the traditional ethnographic sense, seeking social and natural renewal through its collective religious practices, and a refuge for postcommunitarians who need a place of return and of validation and for whom, therefore, the local cultural performances in the annual festival generate both symbols and attached feelings of nostalgic recognition, which they may use to construct personal meaning and identity.

For the actors encountered in this story, neither an abstracted, nonlocalized set of traits like food preferences and ways of dressing nor a shared ethnicity and history seem to provide an adequate repository for meaningful symbols and reconstitutive symbolic action. It is rather the return to Momostenango and the participation in the place and in the larger local community of living and dead that is performed there annually that provide renewal and meaning. A Momostecan indigenous identity is derived from participation in the Momostecan fiesta, but *identity* does not capture the full measure of the emotional renewal that comes from walking again with family, with the living and the dead, as "the local" and the locale are experienced and celebrated. Thus it is local culture construed as tradition, and participation in it, that provides interpenetrating and mutually reinforcing resort or escape as well as refuge and identity for the actors encountered in this story, even, and perhaps especially, those physically and culturally displaced by a new economy.

This investigation of patterns and processes perpetuating, reconstructing, and revitalizing an indigenous Maya religious tradition occurs intellectually within two rather liminal settings. First there is the rapidly changing and fluid community of Momostecan actors in the story, and then there is the community of academics whose intellectual constructs, models, and understandings have lost the solidity and predictability of the functionalist paradigm that provided a generally accepted format for research and writing about Maya villages and their cultures for most of the twentieth century, or at the very least a clearly articulated model to react against.[3]

Another of the important features of twentieth-century thinking about highland Maya culture was that it was clearly localized and articulated within bounded villages (Tax 1952). Villages were at one and the same time understood as peasant communities and as syncretized but still fundamentally indigenous communities. They had adapted to external forces deriving from an exploitative political economy and to ecological stresses caused by epidemics and depopulation and later to environmental degradation and land shortage caused by population increase (Macleod 1973), but their religions, values, and institutions were also powerfully shaped by "deep generative principles" (Gossen 1986: ix) that derived from several millennia of milpa farming, decentralized living in patrilineal and gerontocratic local communities, and economic roles as tributaries subservient to militarist elites. Periodic cultural adjustments were made during crisis periods, producing several stages within postconquest indigenous culture history (LaFarge 1940, 1962), but each evolutionary episode in this punctuated equilibrium was followed by a period of relative cultural stability once local cultures had "crystallized" (Foster 1960) into new, adapted regional patterns.

Perhaps today we are observing the fluidity and experimentation of one of these liminal crisis periods, but it is problematic to expect that a complex of regionally similar local cultures expressing fundamentally Maya generative principles in their institutions will crystallize on the other side of a transnationalized, neoliberal interregnum, and we cannot know without the advantage of historical hindsight when a crisis is ended and a new, crystallized pattern is established. The community of scholars observes the current flux and it generates a lot of thinking and writing, but so far without a true consensus on how best to think about and talk about what is happening. A dominant paradigm is missing, and academia seems as contentious as ever, but without the clearly defined positions or schools of the ended golden age in which reasonably clear functionalist and Marxist paradigms were in contention. Before advancing an analysis of the cult of the saints within contemporary village life and Maya tradition, then, it seems advisable to perform a thoughtful review of the interpretive issues and current areas of contention within the academic community and to stake out a position so that our perspective is clear.

POST-PEASANTS AND POSTCOMMUNITIES
AND RELIGIOUS INSTITUTIONS

The understanding of the local folk religion of the highland Maya that developed in the anthropological literature in the twentieth century placed it within a historical context of conquest and colonialism (Tax 1952) and saw it as part of the adaptation of a distinctive sort of community that was closed to influences, including marriages, with the world outside of the local village (Wolf 1957). These communities had at least some collective or corporate control of land by extended patrilineal households and even had a clan-like social structure (see, e.g. Carmack's [1966] *alaxik* and Vogt's [1969] *sna*). The local municipalities were construed as meaningful cultural entities (Tax 1937) and as repositories of locally adapted bits and pieces of what had once been a widespread Maya religion that had survived differentially in different communities due to variable patterns of local mortality and to the specific histories of communities with different modes of adjustment to the economic and political forces exerted by the Guatemalan nation-state (Vogt 1964; Mendelson 1967).[4]

There was general agreement, though, that the local folk religions were syncretized blendings of Spanish Catholic and indigenous traits and that they were also the religions of peasants, utilizing the standard definition of rural communities existing in subordination to extractive urban centers within states. They paid tribute, taxes, or rent to the elites and locally utilized labor-intensive technologies in which the household was the primary unit of production and consumption and most families supported themselves via subsistence-oriented farming, with some specialization of some land-poor households in craft production and in regional sales of locally produced goods (Wolf 1955, 1966). Peasant communities had folk traditions that were different from the literate great traditions of the urbanized civilization, or nation-state (Redfield 1955, 1956), and local folk beliefs and ceremonies operated in domestic and personal life, coexisting and sometimes contending with ecclesiastical cults that tended to dominate public space (Farris 1984). Peasants occupied marginal hinterlands subject to the exploitation of their natural resources and cheap labor by metropoles (Wallerstein 1979).

Within this overall framework, communities in indigenous highland Guatemala were typed as more or less traditional according to their articulation with national labor markets. The more traditional ones conformed to the peasant farming/crafts production model described above, while less traditional rural proletarian communities were more vulnerable to market forces and to the influences of the economic and political strategies employed by Guatemala's elite, since their populations supported themselves primarily via exporting wage laborers to the plantation sector (C. Smith 1978; Carmack 1995). These latter communities tended to be the ones that could not afford to maintain local systems of festival sponsorship by the latter part of the twentieth century (W. Smith 1977).

The folk religions of the highland Maya within the dominant twentieth-century model then were nestled and nurtured within local peasant communities, to which they were adapted through a cult of the patrilineal land-controlling ancestors (McAnany 1995) and annual ceremonial cycles closely linked to vegetative fertility (Carlsen and Prechtel 1991; Cook 2000) that conformed to theoretical expectations of "cosmological" peasant religion with a focus on agricultural and human fertility and without concern for individual salvation (Weber 1963).

However, even at the generative moment of the mid-twentieth century when ethnography, finding the discipline's traditional focus on tribal and band-organized societies to lack operationality in a world lacking isolated tribal societies, was developing a substantial literature on peasants and traditional society as an alternative research domain offering the requisite contrast with the industrialized and urban West, there was recognition that much of the world's rural population did not really conform to the classic peasant type.[5] To the extent that rural villagers were articulated with modern mass culture and industrial economies, Clifford Geertz (1961) advocated recognition of proto- and post-peasantries. In fact, similar concerns had been raised during the decade preceding Geertz's coining of the term *post-peasant*.[6]

More recently, in an exuberantly postmodern tract, Michael Kearney (1996) has resurrected the term *post-peasantry*. Kearney is mainly focused on deconstructing Western anthropological dualism and its purported tendency to objectify and essentialize "the other" by creating reified social types (e.g., peasants) that then codify and constrict thinking, reinforcing and abetting the Western ethnocentrism hidden within social science. This ambitious philosophical and political project is not relevant to our limited objectives, but

Kearney also offers a well-constructed explanation for the emergence of new and complex economic formations from what were once peasant communities and societies. Without seeking to engage here the full panoply of capitalist, Marxist, and postmodern theorizing mobilized by Kearney, a nuts-and-bolts summary most relevant to the task of understanding the post-peasantry as a context for the analysis of religion seems useful.

Kearney tells us that "peasants are mostly gone and . . . global conditions do not favor the perpetuation of those who remain" (1996:3). His village-level ethnography in Oaxaca therefore was supplemented with multi-sited work in Mexico and California in the 1980s to depict a seemingly traditional local society that was supported by transnational patterns of production and consumption, indicating that San Jerónimo, the Oaxacan village, was in fact a "transnational community," a "greater San Jerónimo" (17). The explanation for the emergence of a global post-peasantry composed of lots of "greater San Jerónimos" is that rather than following one of the alternatives for peasants outlined by theories of development in the twentieth century—that is, either the modernization of family farming or proletarianization—the peasant communities of the world have developed intermediate forms. These intermediate forms are not, however, transitional to one of these theoretical poles (82) but rather represent what may be persevering adaptive arrangements in their own rights. The labor of these intermediate populations in Mexico and Central America is complexly articulated with capitalism by mixing subsistence farming, local penny capitalism, wage labor, tenant farming, and participation in the growing informal sectors of regional and national urban economies with migration to the United States. Following Alain de Janvry (1981), Kearney sees post-peasants as participating in a "disarticulated economy" in which poverty in the rural areas prevents those areas from becoming a substantial market for consumer goods, with the result that the national economy is export oriented and "the modern sector is thus dependent on the sale of luxury goods and export to developed nations in return for capital investment" (91). Rural population pressure, combined with increasing environmental degradation that comes from heightened levels of consumption in the villages, subsidized by wealth produced outside of the community, forces members of peasant households into urban informal economies, which then grow at an exponential rate. These "disarticulated" economies "result in a proliferation of the informal sector, that is, a growth of post-peasant urban and rural poverty" (94). At various points the post-peasants have also been referred to as infrasubsistence producers, semi-proletarians, semi-peasants, small peasants (a traditional term in the "older agrarian literature"), and peasant-workers (111).[7] Importantly for our objectives here, though, Kearney states, "Fuller anthropological treatment of these semiproletarians and semi-peasants must, in addition to exploring their economic and productionist nature, also inquire more deeply into their cultural and social identity" (111).

Our inquiry here is related to this suggestion. It is an effort to better understand the culture (as opposed to the cultural identity) of a post-peasant community through the lens of its religious life, with a narrow focus on the indigenous tradition or cotraditions. Religious institutions adapted to life in a peasant village and carried mainly by peasants living in the hamlets surrounding the administrative center of Momostenango fifty years ago will either disappear as their post-peasant children and grandchildren convert to the new faiths being marketed by religious entrepreneurs or will adjust to the new setting by developing modified and new institutional forms that work there, and even then only if there are emotionally salient reasons to perpetuate the core rituals and ritual symbols. In an illustrative example, the complex of altars for family welfare (the *warabalja*) and for crops and animals (the *winel*) belonging to locally coresident patrilineage segments (see B. Tedlock 1982; Cook 2000) have no obvious purpose in families that have largely abandoned the land and for whom milpa-based subsistence farming is just one of five or six main strategies to meet basic needs and to articulate with a global economy. These altars are almost totally abandoned today, and few local patrilineage segments, now often divided into Costumbrista, orthodox Catholic, and Evangelical Protestant families, maintain a *chuchkajaw rech alaxik* (mother-father of the clan) to make the offerings at the altars. Yet calendrical divination and offerings at public altars have recently made a big comeback, though in individualistic rather than familial applications. There are important social implications to the construction of post-peasantries, in addition to the economic and broad typological ones emphasized by Kearney. Thus, prior to the investigation of the Momostecan festival as the arena for performance of post-peasant indigenous religion, it is necessary to consider the theoretical implications for community of the massive move to a post-peasant condition in western Guatemala.

Writing of the post-peasantry in Indonesia, Bruner states,

anthropologists should no longer study in villages, and if we do, then our view of that village should be radically altered. As I have shown, the set of beliefs and practices that exists within the physical confines of the village would now be a very incomplete characterization of contemporary real-time Toba Batak culture because so much of that culture is located elsewhere . . . all over Indonesia and the world at large. The village population is demographically skewed as a disproportionate number of widows, children and old people live there. . . . To take the village as the unit of analysis, and then to see forces as impinging from the outside, is no solution because many of the forces already exist within the village and within the consciousness of the villagers. (1999:474)

The implications of this assessment then are that post-peasant villages are no longer communities in the way that peasant villages were, in the way suggested by Redfield's (1955) definition of the little community or in the closed corporate communities of mid-twentieth-century thinking about the indigenous cultures of Mesoamerica. And yet Bruner goes on to consider that there are other meaningful ways to think about community and to relate community to the village. From the perspective of an analyst of Western tourism a village may become a "specially constructed locality, a performance space" (Bruner 1999:475) occupied by tourists and by natives coming from their various communities. These native communities for many are no longer villages as such. The Batak now constitute a "postlocal" or "radically delocalized" community organizing themselves in delocalized enclaves that might be referred to, after Ortner (1997), as postcommunities. Yet the postcommunitarians need the villages as symbolic and ritual centers. While recognizing that for the young a village may be a place of drudgery and isolation to escape from in favor of the opportunities and excitement of the larger world, the village also represents a place of origins of lineage, kin, and ancestors, and even Batak who were born elsewhere often identify with the ancestral village. Of clear relevance to an effort to study the festival in Momostenango and its traditional cultural performances, Bruner provides the following description of the Toba-Batak village in the twenty-first century: "For some wealthy urban elders, it is a place to be buried, to return to the afterlife, to be forever with the ancestors. For yet other sophisticated Batak living in transnational spaces, the village becomes an imaginary place, a sacred center, a site of memory, which they glorify in nostalgic and even romantic terms, much as this ethnographer first did in 1957" (1999:475).

In *Habits of the Heart*, Robert Bellah depicted a modern American society in which our communities are delocalized lifestyle enclaves rather than the cities, suburbs, neighborhoods, or villages where we live. We create these enclaves, often in the form of informal groups of friends, via identification with others occupying a similar stage of life and position in society and also having values, recreational interests, and hopes similar to ours. We are, it would seem, more radically delocalized than the post-peasants, lacking a place of origin to which we can return, and so, though our lifestyle enclaves may represent a model for some forms taken by post-peasant postcommunities, they shed little light on the function of the village in a world of translocalized community.[8]

In analyzing the American high school reunion Ortner (1997) investigates a phenomenon of greater potential relevance to the post-peasant village as an idealized and nostalgic performance space, but in the contemporary American case the main purpose is that of reuniting with a group of people and the place is of little importance. Based on a case study in Newark, New Jersey, she identifies four kinds of postcommunities that develop and persist within an American high school's graduating cohort and that are activated in the reunion process. Neocommunity is constructed by people who have moved away from Newark but not to a great distance and who keep in regular touch with each other, while invented community is formed when graduates living in colonies in Florida construct opportunities to get together. Translocal community involves the maintenance of ties via telephone, letter, and internet contacts. Finally she suggests a more abstract kind of community, the community of memory, a collective sharing of memories of people and events that does not constitute a physical network of interaction per se but is activated within the reunion context and is the main motivation for participation in reunions. Our goal in the investigation of the village festival is not to apply this framework, developed specifically for American society, nor to develop a comparable typology of Momostecan translocal or postcommunities, but rather to seek to understand what specific arrangements among local and nonlocal postcommunities are actually mobilized in perpetuating and strategically revising the indigenous religious performances within the festival, which is understood to be a performance within the village in its primary role for postcommunitarians as a performance space.

While twentieth-century anthropologists thought of highland Maya villages as peasant communities, most also thought of them as indigenous communities, local Maya versions of peasant communities, postconquest neocolonial peasant communities that retained significant continuity with the preconquest peasant communities from which they had descended. During the ideological turn of the late twentieth and early twenty-first centuries this image of peasant villagers living in communities that perpetuated indigenous values and institutions was attacked, and a debate ensued in anthropology as radical constructivist ideologues portrayed the traditional view as an essentializing false consciousness. This produced intergenerational discontinuity among Mayanist ethnographers while also creating intellectual and political tension between the new generation of ethnographers and indigenous Maya intellectuals and activists, who saw that radical constructivism threatened the authenticity of Maya culture, which was of paramount importance to their agenda (Nelson 1999:133; Fischer 2001:10–11).

If the village in the fiesta is thought of in its role as performance space, then clearly the question of the nature of the performance is of great importance. Will the performances emphasize traditional reenactments motivated by supernatural beliefs and a worldview that emphasizes renewal of an eternal order and appeals primarily to the nostalgia of postcommunitarians, or will performances emphasize enactments of newer, post-peasant themes that are probably influenced by Maya tradition and its guiding cultural logic but are fundamentally expressions of the needs and concerns of status groups that have emerged recently and whose articulation with the transnational economic order eliminates the salience of cultural performance as even nostalgic re-creation of an inherited social and natural order? A polarizing debate about constructivism is and always has been counterproductive and is tangential to our purposes, since the roles of both perpetuation and construction of culture within the indigenous religion are central issues. The debate is nevertheless an important element in the academic history that we seek to set forth here as context.

CONSTRUCTIVISM

The initial approach in ethnology to the understanding of the evolution of indigenous religion was to identify a syncretised and enduring indigenous tradition that made successive adaptations to new contextual constraints but retained a core of continuity (e.g., LaFarge and Byers 1931; LaFarge 1947; Oakes 1951; Bunzel 1952; Mendelson 1959); this emphasis was dominant through the 1970s and persisted well beyond (see, e.g., Holland 1964; Mendelson 1965; Carmack 1966; Vogt 1969; Gossen 1974; Hunt 1977; Bricker 1981; B. Tedlock 1982; Gossen 1986; Hill and Monaghan 1987; Freidel, Schele, and Parker 1993). However, there was a countervailing thesis driven mainly by Marxist theory within anthropology but also supported by the Mestizo nationalist agendas of Mexico and Guatemala (Hale 1996), according to which Indians were defined as a rural proletariat and local Maya cultures were interpreted not as expressions of an evolving indigenous tradition but rather as adaptations and accommodations by a marginalized class to economic exploitation and political oppression.[9] By the late twentieth century this difference in perspective had become a rancorous debate, with Maya activists and many anthropologists seeking and finding extensive cultural continuity within the historical changes in Maya villages and their institutions while the new generation of ethnographers, championing both the constructivist models mentioned above and postcolonialist critiques of culture as a misleading and politically conservative reification, not only depicted the other camp as romantic essentialists but in some extreme cases argued for elimination of the culture concept.[10]

Mayanist scholarship in the 1990s recognized new forces at work in the highland Maya world in Guatemala, especially the explosive growth of Protestantism and the emergence of a pan-Maya movement. In response to the desire to establish a new research agenda that could apprehend broader issues and wider contexts than the typical village ethnographies of the past, some Mayanists advocated a shift in emphasis to the interpretation of national social and political movements (pan-Mayanism or Maya cultural activism; see Fischer and Brown 1996; Warren 1998) and to issues of identity formation, ethnicity, and cultural politics (Watanabe 1990, 1992; Fischer 1993, 1999, 2001; Wilson 1995; Nelson 1999).

The end of the 1990s embodied a desire to move beyond the overstated, unfruitful, and politically charged constructivism debate (see, e.g., Fischer 2001:9–14 for a salutary if partial retraction of the overdone critique). Concerned with the potential for conflict between the agendas of constructivist anthropologists and Maya activists, Fischer (1999; 2001:15–19) attempted to bridge the divide with his ethnographically illustrated concept of a cultural logic that shapes cultural construction during episodes of cultural change, similar in inspiration to various earlier, structuralist searches for the "armatures" of a resilient Maya tradition (Hunt 1977; Bricker 1981; Gossen 1986; Carlsen and Prechtel 1991; McAnany 1995). Similarly, Watanabe (1995) argued for an anthropological responsibility to move beyond self-serving and untenable postmodernism and also to move beyond what he called the romantic (essentialist) and tragic (constructivist) argument about Maya culture to an investigation of Maya identity. Since the Maya still see themselves as a people apart and have not disappeared, he asserted, anthropologists have turned from "objectifying Maya culture as some romanticized primordial essence or tragic contrivance of colonialism to questions of the nature of Maya identity itself" (35).

But not everyone abandoned the "objectification" and study of culture for the study of identity. A new emphasis emerged in the 1990s with a focus on the impacts of transnational economic forces on the village-level Maya and their institutions (Goldin and Metz 1991; Goldin 2001; Green 2003; Burrel 2005; Little 2005). Our goal is to contribute to this latter agenda, with a specific focus on religion in the new Momostenango, investigating the processes of adapting and reproducing Maya tradition and institutions in this new, emerging, and still very liminal world. For this purpose highland towns like

Momostenango, which once were depicted as closed communities with local, distinctive cultures (Tax 1937), now represent settings within which actors engage each other in the dual and complexly related processes of transmitting and constructing local cultures. *Cultures* because, for several centuries, and in spite of widely shared *municipio*-level culture, Maya towns have been ethnically pluralistic and also divided by class or status groups within the indigenous population (see Carmack 1995; Grandin 2000), with important Weberian implications for the construction of institutions and, since the mid-twentieth century, if not earlier, for receptivity to new religious ideologies appropriate to the needs and interests of emerging "status groups" with different ways of engaging the social and natural worlds and so with different worldviews and different models for community.

Villages are pluralistic in new ways, too, with very complex local economies, new patterns of consumerism and new identities, major intergenerational cultural differences, and radical and increasing openness to the world, and traditional ethnography utilizing the conceptual framework of a Momostecan culture cannot creatively engage with the potential for development of nonvillage-based, nonlocalized Maya culture.[11] To attempt this latter project, as suggested by Watanabe (1995), it may be time to shift from the study of culture to the study of identity. But here it is our endeavor to use on-the-ground findings in a specific, well-documented community to help delineate the new cultural dynamics of the new kind of village and its local cultures. And more, we wish to present some initial observations and findings about how, under the new economic regime and in a context of increasingly transnationalized culture, and again within the specific context of religious institutions, the process of reconstitution of village-located Indian culture(s) is unfolding.

HYBRID CULTURES, SYNCRETISM, AND PROCESSES OF RELIGIOUS CHANGE

The question of how the indigenous religious expressive culture in Momostenango is changing as a result of the agency of its carriers as they respond to new constraints and opportunities in a new, transnational order is a specific application of the question of how best to conceptualize the adaptations, accommodations, and innovations in any indigenous religious tradition responding to the impacts of any externally situated forces deriving from articulation with a larger, dominant economic order. Interpretation of this kind of religious change began with consideration of how traditional societies responded to colonialism and neocolonialism via acculturation theory (Redfield et al. 1936). This approach delineates several alternatives: complete loss of the indigenous religion during assimilation or modernization, accommodation of the religion through borrowing selected traits while retaining some of its original themes and institutional arrangements (the syncretism process as usually depicted), and a more disruptive or revolutionary revitalization process (Wallace 1956) via creation of "crisis cults"(La Barre 1970), a process that was not usually referred to as a syncretic process but one that nevertheless, in the long run, also produces syncretized religious institutions when it is successful. Thus a theory of syncretism lies at the heart of the traditional anthropological approaches to the problem of religious transformation within the cultures of colonized, marginalized, and oppressed indigenous peoples.[12]

Yet today *hybridization* increasingly replaces *syncretism* as the preferred term in postcolonial or postmodern writings designed to emphasize the roles of sometimes countervailing processes of resistance to hegemony on one hand and adapting to religious commodification and consumerism on the other (Kitiarsa 2005:461).[13] With specific reference to the Maya in Guatemala, a "pluricultural" ethnography was advocated that would study "hybridizing" processes in place of traditional ethnography, as both ethnicity and local cultures are contextualized within globalized economic systems and the construction of national ideologies rather than in simplistic modernization models or in acculturation's "contact" with a generalized West (Watanabe and Fischer 2004).

Additionally, "concerned that the term 'syncretism' evokes a presumed purity of the traditions being mixed, Bastian (2001) avoids the term altogether in favor of 'hybridity' and 'bricolage'" (Zehner 2005:190), and certainly the simple fact that Christian theologians have used the term *syncretism* for centuries to refer to a negative result of ineffective missionary work suggests that a term with less evaluative connotations would be desirable. At least one influential Mayanist ethnographer simply finds the notion of syncretism to be "rather tired" (B. Tedlock 2002:607) and presumably therefore in need of some juicing up by new theoretical constructs marked by a new jargon.

On the other hand, Droogers and Greenfield (2001:31) do not reject the use of the term *syncretism*, instead advocating identification of objective and subjective "views" of syncretism, corresponding to scientific/anthropological and political/missiological usage respectively. Mackenzie (2005:347–56) ends a particularly engaging and thoughtful review of the syncretism concept with a finding in favor of continuing its use in analyzing religious contention when distinct traditions are involved, a situation that pertains in Xecul, a K'iche' speaking village, and that fits the area of inquiry in this study of Momostenango.

Ultimately, though, whatever word is used for the process—and *hybridity*, which for some lacks the implications of dualism in *syncretism*, may have some advantages in referring to an extremely pluralistic and multicultural transnational situation—the conceptualization of an adapting local religious tradition that may adopt some "external" content or institutional forms in accommodating to new realities still involves stark and pretty simple alternatives: perpetuation of the religion without change; selective perpetuation of some of the original form, possibly under transformation, with adoption of new material that better fits the new circumstances; or termination. Perpetuation under transformation, the theoretically interesting alternative, may of course involve many processes and follow many paths, but in the long run will produce syncretisms, that is, locally blended mixtures of indigenous (and traditional) institutional forms and cultural models with those adopted from "external" sources such as the state or international entities like NGOs and churches and via the transnational experiences of community members. The issue in theorizing change within an ongoing indigenous religious tradition, then, is not advanced appreciably by rejecting the concept of syncretism or calling it something else; instead, it is best approached by describing and analyzing the variety of motives and processes that ultimately produce various differently syncretized/hybridized results and recognizing that the context in which the process unfolds today is far less monolithic than the two-party dialectic proposed in traditional acculturation theory.

INDIVIDUALS AND CULTURE,
OR AGENCY AND STRUCTURE

Another element in the contemporary take on syncretic processes, in addition to recognizing more complex contexts and interrelationships, is to emphasize that syncretisms are created through active agents motivated by local political objectives and individual psychological drives and cognitive schemas, operating with limited numbers of potential cognitive models.[14] While this emphasis was not entirely lacking in earlier work in the anthropology of indigenous religious traditions—for example, Radin's (1926) study of the Peyote religion through an autobiographical text or Wallace's (1969) analysis of the code of Handsome Lake as the product of the prophet's life history—it was far more prevalent in studies of crisis cults and religious movements than in studies of less-dramatic syncretisms, as in the Mesoamerican cases, where again the few studies to really engage agency in religious change did so in connection with often dramatic and politically important, and hence memorialized, messianic movements (see Bricker 1981; Reed 2001).

Current models for analyzing the syncretic process within postcolonial settings with neoliberal economic orders advocate interpreting entrepreneurship in broad terms as the individual creation of new structural combinations: not just the creation of new businesses but innovative individualistic social engineering generally (Droogers and Greenfield 2001:36–37). Syncretisms, then, are new structural combinations within religious institutions, made by entrepreneurial actors in intercultural arenas, actors referred to by Motta (2001:72) as religious entrepreneurs, in an analysis inspired by Berger's (1967) concept of a market of competing alternative ritual and belief systems in modern societies, that is, "reality defining agencies" without coercive power to force allegiance. This analysis reflects back on the preceding discussion of pluralism and societal complexity. Syncretism or hybridization today, and in this study, is understood as a result of processes unfolding locally in pluralistic settings through transcultural agency within a globalized marketplace of religions. This framework is applied here to explain some key events and trends within the recent struggles of local Maya villagers to define and defend and to produce and reproduce religious tradition.

INDIGENOUS RELIGION AND
TWENTY-FIRST-CENTURY MODERNIZATION

While studies have treated the adaptations to the new economy made by Maya families and households (Goldin 2001; Little 2005) and their implications for gender roles (Green 2003), and while there is a considerable literature devoted to the growth of Protestantism (Stoll 1990; Goldin and Metz 1991; Sherman 1997; Garrard-Burnett 1998), there has been very little attention paid to the impacts on the formal expressive culture of traditional indigenous religion, possibly because modernization theory suggests it will simply fade away. This tendency informs some sophisticated recent analysis. For example, Fischer ends his brief description of the declining cofradía systems in Tecpan and Patzun by asserting that "with little interest in them among the under 30 population, they seem doomed to die out with the current generation of older adherents" (2001:185). He also notes that attempts by more sophisticated urban cultural activists to reorganize the cofradías to strengthen them have so far met with indifference from the rural *cofrades* (187). In connection with Fischer's (2001) programmatic attempt to define a Maya cultural logic that is expressed within changing Maya culture as it responds to globalism and transnational economic factors, it is noteworthy that a text of 251 pages devotes 54 pages (83–137) to pan-Maya identity, 17 pages (149–66) to Maya conceptions of self and soul, and 43 pages (240–83) to agriculture, while formal religion (that is, collective expressive culture and religious practice), including Catholicism, Protestantism, and traditional Costumbre, is condensed in 11 pages of text (179–89), including two full-page photos, without noting the effects of the postulated cultural logic on organized religion or its expressive culture. The analysis presented here is, in part, an effort to address this gap in the documentation and provide an understanding of how the premises and traditional themes of Maya religion are given ongoing expression in the contemporary reproduction and in the production or construction of Maya religiosity, specifically within the performative complexes of festival-based expressive culture.[15]

The assumption of continued decline and imminent disappearance of the cofradías is reasonable and seems to be a likely outcome of recent trends. However, social scientists have often been fooled by the resiliency of religion. For example, the widely shared positivist belief in the general decline of religion as part of modernization, the secularization hypothesis, which derived some support from trends in Western Europe, is now actively debated and seems to be well on its way to refutation (Swatos and Olson 2000), prompting one analyst to comment, "If religion does decline under conditions of modernization, we must ponder the social, economic and cultural conditions that bring about secularization" (Froese 2008:168). Within anthropology, some forty years ago Douglas Sharon (1974) noted an increase in witchcraft and shamanic curing with modernization and urbanization in mestizo Peru, and June Nash (1967) found similar events in Amatenango, while more contemporary international studies find increasing supernaturalism in "modernizing" post-peasant societies (e.g., Houk 1996 in Trinidad; Kitiarsa 2005:466 in Thailand), though often in the form of antisyncretic revitalization related as much to identity politics movements, it seems, as to religious concerns (Motta 2001:79; Romberg 1998; Stewart and Shaw 1994). The trend of decreased local importance of and support for cofradías is real, but the trend could easily be flattening if the fat has been cut away, leaving just the cults of images that actually matter in local communities. Note, for example, the interesting coincidence that there are now seven or eight remaining cofradías of much-reduced scope in Tecpan and Patzun, which is precisely the pattern in Momostenango.

Other factors that might lead to retention of possibly transformed versions of core cofradías in many communities would include the importance of the festivals of a few specific tutelary deities that have retained attributes of Maya gods as symbols of Maya identity and the consequent, somewhat paradoxical, desire of cultural activists to support this one highly syncretized system, as has apparently already been tried without much success in Patzun and Tecpan (Fischer 2001:187) and is currently underway in Momostenango in connection with the festival of Santiago, as will be described. Should support of the few remaining cofradías provide recognition and status to sponsors within a local and regional activist community the erosion might be ended or reversed, though the tradition could be significantly transformed as it is passed on to participants with activist agendas and worldviews deriving from the new Maya Spirituality movement rather than from local tradition. It is also possible, in those cases of images with miraculous powers, that the quest for personal supernatural power and patronage will remain important to a large enough cadre of younger men, and perhaps women too, especially in the cultural activist faction, to keep the remaining cults alive and to perpetuate some of their significance as Native American medicine societies.

CULTURE, IDENTITY, AND TRADITION

The relationship between culture and identity mentioned above and the pluralism that has produced two distinctive groups of indigenous religionists, Costumbristas and activists, in Momostenango relate to two recurring problems in the recent ethnographic agendas and conceptual frameworks for studying Maya culture. First, culture and identity seem to become confused: "For some, it has become acceptable to treat culture and identity as interchangeable, a view that neatly dovetails with instrumentalist conceptions of cultural construction" (Fischer 2001:12–13). And also recall Kearney's mention of "cultural identity" (1996:111) rather than culture, noted above. This confusion has led some more radical constructivists to reach the rather odd conclusion that culture is a perpetually renewed and fluid construction (as in Nelson's [1999] conception of fluidarity) and therefore to disregard tradition and cultural continuity and to reject the hypothesis of substantial cultural continuity within Maya tradition on the grounds of dependency theory (Wilk 1991:21–23) or, more recently, as essentialism (discussed in Watanabe 1995; Watanabe and Fischer 2004).

A second problem with some very recent ethnographic studies of highland Maya religion is the failure to recognize that there are two distinctive communities of indigenous religionists with very different kinds of traditions, a distinction indicated in Fischer's depiction of urban activists and rural cofrades mentioned above. Thus both Hart (2008) and Molesky-Poz (2006) have recently published monographs that seek to describe Maya Spirituality without clearly separating the local village traditions of Costumbre from cultural activist attempts to develop a revitalized Maya religion without the blending of Spanish Catholic practices and concepts that has been typical of syncretized local religions for the past five centuries. These differences between what Stewart and Shaw (1994) labeled "syncretism" and "anti-syncretism" are rightly emphasized in Mackenzie's (1999, 2005) important writings on contestation between Costumbristas and practitioners of Maya Spirituality in K'iche'-speaking San Andrés Xecul and in similar work done in Momostenango (Cook and Offit 2009). They have also been addressed by some insightful comments in a recent monograph that focuses on the syncretized religious practices of traditionalists in the Q'anjob'al-, Akatek-, and Chuj-speaking communities of the Cuchumatan mountains:

> The buzzword of today's cultural activists is *guia espiritual* (spiritual guide), a designation that encompasses K'iche'-style Maya priests, shamans and diviners as well as Q'anjob'al Prayersayers. As more and more young people take courses in Maya religion, more and more so-called spiritual guides are emerging. In all likelihood, when the current Prayersayers and elders of soloma, Santa Eulalia, and Chimab become too old to continue serving, the office will pass to a New Age Maya *guia espiritual*, as happened in San Juan ixcoy. If this happens, Q'anjob'al *costumbres* will be given a K'iche' cast, and a new type of intellectualized pan-Maya religion will emerge. Perhaps then the K'iche' people will achieve what they were unable to do in the fourteenth and fifteenth centuries, that is, to conquer the Q'anjob'ales and extend their influence throughout the upper reaches of the Cuchumatan highlands. (Deuss 2007:283)

Deuss (2007:240–42) earlier presents a brief but very provocative description of the takeover of the Ordinance cult, the rituals associated with a sacred chest containing powerful relics, by a new age spiritual guide in San Juan Ixc'oy. While her concern is with the loss of Q'anjob'al culture as it is replaced by generalized K'iche' culture, the concerns would also apply to the replacement of experts within the local Costumbre tradition in any community by *guias espirituales* trained in a more generic Maya cultural activist tradition. As Fischer indicates, "The pan-Maya movement is an example of 'self-directed change in Maya culture (albeit in the context of external political-economic contingencies),' intended to 'encompass and perhaps ultimately replace the long-standing community-based allegiances characteristic of Maya groups'" (2001:246). The implication for Maya religious tradition of the replacement of local cultures by a generalized culture of identity or ethnicity is that local syncretized traditions, like the Costumbre in Momostenango, will be replaced by a uniform, generalized, and purified (i.e., less syncretized with Catholic liturgy and folk-Catholic theology) new Maya Spirituality. There is no doubt that purified and activist Maya Spirituality is derived from Maya conceptions, and the adoption of Fischer's cultural logic approach should be strongly influenced by widely shared cognitive schemas that derive from collective Maya historical experience. But equally, as in the cases of identity/culture confusion mentioned above, purified or reform Maya religion is being constructed as part of an identity politics movement. As it spreads, unless it enters into a dialogical relationship with local traditions in a mode similar to the give-and-take between local traditionalists and orthodox Catholics advocated by inculturation theology in the Catholic Church, it will eliminate local differences and local customs that have constituted the local cultures of villages. These cultures, documented by ethnographers throughout the twentieth century, have resisted assimilation thorough effective contra-acculturative strategies over the past several centuries and, along with the *Popol Wuj* and other native chronicles and the writings of some archaeologists, epigraphers, and ethnographers, have provided the basis for the revitalization movement itself. It is perhaps especially important to note here that Momostecan cultural activists involved in Maya Spirituality, though they are not divorced from the larger community and often have access to Costumbrista traditions through spouses and relatives, were not raised and socialized in Costumbre, the local indigenous religious tradition, as they come mainly from orthodox Catholic (Catholic Action) families. Thus, while this critique does not question the authenticity of the new Maya Spirituality, the notion of a continuing tradition of Maya religious thought and practice as put forward in Hart (2008) and Molesky-Poz (2006) is more problematic—at the very least much more complicated—than their conceptual frameworks suggest.

So, within indigenous religious practice in Momostenango today there are two coexisting and sometimes interpenetrating traditions. One, though it has long made use of specialists to read from the Catholic missal and today also relies on published Maya calendars, is a predominantly oral tradition that carries the locally constructed and thoroughly syncretized beliefs and practices of Costumbre and is communicated informally through public expressive culture and through local apprenticeships and initiations. The other is a tradition learned in formal educational programs with manuals and texts from indigenous teachers, based on reading the *Popol Wuj* and published calendrical/astrological literature and seeking both to remove Catholic traits from Maya religion and to promote a universal, nonlocalized Maya religious tradition.

In connection with a possible dialogical and perhaps dialectical relationship developing between them, the syncretized Costumbrista tradition was carried until the 1970s by and has mostly been transmitted within the part of the population that lived mainly through agrarian pursuits, craft production, and activity in local and regional marketing of local goods, that is, that still lived within the social and ecological settings to which Costumbre is well adapted. The indigenous religious tradition of Costumbre, or at least its outward manifestations in veneration of Santiago and in performing public costumed dances and processions, also remains critical as a sort of mine of icons and nostalgic memories to the activists who seek to construct an authentic revitalized Maya culture. At the same time there are many displaced village Maya who continue to pursue identities not as abstract or generic Maya but as Momostecans, while in internal Guatemalan or international diaspora. For them the continuation of local religious practices remains a central concern to the extent that the performance of indigenous religion defines home and provides them with rootedness and a sense of belonging to an enduring and coherent world, especially to the extent that cultural performance in the village as a performance space for a nostalgically viewed tradition becomes a central function of the village for its postcommunities.

THE ETHNOGRAPHIC AGENDA

Our concrete ethnographic agenda, then, is to explore how several specific collectively organized and produced and publicly performed complexes of religiously important expressive culture are operating today and how they are responding, through the strategic activity of the carriers of the traditions, to the forces and options that define the new social and economic order and to the needs of their potential audiences and sponsors. We do not intend another study of Maya identity but rather a study of the local Maya village culture that provides the material and perpetuates the systems of meaning that may be mobilized in identity construction.

The village of Momostenango at this particular time is here understood as an infrastructure inherited from the peasant past. Its local population, descended in a few cases from rural Ladino ancestors but in the vast majority of cases (well over 99 percent) from indigenous peasant ancestors of a variety of social classes, is currently implementing numerous, complex post-peasant adaptive strategies. A few older couples and a few families that have substantial land, living out in rural hamlets, continue to live as peasants, but no longer in a peasant world. Here then, too, in this complex new world is a larger population, not all of whom are currently residing in Momostenango, though they derive from there, a population for whom the village is experienced as both a people (pueblo) and as an infrastructure of plazas; roads and paths; religious, civic, commercial, and residential buildings; and mountain altars, all understood as both economic and cultural capital; for these people the village is of economic and psychological/emotional importance. This population includes both the local residential component and a number of postcommunities, probably of several kinds presently lacking in definition, for whom the village is the most important social nexus and for whom the festivals (especially the feria in July and Holy Week) represent very important rituals of return to the village. That is, the festival in Momostenango performs exactly the same psychological and social functions as the high school reunion studied by Ortner (1997) for mobile contemporary Americans in constituting and reconstituting networks and lives within postcommunity.

Finally, this larger population of villagers and postcommunitarians is experiencing not just emotionally wrenching displacement from places and people but also a time of disorienting change. Alvin Toffler (1970) conceptualized late-twentieth-century future shock, the psychological impacts of rapid, accelerating societal change driven by business and technology. When we live in a time of dissolving paradigms, feel that we have not inherited a stable world, and believe that we cannot pass a stable world on to our children, we tend to interpret it as a transitional period, as Toffler did in his later volume, *The Third Wave*, which predicted massive dislocating transformations in the late twentieth and early twenty-first centuries, ushering in the demassified, high-tech and green but reasonably stable civilization of the twenty-first century. We humans do seem to expect, as in the twentieth-century models of Maya culture history described above and as in the Maya's own cosmogonic model of repeating creation cycles constructing four ages, that we will pass through this chaos to another cosmos. The agents of Maya traditionalism and of cultural activism are seeking to formulate cultures of passage, in an effort to restabilize their worlds and get to some kind of new equilibrium, or at the very least to retain participatory access to the forms and concretized memories of a Maya world.

The remainder of this work, then, is devoted to describing indigenous religion within the contemporary cult of the patron saint and the cultural performances of that cult within the annual festival in Santiago Momostenango. The changes as Momostenango has shifted from a peasant village to a post-peasant transnational community are documented. Religious entrepreneurism and the interplay among tradition, existing culture, and the new options represented in a pluralistic social structure and connections to a wider world are explored in order to understand how indigenous religious expressive culture is being shaped by a new world order. Chapter 1 provides a historical overview of the festival of the patron saint within the twentieth century, identifying a sequence of stages and the forces that have led to its evolution. Chapters 2 and 3 describe the current confraternity of Santiago and the Monkeys Dance and the ways they have changed since the mid-twentieth century, while chapter 4 describes a new costumed dance in Momostenango, the *disfraces*, that is sweeping the indigenous highlands. These three ethnographic chapters depict three somewhat different responses of the larger community to the new order, two of which seek to retain tradition and reproduce culture in a new and challenging setting, while a third seeks to produce a performance that expresses a new, revitalized, modern but indigenous culture.

Specific events that provide insight into how individual actors function as creative agents of change and of continuity within change are examined when chapter 5 investigates three case studies: the response of the Monkeys Dance team to the murder of its leader, the creation of a new shrine to San Simón within the cofradía of Santiago, and the improvement of a vigil for Santiago involving the cooperation of cultural activists and traditionalists. In the conclusion we take stock of the evidence and formulate some general findings about continuity and change within indigenous Maya religion as Momostecans construct a pluralized expressive culture that meets their needs in a transnationalized post-peasant local world.

Throughout this book pseudonyms have been employed to protect the identities and privacy of specific living and recently deceased individuals and their families. The actual names of important public figures in the history of the community—for example, Diego Vicente, a community founder, or Teodoro Cifuentes, the political boss of Momostenango during the early twentieth century, are, however, employed without disguise. The only notable exception to this principle is that in recounting the history of the Monkeys Dance in chapter 3 the authors realized that the patronyms of the two families that have contended with each other for control of the dance and cooperated with each other in producing it since about 1900 might be considered sensitive, since the same two families remain involved today in the same complex relationships. Therefore, readers should be advised that the surnames Raxc'oy and Ixbatz employed in discussion of this dance do not identify the actual families.

CHAPTER ONE

The Fiesta Patronál in Historical Context

The Festival System and Anthropological Theory

D efinitive works on Maya festival organization and sponsorship were produced within the mid-twentieth-century florescence of community studies (see Tax 1952; P. Carrasco 1961; Reina 1966), including Cancian's (1965, 1967) classic functionalist depiction of the cargo system as a leveling mechanism. Waldemar Smith (1977:9) distinguished a functionalist explanation for the festival cycle—seeing the system as maintaining an internal equilibrium by building community and by reducing the potential for class differentiation and insulating the community from external forces—from a Marxian interpretation of festivals as colonial/neocolonial inventions designed to drain off resources, control labor, and fragment the population into weak villages. A third "colonialist" perspective understood the program of festivals as stabilizing the colonial system by keeping communities isolated and, via competition for patronage, encouraging individuals to seek patrons rather than building communities of interest to seek common cause. Smith (1977:15) convincingly argues that the fiesta does not level wealth but rather motivates savings. In a balanced response to the controversy over whether to understand village institutions in terms of indigenous tradition or as adaptations to political economy, Smith argues that the system is "Indian in its ideology, participants and motivation, but is ultimately perpetuated by an outside world that benefits from its existence" (1977:19).

Smith defined the religious core of the traditional festival as a series of sponsored ceremonies. In the 1970s sponsored ceremonies declined in importance in unusually poor communities, where funding was absent, and in those with increasing affluence, since heightened consumption and opportunities for investment decreased the motivation to participate (W. Smith 1977:7, 21). In those communities that successfully maintained sponsored ceremonies, some combination of three new strategies was involved (W. Smith 1977:6): a truncated strategy in which costs are reduced via simplification, an appended strategy in which costs are spread via multiple annual sponsors, and an administered strategy, copied after Ladino *hermandades*, where a permanent fund-raising body is established.

Since Smith's assessment there have been some important discoveries about the origins and earlier history of the fiesta system and of the cofradías linked to it. Chance and Taylor (1985) documented the postcolonial, late nineteenth- and early twentieth-century origins of the "traditional" Mesoamerican system of rotating festival sponsorship, showing that this system developed when privatization of communal lands, and their appropriation in many cases by national elites, and the administrative centralization of indigenous communities for ease in appropriating labor eliminated the colonial-style cofradías in which collectively managed estates supported the ceremonies. Hill and Monaghan (1987) showed that in highland Guatemala the important cofradías had descended from colonial period prototypes in the cults of the tutelary deities of *parcialidades* or *chinamits*, local indigenous communities dominated by elite families that sponsored the cults by utilizing profits from collectively managed land, while Rojas Lima (1988) described a process of colonial "indigenization" that adopted the imported cofradía as a form acceptable to Spanish administrators in order to legitimize perpetuation of local communities with collectivized systems of production managed by indigenous elites. The cargo system/fiesta system evolved from indigenous roots, took advantage of colonial period openings to adapt the cofradía to indigenous economic needs, and only took on the "traditional" form described by mid-twentieth-century ethnographers as a result of the imposition of a liberal agenda about a hundred years ago. The core changes in the mechanisms of festival production involved replacement of an endowment of collectively managed property dedicated to support of the festival by a strategy of spreading the costs among many individuals and centralization of the system with bureaucratic administration.

Thus large, commercialized municipal festivals in honor of patron saints and cofradías with rotating sponsorships were invented in the postcolonial liberal nation-state and apparently were at least partly designed by local and national actors to subvert the influence of rural indigenous elites and to further the control of centralized bureaucracies over the quintessentially decentralized Maya. These twentieth-century "liberal" systems, already succumbing to economic and political modernization by the 1970s, as indicated by Smith's study quoted above, would then seem likely to be greatly weakened and, should they continue to exist at all, significantly changed by recent and current neoliberal agendas designed to reduce government and bureaucracy, increase incentives for consumption and investment, and eliminate compulsory mandated religion in favor of a religious marketplace. In an early effort at defining the new reality, Burrel (2005:12–13) situates a contemporary highland Maya village festival within a "trans-national social field," a term she borrows from Levitt (2001), and considering the goals of participants who have worked in the United States and sponsors who may still be living there suggests that this new transnational community element that is freed from local labor relations and seeks to perpetuate a world to which they someday hope to return is reshaping the festival.[1]

Here we compare the current fiesta in Momostenango as it is coming into focus as a result of recent fieldwork—a cultural performance enacted within a transnational social field and within a post-peasant society—with the so-called traditional cargo system version as it was documented in the mid-1970s, before its precipitous decline, in order to understand how a transnationalized and post-peasant village festival differs from a twentieth-century peasant village prototype. This endeavor seeks to identify complexes and elements that are being perpetuated, those that are gone, and those that are under construction. Later chapters will investigate how indigenous status groups and specific community elements and postcommunities are acting and interacting in this process.

In his interpretation of an annual system of festivals in rural Venezuela as cultural performances, David Guss notes that traditional expressive forms of behavior in little communities are not necessarily "dissolving into a market driven global culturescape" and that "these forms may actually enlarge their semantic fields" under conditions of modernization. He redefines authenticity as based not on continuity of tradition but rather on creative hybridity, that is, through creating rather than recapitulating or reenacting history (Guss 2000:4). Cultural performances are authentic when they are alive and meet the emotional, social, and economic needs of the performers. Following his interpretation of García Canclini's work, then, Guss seeks to understand cultural performances in Latin American festivals as "double enrolled," that is, as producing culture by simultaneously providing for identity through historical rootedness while adapting to "dependent capitalism" (2000:5). In this way there is a "rearticulation of tradition" (after Yudice 1992:18) in which expressive forms once adapted to small, rural communities adapt to and thrive in different circumstances. In our case, in analyzing the cultural performances of a festival in Momostenango we seek to explore how a festival and the individual expressive complexes that are its components—which were once adapted to an agrarian economy, cultural patterns of personalistic patronage, and the social structure of a peasant village—are being perpetuated or recast to operate within a post-peasant context.

Guss (2000) seeks to move beyond functionalist interpretations of cultural performances that show how the performances fit with the cultures in which they are embedded at one point in time to diachronic analysis, showing how the performances change over time as the context changes. He recommends Abner Cohen's (1980, 1993) study of the social history of the Notting Hill Carnival as a model. Cohen's dramaturgical approach "shows how the carnival has responded to various socioeconomic changes, taking on new meanings with each performance." It is always multivocalic and cannot be reduced to any one interpretation, but still "certain motivations and ideas emerge to dominate different phases" (Guss 2000:8; e.g., a polyethnic phase, a Trinidad phase, a reggae phase, an institutionalized phase, a regimented phase, and a tourist/commodified phase). The dramaturgical approach means that the focus of analysis is on production of meaning within a context of potential or actual contention.

In this chapter we seek to understand three stages in the history of the festival for Santiago in Momostenango. Then, in chapters 2–5, we seek to understand how specific institutions organized to produce components of the festival are changing with the times. The twentieth-century fiesta was constructed during the liberal period between the 1870s and the 1920s through privatization of collective lands and political and symbolic centralization favoring a "modern" Ladino-style bureaucratic administration over the decentralized colonial cacique system. This had crystallized as a typical "Recent Indian Stage" (La Farge 1940, 1956) local culture by the 1920s (Carmack 1995:125–219). In the 1970s much of this local crystallization was still performed in the festival, but it was beginning to suffer attrition as a result of polarized local politics resulting from increasing proletarianization of Momostenango and the related struggle between Catholic Action and traditionalists for control of the religious infrastructure (Carmack 1995:223–374). The contemporary festival no longer reflects mid-twentieth-century polarization, but it is adjusting rapidly to a more complexly pluralized social setting, a transnationalized/globalized cultural setting, and a neoliberal, antibureaucratic political economy. It is our goal to describe and interpret social action today by assessing the changes in the festival's institutional structures and functions and by analyzing the strategic behavior of the actors—various competing religious entrepreneurs in the new Momostecan religious marketplace. The historical framework for understanding changes in the fiesta is prefaced here by a brief comment on the institutions—the components within the Costumbrista performances in the festival in the 1970s and today—and an introduction of the ritual symbols at the center of the Costumbrista performances.

THE INSTITUTIONS AND RITUAL SYMBOLS IN THE COSTUMBRISTA FESTIVAL FOR SANTIAGO

During the past century, and still today, there are two main embodiments of the Maya tradition of religious cultural performance, the cofradía and the dance team. The cofradía is a group of men arranged in a hierarchy with differentiated responsibilities, often affiliated with a similar though smaller group of women, that produces festivals, vigils, and opportunities for visits and processions with a *wachibal* or *imagen*, a physical representation, manifestation, and localization for a spirit being (*nawal*) that walked the earth with Jesu Cristo in a liminal period before the founding of the human community. The image that is the center of the cult and the ceremonies and offerings associated with the cult have been inherited from the *primeros*, or founding ancestors.

In mid-twentieth-century Momostenango there were twenty-one cofradías, but the only ones that really mattered to the community were the dualistic tutelary complex of Santiago and his companion San Felipe, who together symbolized and protected the town, Niño San Antonio who controlled animal and human fertility, and two images of Jesu Cristo: a Cristo Crucificado called Capitagua and a Señor Sepultado called Corpus, who together served as lords of the dead and owners of the cemetery while also having some sun god and maize god attributes (see Cook 2000). The dance team is a group of male volunteers in rented costumes who, in the traditional form, enact a story owned by a dance master and of thematic relevance to the community in order to entertain the saint and the souls of the dead as well as the living human audience. Examples of the current situation of these two kinds of traditional Maya cultural performances are presented in chapters 2 and 3, while a new take on the dance team and dance is presented in chapter 4.

Of all the ritual symbols manipulated in the tutelary deity cult institutions, the paramount objects are the carved wooden statues known as

Santiago and his secretary San Felipe, a bipartite complex representing a distinctive K'iche'an concept of protective power at the societal level:

> The Santiago and San Felipe pair reflect the Quichean cultural pattern of dualistic authority. . . . This might be a southern Maya pattern. For example, a chest called Ordinánce found in San Miguel Acatán . . . (Siegel 1941) and the San Martín Bundle in Santiago Atitlán (Mendelson 1965) are associated with rain and wind ceremonies, and each is also an element in a dualistic complex (Ordinance-Gaspar, San Martín–Yashper) functioning as a community protector and rain-wind deity. The ancient Quiché combined an image (Tojil) and a sacred bundle (Pizom Gagal) in their corporate iconography, while in the colonial *parcialidades* saints and *titulos*, the latter often stored in chests, came to play these roles. (Cook 2000:87)

The meanings of the images of Santiago and San Felipe in 1970s Momostenango are explored in Cook 2000 (75–98). Santiago is dominant and is referred to as captain, a role symbolized by his brandished sword, while San Felipe, who carries a book (the Bible) is his secretary. Momostecans still make this distinction, though claims that, like Momostecans, Santiago could not read nor speak good Spanish are not accurate today and are not commonly expressed. The pair's combination of charismatic power with managerial/secretarial functions reflects both the municipal authority system where an elected alcalde and a professional *sindico* share power and ancient K'iche' bipartite ruleship with an *aj pop* and *k'alel* presiding over each fortified center, or *tinamit* (Carmack 1979a:143–144, 1995:29).

Like the *cabawil*, the tutelary god image in the *Popol Wuj*, Santiago's image has an associated spirit, or nawal. Field data from the 1970s showed that this nawal sent signs to dancers and cofrades during the ongoing communication of offerings and rituals, and this is still clearly the case today. A contemporary example is provided by don Apolonio, the alcalde of Santiago in 2006 and 2007:

> The patrón has his miracles, and when one says he will go with him he must, because the patrón exacts justice [or revenge, *juicio*]. He is very *delicado*, because one time a man did not observe his day, he fired a *bomba* [percussive sky rocket fired from a mortar] and boom, he was killed, his face here [gesture showing removal of his face]. So in our case we observe forty days for the fiesta, we do not touch women. This is how he is, our patrón.

There is a story of Pueblo Viejo. At his fiesta there if the costumbre is good the spring flows, if not it is dry. If the water does not flow there is danger there. There will be dissension there if the water is not born there in Salpachán. But if they do costumbre and the water flows it will be okay.

The nawal of Santiago also appeared on the battlefield to lead the Momostecans to victory (Carmack 1995:194; Cook 2000:96), and he also appears in dreams, usually to elicit some service but sometimes to warn his adherents of dangers or of approaching calamities. Finally, like Tojil in the *Popol Wuj*, Santiago has a celestial association with Venus in its morning star appearances and combines the war god and protector attributes of a tutelary deity with specific weather and storm attributes. Don Valentín, the deputy of Santiago, related the following in 2008:

The image used to move and to speak to the ancestors who founded our town. It still has power, but now it gives signs to the chuchkajaw in his blood and in dreams. My wife was widowed in her seventh year of a novena [vow to serve for nine years] to sponsor the rockets [skyrockets fired at stops during the procession with Santiago]. I have helped her for the remaining two years because if not the patrón would send dire punishment.

Question: Is Santiago the Morning Star? Have you heard of any link between Santiago and the Milky Way?

The old ones said that the great star [*nima chu'mil*] that appears in the morning before the sunrise is Santiago. I do not know about Santiago and the Milky Way. It is said that the Milky Way is a sign of frost. It is also a sign of the time when winds [*aeres*] are dangerous, when hail and wind may destroy the milpa.

This account relates the Milky Way to two critical times in the Monkeys Dance. Practice sessions begin when the Milky Way runs across the sky from north to south in January, the time of frosts, and the festival for Santiago and the dance performance occurs in July, the greatest time of danger from winds and hail and the other period during the year when the Milky Way runs from north to south across the center of the sky. In Momostenango in the 1970s, as in Chichicastenango (Bunzel 1952:58, 268), Santiago was a milpa destroyer and sender of hailstorms. Santiago also brings or withholds rain. When rain is needed his image is dressed in green and leads the procession of saints with San Felipe, San Miguel (the archangel), and San Francisco, founder of the religious order that evangelized Momostenango, that leaves the church to visit parched fields during a drought . The dressing and undressing of the image during clothing ceremonies, with their Maya and general Native American sacred bundle aspects, and the role of Santiago as a traveling saint and owner of distinctive altar complexes are described and discussed below in the section on the cofradía and its ritual symbolism.

The communalistic cult institutions for the patron saint are the means through which the larger community of Momostecans has delegated its responsibility to its powerful protector. They allow individuals with strong needs for personal power and supernatural protection to cement long-term dyadic contracts with the spirit, or nawal, that is the owner of the town, embodied in a living object that has accumulated great power in its passage through time and the hands of many generations of ritualists. The festival is a rite of intensification and renewal for the community, and the service of the cofrades and dancers takes the form of a classic rite of passage. The service, while dangerous in its own right, makes them impervious to the envy or hostility of their peers. The company in which the symbolism of the rite of passage is most obvious and in which the service is literally most dangerous, with rewards that are commensurably greatest, is the Monkeys Dance. Description and interpretation of this dance in 2006–2008 is provided in chapter 3 and follows the similar treatment of the contemporary cofradía of Santiago in chapter 2. The remainder of this chapter seeks to describe the annual festival that is the context for these Costumbrista religious productions and to assess how this context has itself been reshaped as Momostenango has become a post-peasant village.

THE PEASANT VILLAGE FESTIVAL
IN THE EARLY TWENTIETH CENTURY

Information provided in the middle 1970s by the sacristan and by elders of the Herrera family, whose ancestors had controlled the image of Santiago in the nineteenth century, allow the Momostecan festival of the patron saint to be situated within a modernizing town at the beginning of the twentieth century (see Cook 2000:75–87). Fortunately this local oral tradition is now also supplemented by published histories of the early twentieth-century K'iche' people of the Quetzaltenango region (Grandin 2000:130–58) and of Momostenango itself (Carmack 1995:125–222). Neither of these sources describes the festival system per se, but they do allow the festival's changing political and economic context to be established in the period of liberal reforms and nationalism between the 1870s and 1920s.

Several important parallels in the analyses of Grandin and Carmack suggest a basic framework for understanding the origins of the twentieth-century festival pattern in Momostenango. First the privatization of land, rationalized nationally by coffee production, became more acceptable to the rural indigenous population for reasons that are not clear but that might be related to a desire to weaken the power of rural indigenous elites ("principales" in Grandin, "caciques" in Carmack) who controlled the commons and distributed land use rights to households and families. This privatization also meant that cofradías lost their collectively owned and managed estates, ushering in the cargo system of Mesoamerican ethnography (Chance and Taylor 1985). If the colonial-period cofradías were used by cacique families to maintain control of large collective estates, as in Rojas Lima's (1988) analysis, then the privatization of these estates would eliminate the economic functions of the cofradías in rural social organization. They would disappear or take on new roles within a new mode of production.

The national economy needed a large seasonal labor force for the coffee plantations, and somewhat later also for bananas, sugar, and cotton, and its managers were well aware that a labor force that could meet most of its own subsistence needs during the off-season could be paid very little and hired only as needed. The early twentieth-century peasantry, then, was, in its role in the national economy, a surplus population that because of its huge numbers in relation to the available wage labor needs would keep the costs of labor very low while as a result of demographic expansion and increasing scarcity of tillable land would be forced by economic necessity to adopt subsistence strategies in addition to farming. As Grandin (2000) explains, the best national strategy for managing the growing indigenous population was to allow and encourage local identifications and identities that would preclude mass organization and ensure that insurrections responding to land shortages and economic desperation were local and controllable. Thus developments in the liberal period exemplified the colonialist perspective within the broader Marxian vision defined by Waldemar Smith (1977:6–9), according to which isolated and closed local peasant villages with active festival cycles were developed and maintained both because of local indigenous cultural conservatism and because of their good adaptive fit with the neocolonial agrarian regime. Strong local identities precluded broader, class-based political movements, thus stabilizing the labor extraction system. Village festivals strengthened local identities and also diverted capital from local populations to the purveyors of alcohol and fireworks and heightened the consumption of clothing and food, thus enhancing regional markets and encouraging the accumulation of capital. Similarly, the debts incurred by festival sponsors and many festival participants favored the interests of local moneylenders, local landowners seeking to enlarge their positions by taking advantage of bad debt, and labor contractors who relied on debt peonage.

A strengthened municipal governance system provided employment for Ladino administrators and, in a context of surplus rural labor, facilitated the planning for labor mobilization for major infrastructure projects like roads, bridges, and railroads that were part of the liberal plan to encourage efficient movement of laborers and construction of an internal market. As Carmack (1995) makes clear, abetted by and reinforcing the general tendency toward more centralized and bureaucratic administration, alliances were formed in Momostenango between Ladinos and members of a small, emerging indigenous elite different from the traditional landed elite of rural caciques. The new indigenous status group lived in the town center and had connections of patronage through the Momostecan militia to the early twentieth-century caudillo Colonel Teodoro Cifuentes (later a general), an ally of President Manuel Estrada Cabrera, who ran the department of Totonicapan through the 1920s, and served as Guatemala's army chief of staff and whose son Everardo was the political boss (*intendente*) of Momostenango a generation later under President Jorge Ubico (Carmack 1995:192). These acculturated urban Indians, whose descendants constituted an indigenous petite bourgeoisie self-styled as "civilized Indians" by midcentury (Carmack 1995:264–68), took over the role of cultural brokers between the Ladino state and the less acculturated peasants, at the expense of the caciques and rural *principales* in their economically and politically marginalized rural enclaves. The acculturated faction benefited directly from centralization of authority and from developing a cult of the patron saint and an annual festival that symbolized the new and modernizing world that it played a central role in creating.

Prior to the redesign of the fiesta in the Cifuentes period, the images of Santiago and San Felipe were kept in a rude little house that served as an *ermita*, or cofradía house, that belonged to the Herreras, a cacique family from Pueblo Viejo in Aldea Tunayac where the pre-Hispanic tinamit of Chuwa Tzak, the administrative center for what later became Momostenango, had been located. Santiago was in their keeping and did not reside in the church, which at that time was a dilapidated building that had been constructed by Diego Vicente sometime around 1600 and subsequently damaged by an earthquake and which stood where the municipal building stands today. The fiesta as described by elders in the Herrera family was restricted to an all-night vigil on July 23 at the ermita, accompanied by a marimba or fiddle, followed by a procession around town. The Dance of the Moors was performed, a dance that officially commemorated the reconquest of Spain but in which the Spanish king was decorated with a quetzal bird, linking him to Tecum and so opening the possibility of a nativistic gloss. The Dance of the Monkeys, which was produced by a team from Aldea Jutacaj, was sometimes also performed.

General Cifuentes desired an enlarged festival and an infrastructure that would conform to liberal notions of progress. He initiated and oversaw construction of the existing church and municipal palace between 1910 and 1920, employing a substantial local labor force and replacing the decrepit, earthquake-damaged colonial church that had sufficed for two centuries for a smaller and decentralized, K'iche'-style peasantry. Local informants who were elders in Momostenango in the 1970s could remember the Cifuentes period and noted that the new church was built on the site of the village cemetery and that the *calvario* was also constructed in the relatively new cemetery east of the town center, while the old church was demolished to provide a site for the new municipal palace. Because this had been sacred ground an altar complex was retained in a room in the new administrative edifice. Importantly for this study, and in conformity to the national needs and political trends of his day as outlined above, Cifuentes "centralized" the cofradías, thereby forcing principales and rural peasants into implementing complex and expensive ritual cycles organized around images in the church and performed in the town center. He also initiated the festival for Patrón Santiago and moved the conquest dance that had previously been given at Easter to the fiesta of Santiago in July.[2] A patron saint that had figured in parcialidad-style cofradías in hamlets removed from the town center and that had recently served as the war patron for the Momostecan militia during Cifuentes's political rise now became patron saint for a Guatemalan municipio and for all its people. The festival became a major celebration of local identity and participation in the relatively new nation of Guatemala. In this way the traditional, closed corporate community of twentieth-century ethnography, with its cargo system of festival sponsorship, was built in Momostenango.

In the 1970s Santiago was portrayed as a monolingual war chief, a Tecum-like deity. The origin stories then embodied what Eric Wolf (1959) called the epi-Toltec myth and portrayed the image of Santiago as the concretization of the protective nawal associated with Diego Vicente, the official founder of Momostenango, a cacique grandson of the last pre-Hispanic ruler of Momostenango, who obtained the image at a shrine complex on the edge of the distant city of Spain (Cook 1983, 2001a). The later twentieth-century understanding of the character of Santiago may have developed as a projection of the forms of intimate but dangerous and sometimes terrifying (delicado), personalistic patronage that existed between the later foundational figure of General Cifuentes and the local militarist and commercial leaders within the indigenous community.[3] With its roots in the late nineteenth-century neoliberal transformation of Guatemala and its formal construction in the Cifuentes social engineering of the early twentieth century, the "traditional" *fiesta patronal* of the mid-twentieth-century peasant village was established, a festival that is currently undergoing a second transformation as it becomes a rite of renewal and intensification for a post-peasant village.[4] The current festival, a fluid and always adapting institution, is illuminated through a comparison with its more clearly crystallized, "commercialized" peasant prototype, as exemplified in the findings of ethnographic research from thirty years ago.

THE TERMINAL PEASANT FESTIVAL IN THE 1970s

By the 1970s the "civilized" faction of petit bourgeois Indians was well established in Momostenango and had a reasonably cooperative relationship with local Ladinos (see Carmack 1995:262–76, 312, 380–82). Though some of the urban indigenous bourgeoisie had become Mormons and Adventists, the majority were still nominally Catholic in the local Cristo-pagan tradition. Through their command of K'iche' language and patterns of patronage with rural principales, their control of the system of military commissioners, and a related alliance with the Movement for National Liberation and Institutional Democratic Party (MLN/PID), allied political parties that dominated the country, they had become the de facto cultural brokers between Momostenango's rural artisans, peasants, and proletarians and the nation-state by the middle twentieth century, after the Castillo Armas counterrevolution. They shared power with Ladinos to an increasing extent within the elected municipal government, and they dominated the *auxiliatura*, the administrative structure of alcaldes and councils in the hamlets that mediated between the elected municipal and national governments on one side and the rural principales and rural population on the other.

There were, however, two main factions of indigenous actors in mid-twentieth-century Momostenango. A huge contingent of Catechists and other followers of the Catholic Action movement (Carmack 1995:227–29, 237–41, 274–76, 289–91) opposed the Costumbristas in about equal numbers. The rise of Catholic Action since the mid-1940s challenged the traditionalist indigenous faction and its acculturated Indian/Ladino urban leadership by creating a de facto competing administrative and financial structure through the Catholic Church (Carmack 1995:290), and by the 1970s the Christian Democratic Party (DC), the political wing of the movement, was contending seriously with the MLN/PID for control of Guatemala. Accommodations between the factions in Momostenango over use of the church and over the rights of Costumbristas had been reached after a crisis period of showdowns in the 1940s and 1950s (Carmack 1995:227–41), but neither side had really accepted this as anything other than a temporary truce, and there were constant skirmishes in a local "culture war" as the Catholics sought to eliminate paganism from church-related activities and to promulgate a modern Catholic theology and understanding of Jesus and the saints. Thus, in the 1970s, the prominent Costumbrista deputy of Santiago's cofradía, after serving as chief ritualist for eighteen years, was removed and replaced by a Catholic Action convert in a little coup, in which the Italian missionary priest and his sacristan outmaneuvered the Costumbrista cofrades and the principales (Cook 2000:43–45, 231; B. Tedlock 1982:42–43).

The community then had a social structure including a Ladino/Indian caste system. Ladinos still controlled the bus lines, the larger stores, and the official agencies of national government, but their control was locally contested and was beginning to slip by the 1970s. The festival in the 1970s occurred, then, in a modernizing neocolonial society in which an oppressive and reactionary national elite was being challenged by a reformist Catholic Church–based social and political movement. Locally the village was rapidly outgrowing its land base and the institutional arrangements established under the Cifuentes regime, and though cultural lags and social unrest were increasingly evident, Momostenango was still, formally at least, an indigenous peasant village (Carmack 1995:xviii), though one in which power was increasingly contested between two religiously defined factions with national-level political affiliations.

Primarily as a result of land shortage, the true peasantry was declining in numbers and influence, and proletarianization and the emergence of a mercantile indigenous petite bourgeoisie were occurring simultaneously. Thus it could be argued that the festival of Santiago observed in 1975 or 1976 was in many ways an anachronism that retained the outward forms of a spectacle that had been constructed over several decades as part of liberal social engineering and had crystallized a good half century before. The Costumbrista institutions embodied in the festival were not openly and publicly contested by the other faction, and the community appeared to its anthropological observers (D. Tedlock 1993; B. Tedlock 1982; Cook 1986, 2000) to be a conservative repository of indigenous religiosity. But in hindsight it is increasingly clear that the cofradías, the dance teams, and the religious complexes of rural patrilineages (alaxiks) whose chuchkajaws performed ceremonies for the ancestors at inherited family altars were all undergoing the early stages of what became massive damage because of their lack of fit with the practical, emotional, and spiritual needs of the land-scarce and financially pressed proto- and post-peasants who made up an increasing proportion of the population. During the crisis of the civil war and violence many of these culturally, if not geographically, displaced Momostecans would convert to Pentecostalism and to radical evangelical sects, often with roots in the United States. This damaged but still functioning peasant village and peasant village festival, then, is the context within which cultural performances to honor Santiago took place in July 1976.

Though the indigenous factions were joined by the Ladinos in lavish competitive productions during Holy Week in the 1970s (see Carmack 1995:291–92), there was little obvious symbolic or performative competition in the fiesta patronal. Catholic Action celebrated a mass for Santiago, but reflecting its reformist ideology and campaign to reduce the significance of the cult of the saints, it did not mount competing processions nor sponsor bands or dances, which left the public religious performances to the Costumbristas. The religious performances were staged within a two-week period of daily gigantic markets in which the local population interacted with vendors from far and wide, mainly selling typical market food (soups, stewed chicken with rice and beans, broiled meats with *tamalitos* or tortillas), augmented by the seasonal roasted ears of corn (*elotes*) with lime juice and coarse salt and cotton candy, and providing a few small, decrepit carnival rides on the edge of town near the soccer fields and lots of beer and "fire water" (*agua ardiente*, called *aguardiente* or *guaro*). An observer of the public performances in the 1970s saw traditional cofradía processions and vigils and colorful, costumed, folkloristic dances and, based on the public performances, would never have guessed at the deep divisions within the indigenous population nor at the struggle between the DC and the MLN/PID for Guatemala's future, the institutional manifestation of the deep-seated conflicts that were just a few years from devolving into murderous civil war.

The main religious cultural performances were cofradía functions and costumed dances. The cofradía, an obviously religious institution, produces a house party where the images are displayed for both public visitation and private cofradía ceremonies, as well as the processions with the images of Santiago and San Felipe. The dancers perform according to vows made to Santiago to complete novenas (nine performances), and all the dances involve offerings and invocations at specified altars by calendar priests (chuchkajaws) serving as representatives of the dancers. Additionally, as pointed out by Harry McArthur (1972) in the town of Aguacatan, the dancers in Momostenango reported that the dance was performed for an invisible audience of primeros, the souls of the deceased dancers who had founded the dance or had performed it in previous decades. While this was clearly of more relevance to the older dances (Dance of the Moors, Dance of the Conquest, and the Monkeys Dance), all of the dances performed in the 1970s had at least several decades of local history and so were performed under the critical aegis of supernatural observers.

An observer on the roof of the Catholic church in 1976 looked west across the main plaza, which was surrounded on three sides by stores and cantinas. In the northwest corner of the plaza the Dance of the Moors was accompanied by plaintive flute and drum music with long, unintelligible soliloquies and slow, graceful stylized dancing with brandished swords. It never attracted a large crowd and probably had the longest association with the festival of Santiago, who had, after all, been patron saint of the *reconquista*. It was being displaced by the Dance of the Conquest, which embodied a similar theme of war and conquest but was far more elaborate and lively and included lots of entertaining clowning.

Along the western edge of the plaza, south of the altar and directly across from the church portal, three dances were performed simultaneously every day, in order from north to south: a Mexicans Dance, a Vaqueros Dance, and a second Mexicans Dance, each accompanied by a small brass ensemble (Mexicans) or a marimba, with rustic *rancheria*-style music. Informants reported that the Mexicans Dance had first been performed in Momostenango in about 1940 and had become so popular with dancers and the audience that two dance teams now performed it. The Vaqueros and Mexicans Dances told similar stories of bullfights, sexual jealousy, and the deaths of patriarchs and the ensuing conflict over their estates, but the Mexicans had more colorful costumes, with Mexican sombreros and cap pistols, which they fired frequently. Momostecans reported that this was a faithful representation of Mexicans.

The center of the plaza was dominated by a tall wooden scaffolding and platform of cedar and pine poles and rough-hewn planks. A lashed pole tower thirty feet tall with a ladder and small platform was attached to its northeastern corner. This complex was referred to as the palace and represented the home of the K'iche' dancers in the Dance of the Conquest. The paired *chirimía* (shawm) and *tun* (native Maya drum) musicians who provide the music for most of the dance action were seated on the palace platform. Additional musical accompaniment was provided sporadically later in the day by a bugle and little snare drum carried by the invading Spaniards. Some special features of the Dance of the Conquest as it was performed in 1976 included the entrance of Alvarado into town on a white horse during the two biggest days of the festival, July 21 and August 1, and the climbing of the tower by the Aj Itz or Tzitzimite character, representing the priest and diviner who assists and seeks to magically defend the war chief Tecum. At the top of the tower he decries the Spanish invasion and signals to the·audience. There was also a little emblem of a peace or victory sign made from an American flag sewed onto the Spanish flag carried by Alvarado. This, combined with active questioning by some thoughtful young men about whether or not Guatemala was a colony of the United States, signaled growing cosmopolitan sophistication within the local population.

Though on ordinary Sundays there were produce and blanket vendors in considerable numbers selling their wares in the plaza in front of the church, the plaza was cleared of vendors during the fiesta, except for some blanket vendors along the south edge, leaving lots of room for spectators and for the action of the dances. On July 31 and August 1, the big days in 1976, buses full of American and German tourists rolled into town, and the tourists photographed the dances, bought blankets, and left within a couple of hours.

The cofradía of Santiago in 1976 was still a part of the "traditional" and "official" cofradía system and was staffed by an alcalde, a *diputado*, and four *mortomas* (*mayordomos*), with a women's group of four *chuchaxeles*.[5] There were twenty-one cofradías in 1976 (see Cook 2000:35–40), organized in a hierarchy with the first five—Corpus (the entombed Christ), Santiago and María Concepción, Santa Cruz, and Capitagua (the Crucified Christ)—constituting the directorate or *c'amal be* (literally, "road guide"). The alcaldes of these five met after mass every Sunday, supervised all cofradía activities, and approved requests for temporary excuses from service.

On July 23 the images of Santiago and San Felipe were taken in procession from the church to the cofradía house in barrio Santa Isabel for an all-night vigil and fiesta. In the morning the incoming alcalde and any other new cofrades and chuchaxeles were received there at breakfast and then accompanied the outgoing officers to church, where those who were leaving the service adorned their replacements with flower crowns (cofrades) and necklaces (chuchaxeles) while kneeling in front of the main altar. On July 30 the new cofradía took Santiago in procession back to the cofradía house for a second vigil, during which his clothes were changed by the new alcalde at midnight, thus signaling the start of a new year for the alcalde and his patron. Early in the morning on July 31 Santiago and San Felipe were carried to the calvario and then, in the early afternoon, there was a big procession around town accompanied by all of the costumed dancers. The final public displays of the images took place on August 1, with a major procession around town, ending with a return to the church after dark. In addition to these public and quasi-public religious performances in honor of Santiago during the festival, his alcalde and diputado were also responsible for making offerings at specified altars on specific days of the Maya calendar throughout the year, and the cofradía was also responsible for carrying the images to festivals in San Vicente Buenabaj (a reunion with the image of Santa Isabel) and Pueblo Viejo, Tunayac (a reunion with Santa Catarina), in November each year (Cook 2000:78–80).

THE POST-PEASANT FESTIVAL IN 2005–2009

Visiting Momostenango in 2005 to witness the festival for the first time since 1976, Garrett Cook was initially struck by the tremendous expansion and the change in character of the operation of the street vendors' market. In 1976 it had occupied the southern margins of the church plaza and the paved streets around the little *parque central* east of the municipal palace, extending for a block or so along, beyond, and behind the church convent complex. In 2005 vendors not only completely filled the two covered market complexes, the church plaza and the central square, as in 1976, but then extended for three blocks beyond the church convent, heading east on the bakery road, and up and down all the side streets. The market extended the same distance east of the Paclom intersection on the cemetery road. It also extended, though sporadically, for three or four blocks along the streets south of the cemetery road, from the first block east of the Paclom intersection to the main entrance/exit road. The side roads in this expanded commercial zone were all closed to vehicular traffic by sidewalk vendors selling their wares from little easels, on blankets on the ground, or on tables and partially enclosed wooden booths. Blue plastic tarpaulins with guylines crisscrossing in all directions, about head high for a six-foot gringo, hovered above all the side roads, converting them into arcades and sluicing the afternoon rain water into little waterfalls and a complex deltaic pattern on the cobblestone streets. To the north vendors' displays extended all the way down the *salida* to the spot where the road forks to Canquixaja and El Salitre on the left and to Xequemeya, Santa Lucia La Reforma, and Quiché on the right. The blocks west of the plaza that run downhill into barrios Santa Ana and Santa Isabel lacked vendors but provided numerous *parqueos* for the cars of visitors and a way for through traffic to bypass the center of town. The area devoted to vending had increased by three to four times over the past thirty years, or doubled in each fifteen-year period, a rate of growth that approximately duplicates the rate of natural increase in Guatemala.

Food sales on the side street between the covered market plaza and the bakery road included a vast expansion of the usual market fare, *comida típica*,

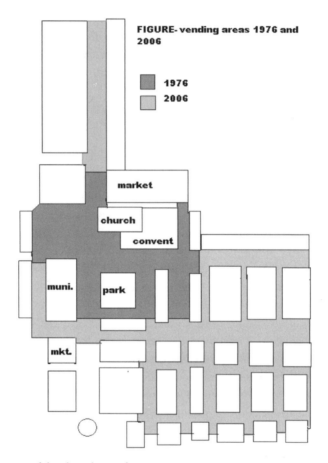

Figure 1.1 Map of the plaza during fiesta season, 1970–2010, Momostenango.

the same as that which was sold during the fiesta in the 1970s, that is, roasted and stewed meats, soups, rice and beans, tortillas, and tamalitos, as well as *arroz con leche* and various local breads. But the church plaza in 2005 was dominated by carts and wagons and more formal booths like those that would be found at a fair in the United States, selling fried chicken and french fries; shaved pork tacos; steamed hot dogs and buns with diced onions, cabbage, mustard, and ketchup (*cheverres*); pizza; and sweet corn which is boiled in huge vats and served with interlaced ribbons of mayonnaise, mustard, and at least two chili sauces squeezed by the proprietors from plastic bottles. There was a whole aisle of funnel cake vendors, numerous cotton candy machines, and several vendors of fried plantains. By 2008 an official Pollo Campero stand, Guatemala's most successful nationally advertised franchise operation, had joined the other vendors of chicken and fries.

The central location, the southern half of the church plaza adjoining the municipal palace, and the main street separating the palace from the central park are now dominated by fair foods that were not available at all thirty years ago. The corn on the cob is the most noteworthy change, as it has completely replaced the roasted elotes served with lime wedges and salt that were the dominant festival food thirty years ago; they represented the agricultural cycle and fit with the timing of the festival as the season of elotes. Only one daily vendor of traditional elotes was located in 2008, while a couple of the plantain vendors sometimes sold roasted ears in the late afternoon. At the same time, there were six vendors devoted to sweet corn, each selling dozens of ears every hour from twenty-gallon steel pots heated by propane. The corn on the cob is not local but a hybrid imported from the southern coast and Peten. The core of the festival dining complex, understood as a cultural performance in its own right, now presents a U.S.-style midway experience, while the typical rural Guatemalan festival foods, with the exception of some tacos and fried plantains, have been pushed to marginal locations.

Pirated DVDs and CDs are sold at two booths located near the gringo-style food vendors in the plaza in front of the church and at scattered locations elsewhere. They play music or movies constantly with volumes set at a high level, making a minor contribution to the noise in the central plaza. Additionally, there are small theaters set up in several locations, where ten or twenty young men can sit packed together on benches in sheet metal and canvas-walled shacks watching action DVDs projected on large screens. One interesting twist is that in 2006 the authors made a DVD of the Monkeys Dance, including ceremonies, practice sessions, and the raising of the dance pole, and returned in 2007 to provide gift copies of a two-volume set to the dancers and dance sponsors.[6] One or more of the recipients later sold copies to DVD piraters. The result was that during the festival in 2007, a year when the Monkeys Dance was not performed, there were copies of the video for sale on the plaza. In 2008 the dance was performed again, and it was strange to stand on the plaza and observe a costumed dancer doing acrobatic tricks on the tightrope while a video of the same performer in 2006 was playing below. A second video that just showed the tricks on the rope in 2008 was produced at the dancers' request and distributed before the end of the festival. Dancers report that it was available for sale in a pirated edition on the plaza within two weeks.

In the 1970s the music on the plaza came from musicians accompanying the costumed dances that were being performed. The music from different locations sometimes blended together, but it was generally possible for the dancers and the audience to easily hear and follow the dance music pertaining to a particular performance. Thirty years later several stores located around the plaza play radio stations over loudspeakers at high volume all day long. Additionally, there are now two large bandstands located right in front of the church, and there are times when bands are playing on both; from about eleven in the morning to eleven at night, except when mass is being given in the church, there almost always is at least one band, with keyboards, drums, several horns, electric guitars, and vocalists, playing loudly amplified music through stacked, refrigerator-sized speakers. Often there are two or three fashionably slim, attractive women dancing in short shorts and tube tops, skintight jumpsuits, or microskirts and go-go boots while singing. The speakers are aimed at the church, the portal of which is some forty feet away from the bandstands, since the music is meant to honor and please Santiago, whose image is usually in the church. This creates an overwhelming, consciousness-altering soundscape in between the giant speakers and the church; standing in this area, one's chest and head pound to the music and one's vision is blurred by the buffeting sound waves that seem to thicken the very air. A few seconds there and you are transported into a dreamlike state of dissociation. Here the drunks dance and grapple in the K'iche' version of the clubbing experience, while seemingly impassive crowds look on. Each band is contracted for a full day by a local sponsor, usually an association of businesses from a neighborhood or barrio. Since the traditional dances are performed on this same plaza, it is usually impossible to hear the traditional dance music during a performance, except when mass is being given in the church.

The only traditional costumed dance in 2005 was the Mexicans. This was a surprise to the authors, who had planned to begin a restudy of the Dance of the Conquest in an effort to see how the dance and its local interpretations had changed over a thirty-year period that included a civil war, the explosive growth of evangelical churches, fifteen years of Maya cultural activism, the development of a new, transnationalized labor market, exposure to international popular culture and media, and the development of a neoliberal political economy. It appeared initially, though wrongly as it turns out, that the dance had disappeared. The only other costumed dance performed was locally referred to as *convites* (invitations) and *disfraces* (from *disfrazar* "undressings"), involving pairs of male dancers in elaborate matching costumes inspired by characters from TV shows and movies, for example, two Sith Lords, two Xena, the warrior princesses, and so on. The pairs wore numbers and competed for prizes, dancing in parallel lines to amplified popular music like that on the bandstands in front of the church on a dance ground on the south side of the parque central. Hundreds of spectators packed together in an extremely dense mass watched from the arcade in front of the building on the south side of the parque, while hundreds more lined the railing three or four persons deep on the second-floor gallery of the building. By 2008 a women's disfraces had been added and was also a big hit, drawing a mammoth and enthusiastic crowd. This dance is discussed in chapter 4.

Conversations about how the festival had changed suggested that the time required to practice the traditional dances made them unattractive and that the conversion of so many to Evangelical churches had reduced both the audience for the traditional dances and the pool of possible dancers. The authors interviewed don Celestino, who had performed in a leading role in the Conquest Dance in 1976. He reported that the Conquest Dance had not been performed in Momostenango for two years because the *autors* (sponsors/producers) had died and no one else had come forward to take on the responsibility. Numerous collaborators, including himself, were now sponsoring the bands that played in front of the church as their contributions to the festival. This meant that there was less money available to help produce the dance in the future. He accompanied us to a visit with don Nicolás, the dance master who taught from a book that he had purchased in Santa María Chiquimula, a neighboring town that performs the same version of the dance that was always given in Momostenango. Don Nicolás would teach the dance during rehearsals on the dirt road winding through the pine forest at the base of the hill where he lived, but no one was willing to take on sponsorship. The old men had been talking about maybe dancing for five days, rather than the two weeks of the festival, but production costs were estimated as Q 2,000 to construct the palace, Q 20,000 for rental of twenty costumes, and Q 400 for the two musicians for five days, plus the costs of food for the dancers and at least four days of offerings at mountain altars prior to the dance. They told us that this is what had happened to the Moors Dance as well. "The autors were two little old men, and when they died no one came forward to take their place," don Celestino said. "Ordinarily these responsibilities are passed on in families, but the sons are unwilling to comply. In older times, things were strict, and people accepted their responsibilities. Now, if it rains they run inside."

Broken transmission lines are more likely when families, and generations within families, become divided over religion, with children joining Catholic Action or Evangelical churches. These problems are compounded by the difficulty of recruiting dancers, since the dance autor is both sponsor of the dance and producer in the sense of recruiting dancers, contracting with musicians, and everything else. Several interrelated problems amplify each other and discourage all but the bravest and most faithful from stepping forward. These issues are explored more fully in the context of the Monkeys Dance case study in chapter 3. In 2008 the Conquest Dance was produced again after a lapse of four years, with a completely new team of sponsors and dancers and a new master as well. Don Nicolás had died in 2006.

The Conquest Dance in 2008 was essentially the same as the one performed in 1976, except that the tower was too rickety to be climbed by the Aj Itz and there are no longer any horses available in Momostenango, so Alvarado just appeared suddenly on the dance ground, rather than riding into town. This seemed to reduce the feeling that Momostenango represented the K'iche' world and that Momostenango itself was invaded each year by the Spaniards. The performance is still attended to with great interest and still potentially provides a charter for K'iche' identity and resistance and for the survival of the K'iche' religion (see Cook 2000:118–41). One other interesting change is that the dead Tecum was once carried off to a room in the convent behind the Catholic church, while today he is carried off to a location under the stairs in the municipal building. This may reflect some loss of trust between Costumbristas and the church after several more decades of Catholic Action opposition to Costumbre, but the current priest is indigenous and is committed to somewhat guarded inculturation theology, so it seems more likely that this is just related to the different social networks of the two dance producers.

Processions with the images of Santiago and San Felipe are basically as they were in the 1970s and follow the same timetable. One change that was introduced in 2005 and 2007 was a group of rocketeers who fired off sky rockets at every rest stop and corner during the procession. This was the off-year project of don Pedro Raxc'oy, the autor of the Monkeys Dance. Since his murder in 2007, however, no one has come forward to keep this innovation going, and it lapsed in 2009. The cofradía is organized and sponsored very differently than it was thirty years ago, but that will be discussed in the following chapter.

THE ADAPTATION OF A POST-PEASANT FESTIVAL TO A POST-PEASANT WORLD

The location of events within the spatial plan of the festival is an important part of their meaning. In the festival today, the central place is given over to commerce rather than religious ceremony. The symbolism of gringo-style consumerism as expressed in foods takes central place, while comida típica is marginalized. Symbolism of Guatemalan identity and Guatemalan progress is hard to separate from symbolism of Momostecan identity and progress, as both are exemplified concurrently in the huge parade of all the schools that takes place over two days, a convincing advertisement for the improvement of Guatemalan primary education that at the same time is an opportunity for competition and displays of local civic pride among specific schools from the rural hamlets and urban neighborhoods. The fact that Guatemalan and Momostecan pride are conjoined in this way would likely be pleasing to Teodoro Cifuentes and to generations of Ladino and acculturated Indian nationalists and assimilationists. There is considerable shaping by North American culture, as the marching bands with baton twirlers and pompom-wielding dance lines have a Macy's Thanksgiving Day Parade feeling.

There has been a resurgence of Maya identity and Momostecan pride in the return of the Conquest Dance and the perpetuation of the Monkeys Dance under difficult circumstances, while again the most distinctively hybridized and transnationalized performance of all is found in the extremely popular disfraces, with virtually no Guatemalan symbolism. Here purely transnational, media-inspired imagery is combined with the underlying institutional functions and format of an indigenous dance team, with at least some costumbre being practiced prior to every performance. Unlike the traditional masked dances, which enact stories with dialogue and plots and which provide charters and depict themes of direct relevance to Momostecan institutional arrangements, the disfraces have no legitimizing function in regard to and provide no commentary on the locally lived life. They internalize and interpret the worlds of entertainment media and international politics. The indigenous communities and postcommunities brought together by the festival have developed a series of separated performance spheres, all of which are open to all as spectators, though not equally intelligible to all. The performances emerge as little islands from a sea of raucous commerce, and they can mostly be seen but not heard as a result of the domination of the soundscape by advertisements and by mind-numbingly amplified, popular Latin music.

While Momostenango seems to have lost most of its Ladinos and they no longer dominate the municipal government or the commercial sector, the indigenous community is itself increasingly pluralistic and has developed considerable complexity since the 1970s. Carmack (1995) has identified long-term trends toward commercialization and a rise in power of an urban, acculturated, capitalist indigenous status group, his "Indian petty bourgeoisie," and he also provides a cogent analysis of the local political neutralization of Catholic Action since the 1970s, a change in the character and social action of this large status group that defines a new context for cultural performances. In the first place, he argues that Catholic Action was and remains essentially a movement of proletarianized Indians, since the peasants and the commercialized post-peasants or proto-peasants generally remained with Costumbre and the more successful urban bourgeois Indians, many of whom are descendants of the militarist allies of Cifuentes, tended to align ideologically with

Ladinos and share in the running of the municipal corporation while maintaining their political and religiously symbolized alliance with their constituency in the Costumbrista masses.[7]

During the period of violence between the late 1970s and early 1990s the Catholics in Momostenango were in a dicey position. The urban indigenous powerbrokers and their rural constituency supported the MLN/PID alliance, as explained above. Local Catholics were not political radicals, but the church itself was under threat because of liberation theology. Within Momostenango, then, Catholic Action members did not make common cause with the insurgents but could not readily join with their traditional adversaries (the Costumbristas and *civilizados*) and so they were marginalized (Carmack 1995:404–5). The Pentecostal and Evangelical Protestant movements that swept the highlands during the 1980s and early 1990s made many converts from among these marginalized and proletarianized Christians as well as among the land-poor younger generation within the Costumbrista community while also making some inroads among the emerging capitalist class, as accumulation of capital generally meant ventures that involved living in Guatemala City or the United States, where new Protestant identities were encouraged by very active proselytizing and where abstinence from alcohol and high regard for savings and investment were reinforced to the advantage of converting families (see Annis 1987). Thus to the Catholic Action–Traditionalist division that endured from mid-twentieth-century Momostenango a new faction of theologically radical Evangelical Protestants was added, a community generally committed to a spiritual warfare theology and hence ready to pick up the fight against the traditionalists where the Catholics had left off.

A little bit later, as a result of cultural activism and changes in the legal code following the political awakenings of the quincentennial of the conquest and the coincidental formalizing of peace accords and return to civilian government, the indigenous religion began to enjoy legal protection.[8] Its practitioners, whether they are traditional Costumbristas or activist spiritual guides and Maya priests, enjoyed some increase in status as a result of international attention from anthropologists and from cultural survival and new age constituencies.[9] So as the fiesta unfolded in the period between 2005 and the time of this writing, it was in a very different setting. The priest was experimenting with inculturation theology and not overtly hostile to at least some costumbre. The Catholics were somewhat chastened by the Protestant explosion and by their difficult and ambiguous position within local and national politics and seemed to be amenable to greater cooperation with the Costumbristas, or at the very least to withdrawal from political and symbolic contention for the time being. As noted above, Holy Week was the festival at which religious contention was most pronounced thirty years ago. Since all the religious factions have a stake in the Holy Week celebration it is still very different from the feria.

Santiago is largely ignored by the Protestants, since neither Catholic saints nor indigenous tutelary deities require any respect in their theology and since the current legal system and the complexities of local politics and networks reduces their ability to mount open spiritual warfare. They are free to participate in the festival as a secular celebration of the schools and of progress and modernization and in some cases to benefit from its commercial opportunities. The competing performances of the feria, then, are more about symbolizing progress and tradition and about symbolizing and providing support for several models for indigenous identity than about religious ideology or local politics. The challenge for highland Maya social action and cultural construction today seems to boil down to finding ways to modernize while retaining an indigenous identity and, for many, also a Momostecan identity. These identities are experienced and expressed through participation in what is perceived as traditional cultural performance within the specially constructed performance space of the festival. The identities are real only to the extent that the supportive cultural infrastructure remains in place. The festival then must simultaneously provide performance of these two, as yet not well integrated and quite possibly irresolvable, symbolic poles.

The post-peasant persona, as Kearney (1996) has pointed out, is multifaceted and articulated in complex ways, with numerous strategies for earning money and producing family welfare. Thus the festival replicates the post-peasant condition through public symbolism of a complex world within which Maya tradition and a Maya religious worldview remain necessary for some remaining peasants and commercialized peasants and may be necessary elements in homecoming rituals and identity construction for many more, although for most people and for the larger community they have been insufficient for a couple of generations. The next two chapters explore the strategies and goals of two generations of Costumbristas as they seek to maintain the cult of Santiago in this complexly pluralized and thoroughly transnationalized village within Guatemala's new neoliberal order (Offit and Cook 2010).

CHAPTER TWO

Santiago and the Cofradía

Reorganizing the Tradition

STRUCTURE AND AGENCY

E thnographic research on the cofradía of Santiago between 2006 and
2009 is reported here and in chapter 5 as it responds to two goals. Here
we seek to describe the current institution and to compare its organization with that of 1976. From time to time issues of agency will arise in this
discussion since the individual and culture are involved in unremitting interaction. We seek to portray an ad hoc and adjusting interactive field rather
than a frozen model of local culture. Nevertheless, our emphasis here is to
depict cultural patterns, as these are institutionalized or are becoming institutionalized at the time of this writing. We will return to agency in chapter 5
and explore the drama enacted by individuals engaged in innovation and in
negotiation of the complex hybridized terrain of a twenty-first-century transnational festival in a post-peasant village.

This chapter suggests that the cofradía remains largely successful at reproducing the mid-twentieth-century ritual symbols and the expressive culture
tradition of Santiago, but that to do so it has had to make some significant
adjustments in its social organization, funding, and articulation with the larger
community. On balance, then, at the organizational level the cofradía has been
substantially remade and is undergoing ongoing reconstruction, while at the

level of ritual symbols and meaning we see the cofradía today as reproducing a tradition rather than constructing one. The discussion of the disfraces in chapter 4 documents a more radical episode of discontinuity and cultural construction within Maya cultural performance and ritual symbolism.

THE FIELDWORK

Recent fieldwork on the cofradía of Santiago and its role in the fiesta included observation of the village festival in 2005 and of the specific activities at the cofradía house between 2006 and 2009. In 2006 the cofradía fiesta proper at the cofradía house was first observed when the authors attended in their role as collaborators and videographers of the Monkeys Dance, since the dance team and its sponsors were invited to have lunch at the cofradía house and to return to the town center in the cofradía procession. This first visit to the cofradía house allowed us to meet the alcalde and the diputado of the cofradía as interested supporters of Momostecan tradition and Costumbre. They both agreed to meet with us later and provided contact information.

In July 2007 the authors returned with funding for fieldwork from the Foundation for the Advancement of Mesoamerican Studies, Inc. Two interviews were completed that season with the diputado, a practicing *aj mesa*, one on the roadside after observing his offerings at the shrine of Ventana Mundo and another, longer one in his consulting room. Several additional interviews and numerous conversations have since taken place. The alcalde invited the authors to his ceremonies at a shrine complex on a hilltop overlooking the cofradía house in 2007 and later provided several recorded interviews at his altar table in the cofradía house. We again attended the festival at the cofradía house in 2008 and 2009, as guests of the alcalde and minor sponsors, and again accompanied the procession from the cofradía house to a chapel that used to belong to an hermandad, remaining for several hours to participate in the vigil and meal. We also accompanied the cofradía and images of Santiago and San Felipe in several processions through the principal streets of downtown Momostenango over these several years and added at least one additional formal interview with the alcalde in each season.

The senior author had witnessed the cofradía processions and been invited to a lunch at the cofradía house during the festival of Patrón Santiago in 1976. He had completed two very long recorded interviews with the recently retired diputado of the cofradía, an experienced ritualist who had served as chuch-kajaw for the cofradía from 1957 to 1975 and who had been removed through a Catholic Action plot, as mentioned in chapter 1 (see Cook 2000:44–47, 231;

B. Tedlock 1982:42–43). The findings of this earlier research, which have been reported elsewhere (see Cook 2000:43–47, 75–98), provide comparative and historical context for the analysis here.

THE COFRADÍA IN 2006–2009
DESCRIBED AS AN INSTITUTION

In an effort at retaining some continuity with Cook's (2000) description of the 1976 cofradía prototype and in order to facilitate comparison and allow for an analysis of phases in an evolving tradition of cultural performance as recommended by Guss (2000) and Cohen (1993), the description here follows Malinowski's (1944:47–52) approach to the institution: "An institution is an organized system of activities that fulfill a defined and legitimized purpose, its charter. It utilizes concrete capital and is staffed by personnel whose roles are governed by ideal norms or rules" (Cook 2000:24). The purpose of the cofradía of Santiago is to serve, honor, feed, and entertain the powerful spirits, or nawales, associated with the images of Santiago and San Felipe, as well as the souls of the deceased cofrades and the original founders of the cult. Specific ritualized complexes have been created and maintained to fulfill this function and thereby to insure the protection of the community and the orderly transition of seasons, with a special focus on rain needed for the milpa. The main complexes are called fiestas, but each fiesta is a combination of a procession with the images and a visit or vigil at a house. Sometimes the house is a church or chapel (ro'choch Tiox, or God's house), sometimes it is the official shrine house of the sponsoring organization, and sometimes it is a private house where a visit has been requested by the owners. Visits or vigils take on a minimal form in which the image enters a building, or possibly just a courtyard, and remaining on its palanquin (anda), is placed on a carpet of pine branches and visited there by devotees and supplicants who offer candles and gifts as well as petitions. At every such visit the images are provided with food and drink, as are the cofrades who have transported them and the visitors. The fully developed form of the visit/vigil occurs when the images are installed overnight in a chapel or ermita (cofradía or hermandad house). In these cases the images are removed from their palanquin and placed on a table decorated with flowers and Momostecan blankets. A welcoming ceremony is followed by supplicant visits, with meals served to the images, who are nourished by aromas, and to everyone who is present. Guests may remain for the entire afternoon, night, and morning of the vigil. Marimbas or musicians playing the chirimía (shawm) and drum are engaged for most of the visit, especially overnight, and other bands perform depending on the financial resources of the sponsors.

The alcalde and deputy of the cofradía dance with the images and may allow other guests this privilege. Boots, cloaks (colorful towels, in most cases), and scarves are offered by supplicants and may be placed on the image of Santiago by the deputy or the alcalde, and cloaks and scarves may be also be placed on San Felipe and on Santiago's horse. As new gifts are given the older clothing is stored in chests and bundles.

> They [cloaks, boots, blankets, etc.] are kept in a house and we guard them in a rented house. He [still] has all his clothes. Twice or thrice each year, we change them. We change his towels [colorful beach towels are often used to drape Santiago and his horse] and all of his clothes. For example, tomorrow there is one from above in Los Cipreses. They want to give clothes, but not until now, because last year I gave clothes to him. But this year, tomorrow, there are those who will give him clothing [*ropa*], and tomorrow in the house, well first tonight at nine there is a vigil in the house, and tomorrow we go down and I will change his clothing tomorrow, but they have only bought his cape.
>
> Now he who has the old clothing guards it in his wardrobe [*ropero*]. . . . We just put them there, and there they are. Now all the plumes, here [decorating his altar table] I have some, see. Every year when we remove the plumes I put some here as an adornment. We are also having a discussion about his clothing. Some of it is very old and the older clothing is much better and fancier. It is all kept in chests and guarded. And there it is, all of it. (don Apolonio, 2009)[1]

This material is ceremonially washed from time to time, and its keeping is one of the responsibilities of the alcalde. "For example, in the costumbre of the Patrón, it falls in February that all of his clothes must be washed at the baths in Pala Grande. The clothes are given to be washed and the dates are arranged, and the cofradía and the women go to Pala Grande to wash the clothes" (don Apolonio 2009).

At the time of transition from an outgoing to an incoming alcalde an inventory of the property of the image is passed along. When the municipality was firmly in control of the system this inventory was supervised by the *síndico segundo*, and any missing items had to be replaced or paid for by the outgoing alcalde. It is not clear how this will function in the future since oversight responsibilities, though still clear in terms of tradition and presumably official policy, are no longer clear in practice and since cofrades no longer are changed annually. In fact, the current alcalde made the following interesting comment: "Every year there are many towels donated. I give last year's towels to a hospital with the permission of the Father [parish priest] and with a receipt, but some do not approve of this. But look . . . [he points to four two-foot-tall stacks of blankets and towels lined up along the wall and covered by plastic sheets]. In the municipality the sindico segundo is responsible, but they do not do their part, and some are Evangelicos" (don Apolonio 2009).

Processions involve ceremonial transportation of the images from the church to a specific destination and then back again, or sometimes just taking them for a walk around town, starting and ending in the church. The images are lashed to palanquins and carried on the shoulders of the cofrades or of a larger group, depending on the size of the palanquin and the number of devotees involved. The palanquins are decorated with cut and plastic flowers and also carry a bowl or basket for donations. In the processions associated with the festival in Momostenango proper the heads of the other cofradías accompany the images, walking immediately in front of them or flanking them, as do any dancers performing on the day of the procession, in costume, preceding the images in the order of march and accompanied by their musicians. Women with shawls over their heads and carrying bouquets or candles often flank or immediately follow the images, while devotees and friends and family of the principal participants will follow in a respectful group. Again, the current alcalde offers an interesting comment: "I want to improve the processions to involve children as in the past, girls with red blouses and black skirts with red belts and women with incense. If God permits we will improve it. We will have chuchaxeles (female counterparts of the cofrades) and a *nima chichu* (first dame, a woman who is in charge of the chuchaxeles). We will return to the traditions" (don Apolonio 2008).

In addition to the fiestas there is one other ritual complex, the visit to altars belonging to Santiago by the alcalde and by the diputado on specific days in the Maya calendar to offer incense, candles, and other offerings to the nawales and to the souls of the dead cofrades and primeros. As explained by the diputado don Anselmo in July 2007, there are three altars for Santiago located in Momostenango. These are called Paclom (hilltop altar in the town center), Uja'al (springside altar at the base of Paclom hill), and Ventana Mundo. Ventana Mundo (world or earth window) is the most exclusive of these, restricted by tradition to use for cofradía functions. Don Anselmo reports that except for Niño San Antonio, which maintains its own altar in the aldea Pologua, the important cofradías that still exist—Santiago, Corpus, María, Capitagua (Cristo Crucificado), and Santa Cruz—all pay respects to Santiago at Ventana Mundo. Ventana Mundo is located at the top of the steep climb out of Momostenango to the west on the road to Pueblo Viejo, near the point where that road forks with the road to Pologua. Santiago came to Momostenango from Pueblo Viejo, which had been the original, local forti-fied outpost of the Q'umarkaaj-centered K'iche' polity prior to the conquest, and he continues to visit Pueblo Viejo in a procession on this road in November, with a stop at this altar. The deputy of Santiago makes about Q 70 ($10) worth of offerings there on every day numbered 1, 6, or 8 in the sequence of thirteen repeating numbers in the Maya 260-day divining calendar, and the alcalde makes offerings there every day numbered 9, 11, or 13. Offerings include wax and tallow candles, sugar, copal, incense, and tobacco. Don Anselmo explains that these ceremonies are for the protection of Momostenango and the entire world. Although new religions have developed and not everyone is in accord, the offerings are for everybody.

> There is one patrón [i.e., an altar dedicated to Santiago] at Pila [also called Uja'l], another at Ventana, in Quilaja, Socop, Tamancu and Pipil, in Las Minas there above Chiantla. Las Minas is visited every January 1. I go carrying his copal and his candles.[2]
>
> I am brought by a committee representing the *hermandad del banda*. There is a social group called K'akaj which is from the image of San Antonio. We all go together, because if not how could I afford the fare? It is 500–600 quetzales to rent a car. So this is how it is done at the *volcanes* [i.e., the major and distant shrines] because if I was alone I could not do it. (don Anselmo, 2007).

PERSONNEL AND ORGANIZATION: THE ADAPTING SOCIAL STRUCTURE

Currently the cofradía of Santiago has only three or four official members, an alcalde who produces the festival, a diputado who must be a practicing aj mesa and who is equally responsible with the alcalde for performing offerings and invocations at the altars, and one or two mayordomos (called mortomas in Momostenango) who are expected to contribute some money and who run errands and perform whatever additional labor may be needed as directed by the alcalde. The diputado is the chuchkajaw of the cofradía, but in the event that the alcalde is also an initiated Maya ritualist of aj mesa grade, as is the case currently, the costumbre may be shared. This is espe-cially important in the current situation, since the diputado of the cofradía is also serving as the chuchkajaw for the Monkeys Dance and so is spread very thin during the festival.

The current diputado belongs to a family with very deep connections to the Monkeys Dance, and so to Patrón Santiago. With his wife he has cosponsored the group that fires skyrockets during Santiago's processions for several years. When asked about the cofradías and how they functioned during a recorded interview in July 2007 he reported the following:

> Now then, well, those of the cofradías, now we are not many. I think we are twelve [officers] and no more. Now the images are abandoned. The Patrón and San Felipe, the two together [are one cofradía], San Antonio, El Sacramento [Corpus or Sr. Sepultado], the virgin María, Santa Cruz, Capitagua [Cristo Crucificado]. Those are seven images. There is one called San Francisco, making eight, and another called Santa Bárbara, making nine [nine images but eight cofradías].
>   Question: Is San Simón still with Santa Barbára?
>   Yes, it is the same, they keep watch with him on Friday [of Semana Santa], it is the same, yes. And now there are only twelve, no more than that, as officers of the cofradías. Now the image of Santa Cruz, or Capitagua, their cofrades don't spend much. Bárbara does not spend much. The one that costs a lot of money is Patrón Santiago. The first day of May is the day of Santa Cruz, the day of the Holy Spirit [Espíritu Santo] is the signal to enter the forty days of change in the cofradía [of Santiago]. The twenty-third and twenty-fourth of July is the actual change of the cofrades. But now as there are none, just the two of us, we are forced to say yes. In this year at Espíritu Santo we accepted again because there was no one else. In all we are three, the alcalde, myself, and there is a mayordomo.

An interview recorded a year later with the alcalde of the cofradía, here represented by the pseudonym don Apolonio, confirmed and clarified the current system for recruitment of cofrades while also providing an insider's perspective on the evolution of hermandades in the Costumbrista cult of Santiago.

> The hermandad of the apostle [Santiago] in Barrio Santa Isabel does not exist any longer. They all died. One of the members of the hermandad del banda is from Santa Isabel. Now there is only the image [i.e., it is alone, without its own hermandad]. There were once eighty cofrades altogether and thirteen women who were selected by the juzgado, and

if they didn't serve they went to jail, if they weren't at mass, they went to jail. As it was each barrio did its service, year by year.

Question: When did this change, don Apolonio?

It changed in 1985 or 1986. Before that the cofradía collected money, coins, there was money collected, two hundred quetzales. Now they don't, the municipality ignores the cofradía. It has just been four or three years since the Paclom poured water out, because there in PaXolak [an altar near the river below the Paclom, with costumbres on the days numbered one] the water is very blessed. Because the people there, it is the costumbre of the *chuchkajaw rech tinamit* [Maya priest employed to perform ceremonies on behalf of the municipality]. He didn't do the costumbre [specific ceremony performed to protect the *varas*, i.e., the staffs of office of the municipality and the authority they represent], so the water flowed out and made the whole milpa into a patch of mud right up to the house, and no one could do anything for all the mud. In this case the alcalde, who lives in town, I forget his name but he is a Ladino and an Evangelico who doesn't believe in the costumbre. He didn't attach importance to the costumbre. He said, "If water comes, it comes." The people were afraid because the Paclom is full of water, it is a volcano of water [the spring, or pila, at Paclom is said to be connected to another sacred spring called Salpachán in Pueblo Viejo, an earlier seat of authority and "the root" of the spring at Paclom]. It could have flooded the house.

Don Apolonio, in seeking to implement his understanding of his responsibilities as alcalde, has sometimes struggled with other persons and groups that have an interest in the image of Santiago, and as noted above in connection with stored and inventoried possessions donated to the image, there is not always a clear line of authority nor decisive action taken in the contemporary, less bureaucratized, cult of the image.

When San Vicente Buenabaj [i.e., representatives of the Charismatic Renewal–dominated Catholic community in the aldea of San Vicente Buenabaj] wanted to take the image to their festival in a car I went to the juzgado to stop it. The authorities said that the cofradía was responsible for the image and so those of San Vicente became angry with me, but in reality the officials didn't take any action. So I went to the parish priest, Father Ionel. Father said if they didn't take good care of the image this year it would not go at all next year. So that is to say the municipality and the Father are both in charge of the image. Now the Father and the municipality have both said that the cofradía is in charge of the image. The municipal officials said the cofradía would be issued a document to certify its rights, but the document was not issued because we are only thirteen, and some are not active.

Responding to questions about how cofrades are recruited and about how he became the alcalde of Santiago, don Apolonio made the following remarks:

As it works now if a cofrade needs to be replaced it is by the Sociedad de la Banda. They arrange for this for Santiago on Espíritu Santo on May 1. The question will come, "Will you continue for another year?" Each cofradía has its own month. So forty days before the fiesta begins we ask at the Paclom, Ventana Mundo, Salpachán, and C'oy Abaj.

The Sociedad de la Banda, each is made up of members, they have forty or fifty persons. They do their costumbre in August 2008 to ask for the fiesta in 2009. Each then is asked for Q 100 or Q 200. In this way they get together Q 8,000–10,000. Now each band costs about Q 3,000, each band with many members. All of the members of the society are private persons, volunteers; there is no relation to the church or the municipality. . . .

Before I provided support and did costumbre [i.e., he was serving as chuchkajaw for the hermandad del banda], but I never imagined it [i.e., becoming alcalde] would fall on me. I always had faith in the patrón, and when there came a day in May, May first, and they came here and there were a lot. The Sociedad de la Banda—there were two groups of band sponsors—and the cofradías, and other gentlemen that came with incense and they spoke to me personally.

"Now in the future you are going to take a double, a double," they told me. "You are the chuchkajaw, and now you will also be the Patrón Santiago and San Felipe. You will take charge of all this. And here is the key for the ropa, and all his things, and do the costumbre, and all this, and we are going to deliver his *porobal* [altar where offerings are burned]."

So I said, "I am going to think."

So a year passed and who knew how it would come out? When the year came they returned and called on me.

"Okay, I will go with him, but with all the expenses I want to leave it for another year. I don't want to do it because it will cost too much. But we will see if I am blessed, maybe. Maybe with a good fight [*lucha*, the struggle for life], but this we cannot know now."

Finally, in connection with issues of the transmission of tradition within the cofradía and in connection with the distribution of authority within the current social organization of the cofradía, don Apolonio made the following pertinent remarks in various interviews and conversations.

Question: Don Apolonio, how did you learn the costumbre of the ancestors? Did you have a teacher from the cofradía?

No, for myself I never had a teacher [from the cofradía]. I had a teacher who has died, an elder from Xequemeya who taught me the defenses [i.e., divination and how to make offerings and invoke the powers]. He lived far away. While he was alive he told me do this and do that. He told me how to handle candles for the Patrón, candles and incense. He told me when the Patrón came out, that there were five processions in the year, that he comes out in Espíritu Santo and in Semana Santa, and that offerings are made then. He left me instructed. He told me that a drummer had to be provided, and gourds of *atole* [maize gruel], to give it, to drink it, to give the cofradía [i.e., the festival of the cofradía]. This is the custom of the ancestors, of the earlier cofradía.

On another occasion, while discussing the trip to Pueblo Viejo with the image each November, he was asked, "And when you went in procession to pueblo Viejo the first time, did you have a guide?" He responded, "No, because there in Ventana Mundo is the porobal for his departure from town. Then in Chicoch is his *mesa silla*. There is the one for the Patrón and another for private personal use, for saving them from their illnesses. There are his altars, and another in Salpachán, one for the entire pueblo, to request blessings [for the pueblo] one prays there."

The gist of these responses seems to be that there is really little specialized esoteric knowledge required beyond the training and calling to serve as an aj mesa, that is, the personal charisma and supernatural powers of an initiated ritualist/diviner and the knowledge of how to make offerings and which powers to invoke. Otherwise all that is needed is the schedule of events and the locations of the altars. Some additional comments that touch on issues of legitimation and problems with transmission of costumbre, culled from several conversations, include, "In the church there is an altar, actually within a house behind the convent. Ix Pix C'ar, or Chajal, is the name of this altar. This is because before, it [the church and convent] was a cemetery. I had to explain to the father that I have to do costumbre there for the town. The fathers change every two or three years and do not know the costumbre." And also, "Many chuchkajaws do not approve of my being alcalde. They say that I am too young. But I do a good job and no one helps me. There is envy of me, and I fear that some are working against me [i.e., practicing witchcraft to injure him]. Maybe in May I should resign."

CAPITAL, CHARTER AND RITUAL SYMBOLS: THE STRUGGLE FOR CONTINUITY IN THE RITUAL TRADITION

The main performances in the expressive culture produced through the cofradía of Santiago are vigils with visitation by devotees at houses and processions. The cofradía's role in the festival in Momostenango in July is to carry the image from the church to the cofradía house, where a celebration is held and devotees may visit the image, and then carry it from the cofradía to the hermandad ermita for a second all-night celebration with visitation, and then back to the church. There are also two additional manifestations of this complex, which occur in November—a visit of the image to San Vicente Buenabaj and a visit to Pueblo Viejo, a *paraje* (named subdivision of a hamlet) in Aldea Tunayac. Within the complex of visits the most important discrete ritual symbols are individual petitions made with candle offerings, the serving of meals, and dancing, including the dancing of the images. Also, from time to time clothes donated by the faithful are placed on the images, and once each year, at midnight when the images are in the hermandad ermita, the alcalde and diputado, screened from the attending public by hanging blankets, completely remove and completely replace the clothing on the images, and the old set of clothing goes into storage. This ceremony reflects an ancient K'iche' pattern of bundle ritual. The images, power objects left by holy foundational figures (the primeros), dangerous objects that are ordinarily kept covered, hidden within their cloaks and scarves and towels, are briefly revealed to their custodians, acting on behalf of the larger community. The right and responsibility to undress and dress the images is a jealously guarded prerogative of the cofradía.

In the old days, yes, the cofradía carried the image to San Vicente (an aldea), but not now. Now the people of San Vicente are Charismatic Renewal. They do not accept the costumbre. We have just now entered into an argument with them. At this time when it is time to change the clothes they want to dress him in pants and a black jacket, a plain jacket. It is not *traje típica* [i.e., indigenous or traditional clothing]. This got me mad, and I told the father in the church that we should never lose our tradition. If they want to change the clothes it must be ropa típica, and they cannot change the clothes. Only the alcalde can change the clothes, because for this there is a costumbre. Others cannot, there is a costumbre the day before.

And another thing: They want to bring the Patrón in a car. Before, it was always carried on our shoulders. And now they bring the image in a car and last year they changed the clothes, which is only permitted to the cofradía. And they say the clothes do not matter because when the image came to Momostenango it did not come with clothes, it was just wood. But the tradition here is that we use clothes. Well, we dress it in Conquest costumes, all this, like Spaniards. Well, they do not agree and we do not allow them to change the clothes and so this is the story of those of San Vicente. And they have suffered the consequences over the past two or three years. Cars have gone into ravines. They have paid for abandoning the costumbre of the Patrón. (don Apolonio, July 2007)

Finally, outside of but supportive of the visiting/vigil/procession complex there is a complicated pattern of offerings at numerous altars made by the cofradía officers year-round, and in February there is a ceremony of the washing of all of the clothing belonging to the images.

The capital involved in these ceremonies includes substantial cash outlays, since bands have to be paid. The combos that perform at the cofradía functions cost about Q 3,000 each and there are likely to be two or three at the cofradía and another one at the hermandad ermita. The drum and chirimía cost about Q 400 for the day of the fiesta at the cofradía house and then are also needed for every procession with Santiago and San Felipe. There are also substantial cash costs to buy candles, copal, sugar, sweets, and flowers for the twelve or so offerings that must be made each month year-round and for the many additional offerings associated with the festival in Momostenango and with the visit to Pueblo Viejo. The alcalde of Santiago and his deputy in separate interviews both estimated that total annual costs for the fiesta itself range between Q 20,000 and Q 25,000 (about $3,000). But there are additional costs because of all of the costumbre performed year-round, which requires buying offerings and arranging transportation.

As Don Apolonio explained, "Look, I estimate that year by year [summing up his expenses over his four years of service], I have spent some Q 25,000 [$3,300, or about Q 6,250 ($830) per year], and only on costumbre, incense [*pom*], candles for the town, well, yes. Now the fiesta is even more [because of the additional costs of decorating the house and palanquin, hiring bands, and buying large amounts of food]. The expenses for the festival this year are going to be over Q 20,000. I have had to sell some land to cover the costs."

Additionally there is a requisite material infrastructure of the images themselves, with their clothing as explained above and the silver cofradía insignia that accompanies them in processions and visits to houses, of altar tables within houses dedicated to the visits, and of the houses themselves where the visits and vigils are produced, as well as the four main altars in Momostenango and three in Pueblo Viejo that feature specifically in this cult, and probably several others, as, for example, one called IxP'ix Car, or Chajal, in the convent, the C'oy Abaj (Spider Monkey Stone) altar, and maybe others that have not come up in the accounts obtained over the past few years.

The cofradía house and the hermandad chapel are both used for overnight vigils and visits during the festival. As in the house of any Costumbrista there is a house altar, a table that displays sacred objects. The cofradía house in use from 2006 through 2009 is the actual home of the alcalde and so the saints are placed on his house altar, which already displays numerous objects with spirit counterparts (nawales) and supernatural power. In the hermandad chapel the table just displays the images. The pattern is always for Felipe to stand on the left-hand side of Santiago. Both tables are covered with cloths and banners and decorated with flowers and hold a bowl or pitcher of water since the

Figure 2.1 The front room in the cofradía house becomes a shrine, with Santiago, San Felipe, and two images of San Simón all available for visits by the faithful. Cofrades who are in charge of the shrine are seated on the observer's right, just inside the door to the street.

nawales experience thirst. During meals each image is presented with a dish of food since the nawales savor the aromas.

There is a cleared space directly in front of the table where a carpet of pine needles establishes a sacred space within which visitors may approach the images, displaying the candles they have brought and touching the candles to the images' robes. Then, about five feet back from the table, there is a rectangular area on the floor where candles that have been offered to the images during the visit are burned by kneeling supplicants. For most of the time while at the cofradía house, Santiago and San Felipe rest on the table in the front room of the house. The door is open all night and petitioners may come and go, burning candles on the floor in front of the images. Alms placed in saddlebags by the faithful during visits or placed on the palanquin during the cofradía procession are recovered by the sacristan and go to the church. Thus the fiesta is very expensive and does not directly generate any income to support the cofradía.

When Santiago travels in procession he is preceded by a drum and shawm (chirimía), and by any dance teams that are performing that year, accompanied by their musicians, and followed by a brass band. At the cofradía house hired bands playing dance music alternate with the drum and chirimía so that there is some music playing almost constantly for the twenty-four hours

Figure 2.2 In the usual pattern for visiting a saint during a cofradía vigil, candles are burned on the floor in front of the table where the saint's image is displayed. At the cofradía house a series of nawal-bearing stone objects recovered from mundos (i.e., in the vicinity of a mountain altar) are arrayed in the first row.

of the vigil. For most of this time Santiago and San Felipe remain on the altar table in the front room, while the music is played and guests who wish to dance do so in the inner courtyard.

However, from time to time, under the direction of the alcalde, the images are danced with by the cofrades and their close relatives and invited guests. The performances that we have witnessed involved marimba music and sometimes saxophones and horns, and music was invariably to a quick waltz tempo. Each *santo* was brought from the altar table into the courtyard and danced at least once around the courtyard, with several changes of personnel.

Figure 2.3 The alcalde dances with San Felipe, 2007.

Figure 2.4 The alcalde and diputado dance with Santiago in 2007.

San Felipe would be carried by two, but the alcalde also danced solo with San Felipe. After San Felipe was returned to the altar table it was Santiago's turn. He was usually carried by three people, one on each side and one in the rear, but sometimes was carried by two, with one in front and one in the rear. While most of the bearers were males ranging in age from teenagers to about age sixty, at least one woman, the fiancée of the alcalde, was also invited to participate during performances that we observed. The opportunity to dance with a santo is a great honor. At the same time, as in so much else, it is delicado because it represents an opportunity for a sign (*retal*) to be given. A fall or a near fall or a stumble would mean disfavor and would predict worse things yet to come.

At the cofradía house at about 1:30 in the afternoon of July 23, 2006, while the marimba played, San Felipe was carried from the altar table to the palanquin. Then, accompanied by a waltz played by a band hired for the day Santiago was danced around the courtyard once and then placed in the palanquin. This ceremonious handling of the images was accomplished by the head of the cofradía (the alcalde) and four assistants, while the deputy oversaw the fastening of the images to the palanquin.

Preceded by the deer and monkey dancers in and out of costume and the marimba and wooden flute of the Monkeys Dance and by the chirimía and drum of the cofradía procession and flanked by the alcaldes of the remaining

Figure 2.5 The procession emerging from the cofradía house, 2007. Smoke from the firecrackers is visible in the background.

eight cofradías in Momostenango, Santiago and San Felipe left the cofradía house at about two o'clock. The procession stopped for one formal visit at a neighbor's house and then walked downhill into Momostenango, stopping again at the crossroads just south of the municipal building before arriving at the hermandad chapel at about 4:30. Firecrackers and a bomba marked the exit from the cofradía house and the arrival at the hermandad. A group of sixty or so men, women, and children, relatives of the dancers and cofrades, followed along behind. The procession itself is an important ritual symbol, but within the procession, in addition to the images, the silver pole-top emblems of the cofradías are powerful and sacred objects by virtue of their depictions of holy beings and by virtue of their having been used in cofradía rituals over many generations. Some of the emblems used today are new, though, and made of plastic or wood, since the original emblems were stolen from the church in the 1990s. A few, however, possibly including Santa Cruz (a silver crucified Christ), the nearly illegible, beaten-silver representation of San Francisco, and the silver sun disk of Santiago, are originals and are still highly venerated.

The procession from the cofradía house to the ermita arrived at about 5:00 p.m. in both 2007 and 2008. In both years the arrival was marked by Catholic prayers once the images had been placed on the altar table, and in both years the prayer was followed by individual petitioners passing in front

Figure 2.6 The procession turns the final corner before arriving at the hermandad chapel, 2006. Note the silver emblem of Santiago in the right foreground.

of the images and touching the towels and scarves that covered them with bundled offerings and sometimes dropping some coins in the basket on the altar table before making offerings of candles on the floor. There were, however, some major changes between 2007 and 2008. In 2007 there was no music at the chapel once the images were placed on the altar table; the prayer session, which involved reading and singing from a missal, lasted for only about ten minutes and was led by the diputado of the cofradía; and there was no food served. In 2008 a marimba player was hired to play for several hours both before and after the prayer session. The prayer session was a complete and very formal rosary that took well over an hour to complete and was led by an indigenous female lay leader hired from another town to provide the service. At about seven o'clock a meal of tamales and *cevada*, a sweet tea made by steeping roasted grains, was served to about one hundred people at the ermita. The entire floor was carpeted in pine needles in 2008, while it had been just bare concrete in 2007, and there were electric lights in 2008. A new sponsor had taken over this celebration, and the changes and their implications for Momostecan religious performance in the cult of Santiago will be addressed further as one of the case studies in chapter 5.

Some devotees offer new clothing or towels and scarves to the images at this event. The alcalde or diputado may place these offerings on the image. At midnight, completely hidden by a screen of Momostecan blankets, they undress the images and then reclothe them in new capes and in complete

Figure 2.7 In the hermandad chapel a family has waited in line and touched the images with their candle offering. Now they kneel before the altar to light the candles.

changes of clothes for Santiago if someone has donated a new suit. Individuals who wish to seek a special relationship with Santiago offer cloaks, towels, or boots, which may be worn during the fiesta. If private citizens have not come forward it is up to the cofradía to provide new feathers for Santiago's crown and a new cloak or brightly colored towels and scarves with which to drape the image. In 2007 a family that is known to the authors decided to give Santiago a new pair of boots. It was their hope that the boots could be part of his new outfit that he would wear after the vigil in the hermandad chapel on July 23. Since only the alcalde or the diputado may actually clothe or unclothe the image the plan had been cleared with them, and the offering was to be made at about 8:00 p.m.

Don Eligio and doña Catarina and their children arrived at the hermandad chapel at dusk. They waited their turn to pass before the images on the table to present their candles, which they gently touched to the images' clothing, prior to kneeling and lighting the candles on the floor in front of the altar table.

The candles are lighted with accompanying invocations. At this point an ordinary visit would end, but in this case the family awaited the return of the diputado, who had left on an errand. When he returned he knelt with the family before the image and after some invocations he presented the new boots, wrapped in a white cloth, to Santiago, then to each family member, touching the head and heart with the covered gift and then allowing it to be

Figure 2.8 A family that wishes to offer a pair of boots to Santiago kneels in prayer at the altar while the diputado (center) invokes the powers and requests acceptance of the gift on their behalf.

kissed. Finally, the boots were unwrapped and the diputado carefully removed the existing boots and placed the new ones on the image's feet. Since the ankles do not bend this is a difficult and delicado undertaking and again represents the real possibility that the boots will not fit and thus will be rejected by the image. Fortunately everything had been done correctly and the offering was accepted.

Each year in November the cofradía is responsible for transporting Santiago to the hamlet of Pueblo Viejo, an undertaking the authors have not witnessed. Two accounts were recorded from alcalde don Apolonio, one in

Figure 2.9 The family members in turn kiss the offering, still wrapped in a white cloth.

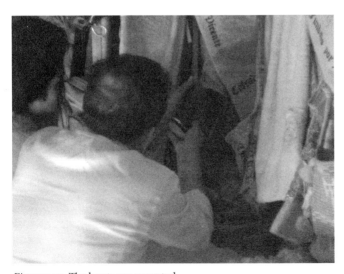

Figure 2.10 The boots are accepted.

2007 and another in 2008. The 2008 account was elicited because there were some areas of confusion for the authors as we sought to understand the details in the 2007 version. Here the 2007 account is provided, with clarifying remarks and expansions from 2008 following below.

> Yes, for example the ceremony on the road to Pueblo Viejo. It [the image of Santiago] goes in November and there is Ventana Mundo. First is Chiquicoch, it stopped there, but nowadays no because they no longer respect the costumbre there. Now it just passes through Chiquicoch, but we do make an offering. After Chiquicoch there is Ventana and then there is Chiquoch and now one sees Pueblo Viejo. After Chiquoch at the Sacramento [a spring or cistern] of Pueblo Viejo there is costumbre. After the image is brought to the church in Pueblo Viejo, after the costumbre in the afternoon at Pa Xoral Mundo, and Pa Ja' Mundo, Salpachán. In Salpachán there in Pueblo Viejo we make this costumbre. There is his water, Uja'l Sacramento, his water in Salpachán, and there throughout all the ceremonies, Herrera, Herrera, Herrera, Herrera, and all of those who have died, we call all their names for the dead that passed on, and that they come as their names are called there in the porobal.
>
> And from there in the morning the mass, the other day, the twenty-fifth or twenty-sixth of November, it is done. There is a procession with the image of Santa Catalina because according to the story there was a long time when he lived there, when with the *antepasados*, with Diego Vicente, the town of Momostenango had its center there. According to the story the Patrón Santiago and San Felipe had their little old house there [*casita viejita*], but they could not be found there because there was no costumbre there. They came to Momostenango because there was costumbre there, Vaqueros [a traditional dance], and I don't know what all else because it was long ago, but they came here to Momostenango.
>
> Those of Pueblo Viejo came to return him again but as he came back by himself it seemed he should stay in Momostenango and so they made his costumbre in Nimasabal, Alajsabal, Puja'lsabal, and he stayed here. And for the other saints as well, Santa Catarina and Santa Isabel and Santa Ana [patrons and namesakes of three of the four wards of Momos], for the women, so for them he stayed here in Momostenango. So he stayed here in Momos, not Pueblo Viejo, only Santa Catarina stayed there [early in the twentieth century the image of Santa Catarina was given to Pueblo Viejo, perhaps as compensation for losing Santiago]. And so for this reason the people of Pueblo Viejo

have fought to have the patrón [returned], but he stays here for the cos-tumbre. For the Maya altars in the mountains [*cerros*] he stays here: Masabal, Alajsabal, Ojerisabal, Pujerisabal, wajchob' Mundo, and all, truly. And Chic'oy Mundo [the altar used by the Monkeys Dance team] well, and all this with its meaning. And the heart of earth with its four cardinal points—Quilaja, Socop, Pipil, Tamancu, and Chumin [Cho u minas, to his mines, a fifth altar lying to the north northwest near Chiantla], this is also his place. These, then, well, thus is the story of the patrón, Santiago Apostól.

And the ancestors it is said, back then they used the costumes of Momos, with white pants, but not now because everything has changed a lot. So now in Momos they make his fiesta. The Vaqueros came, and Mexicanos, and K'akicoxol [the red-garbed diviner in the Conquest Dance] and the Spaniards played in the park here, and there by the Paclom they would fight. Lots of Vaqueros and Conquista, many dancers, like five or six groups of dancers in that time. But now just Mexicanos and the Monkeys every two years. The Conquista may begin again and I would help support it, but we do not know. [It did resume in 2008.] It is great this story of theirs [that of the founders, or primeros], well, and Diego Vicente and the ancestors burned and made costumbre.

In 2007, then, our understanding was that on the road from Momostenango to Pueblo Viejo there is a *mesa silla* altar in Chiquicoch that is an altar at which only priests of aj mesa rank may perform offerings, and then the altar at Ventana Mundo, and then in Pueblo Viejo proper there is a water of the image called Uja'l Sacramento, which is visited upon arrival. Then after the visit to the church in the afternoon there was another altar referred to as Pa Xoral Mundo. This would make two. Then there appeared to be an offering at Pa Ja' Mundo, another Uja'l Sacramento, this one in a place called Salpachán, where the Herrera dead, the founders of Pueblo Viejo and keepers of the image of Santiago in earlier times, are invoked. However, it also seemed pos-sible that there was an altar at Chiquich just prior to entering Pueblo Viejo and then visits to two additional altars, an *uja'l* or *sacramento* in Salpachán, which might be visited twice, and an altar, probably the ujuyubal called Pa Xoral Mundo. In the 1970s a cofrade had reported that the main altar for the Patrón in Pueblo Viejo was behind the church (Cook 2000:46), but it was not named in that account. It was not clear in 2007 which of the altars in don Apolonio's account is associated with the church. In 2008 don Apolonio responded to our confusion and questions with the following clarifications:

In August the Herreras [the dominant family in Pueblo Viejo] make a formal request for the visit of the Patrón at their festival of Santa Catarina, a festival to honor the deceased Herreras. As to the altars of Santiago, he has two "caves" on the Paclom hilltop, one is called Cruz Mesa and has its offerings on the day 13 Kan, and the other called San Simón Mesa Silla with its offerings on 13 Kiej. On the road to Pueblo Viejo the first stop is at Ventana Mundo, followed by Chicococh. Then in Pueblo Viejo there are two altars. Salpachán, also called Paxoral, is at a spring by the river. Water flows here on 13 Amak, and this spring is the "root" [raíz] of the spring of Santiago [Puja'l Santiago] at [the western base of] Paclom Hill in Momos. Santiago passed here in his spiritual [nawal] form and there is a hoofprint from his horse left in the stone. An Evangelical Herrera once tried to remove this stone and he was struck blind, so the hoofprint is still there.

The other altar in Pueblo Viejo is called Sacramento. It is behind the church there. This altar is for the nawales of the people, for Santa Catarina and for the Común Herrera [that is, all the deceased Herreras]. It is not used much but there is still a chuchkajaw [for the Herrera clan].

CHANGE AND CONTINUITY IN THE COFRADÍA: 1976–2010

The biggest changes in the cofradía of Santiago since the 1970s are in the model for funding and in its social organization, including the system for recruiting and overseeing the cofrades. In the 1970s the cofradía was staffed by an alcalde, a diputado, and four mortomas, as well as at least three women, a leader called nima chichu (first lady) and two chuchaxeles (lady helpers). This group bore the expenses of the cofradía part of the festival in July, the trips to San Vicente Buenabaj and to Pueblo Viejo in November, and the regularly recurring offerings year around, with the ultimate responsibility and largest share of the costs falling on the alcalde. In the 1970s new cofrades were appointed each year, except that prior to 1975, and following a pattern common to the cofradías of important and miraculous saints (Santiago, San Antonio, and the calvario complex of Cristos and Santa Cruz) the deputy often remained in office for many years and served as the expert on the tradition and on the offerings. At the end of each cofrades period of service his replacement provided him with a bottle of cane liquor and some cigarettes, in return for which the outgoing cofrade provided some instructions and advice and, in the case of the alcalde and diputado, a tour of the altars at which scheduled offerings needed to be made. The cofrades were appointed by the official indigenous auxiliary municipal government (auxiliatura), headed by the síndico segundo. Specific positions belonged to specific wards in town or to specific aldeas and were filled as they opened under the direct supervision of the principales, elders who had served within the auxiliatura and had retired from the position of alcalde.

Cofrades were appointed under legal authority vested in the municipal corporation, and those who refused to serve were jailed. This system was politicized by the 1970s, functioning then in a town that was polarized into a reform Catholic faction opposing much of what the cofradías stood for—that is, idolatry and offerings made at native altars—and a conservative faction that sought to maintain the syncretism as Momostecan tradition. Some aldeas that had been taken over by catechists and were increasingly dominated by Catholic Action principales sought freedom from obligations to participate in the system. Others were willing to participate but sought to use participation to eliminate paganism from the cult of the saints. Thus the ethnographic depiction was of a system under stress, which still had an official social structure from an earlier era but operated with highly politicized actors with opposed agendas. The shared authority structure of municipal government and Catholic Church was itself polarized. Pluralism has increased during the past thirty years, adding a massive contingent of Protestants to the religious factionalism in Momostenango and then also a small but potentially significant faction of cultural activists seeking to restore a purified Maya religion. These societal changes accompanied the evolution of the creaking and fatally stressed organization of 1976 into something very different.

Today the cofradía of Santiago is staffed by three officers and lacks a women's auxiliary. The cofrades are appointed to one-year terms by a group of Costumbrista elders, the members of several societies patterned after Ladino hermandades that exist to raise money by member contributions to pay for the bands that perform at the vigils and processions. These community leaders have replaced the principales in nominating and certifying cofrades. Oversight of the cofradías is still shared by church and municipality, though neither seems to have much interest in discharging this responsibility. The hermandades do offer significant funding aid, but the alcalde and diputado are still left with frightening financial obligations each year, and though they are free to resign from service each year, they realize that if they do so it may well be the end of the cofradía. In summary, the cofradías overall have been reduced in number from twenty-one to eight, the complement of officers in each has also been reduced substantially, they are no longer integrated into a bureaucratic structure, and the funding model has shifted dramatically.

The cofradía of Santiago has largely resisted what W. Smith (1977) calls truncation in that, although it is a smaller group of people, it has not reduced its sphere of operations appreciably. The current pattern of funding relies on Smith's strategies of "appending" and "administering" costs—that is, by seeking to spread the costs more widely via the several hermandades and by establishing them as permanent entities with ultimate responsibility to ensure funding. Nevertheless, the alcalde and diputado, as in the traditional system, still must make up for the difference between raised funds and actual costs. It is in this context of the need for innovative financial strategies that the new shrine for Maximón in the cofradía house is presented in chapter 5.

Since the cofradía members are no longer appointed annually, the changing ceremonies associated with the induction of *nuevos* no longer occurs regularly, and it is not clear what form it takes when and if it does occur. Thus the new year symbolism of the festival is less pronounced now than thirty years ago. Related to this, there is no longer an institutionalized exchange of information for liquor and tobacco nor a formalized showing of the altars to the nuevos by their outgoing counterparts.

The visit to San Vicente Buenabaj for the festival of Santa Isabel may be more contentious now than it was thirty years ago, since it appears that the Catholic Action takeover of San Vicente that had a good start there has now been consolidated. The walk from Momostenango to San Vicente would take most of a day, and with visits along the way it would stretch into several days, so the apparent takeover of this endeavor by a committee from San Vicente since 1976 might seem to represent a benefit to the cofrades. Still, the alcalde is loath to relinquish his authority and is especially incensed by the moves by the committee in San Vicente to change the clothes of the image without his involvement and without costumbre. Except for some contention related to one of the altars along the road, the visit to Pueblo Viejo for the festival of Santa Catarina seems to still follow the protocol that was in effect thirty years ago.

Processions are much as they were thirty years ago except for two important differences. The twenty-one cofradías of 1976 have been reduced to eight, and the reduction of the complement of cofrades in these remaining groups have dropped from four-to-six each to one to four today. A crowd of eighty men with twenty-one colonial period cofradía ensigns that used to accompany Santiago and San Felipe has now been reduced to a small group of twelve mostly elderly men, and since most of the silver emblems were stolen a few years ago, the impact, power, and perhaps legitimacy of the procession of cofrades has been diminished considerably. The current alcalde would like to reinstitute accompaniment by chuchaxeles and by children dressed in Momostecan *típica*. The accompaniment by children did not exist in the 1970s and may represent a complete innovation, though the alcalde sees it as a return to tradition. Similarly, the more prominent role played by women, who now take a turn as the bearers of the litter, and the opportunity for the alcalde's fiancé to dance with Santiago would appear to be novelties introduced by this alcalde, related no doubt to the need to enlist a wider community in support of the cofradía and the enhanced role of women as leaders in Maya cultural activism.

Finally, the nature of the ermita, or the house at which the all-night fiesta and vigil takes place, seems to have changed in several respects. In the first place, in the past the house was often a rented structure since alcaldes were frequently recruited from one of the aldeas and might not own a house in town, but more to the point, the house changed year by year as new alcaldes accepted their burdens. In the 1970s there was an all-night vigil at this house on July 23 followed by a ceremony inducting the new cofrades at church on the following morning. Today there are two festivals, one at the alcalde's house lasting through the night of July 22 and a second, corresponding to the original cofradía festival, on the following night at the former hermandad chapel.

While in the past an altar table at the cofradía house might have displayed relics and talismans belonging to the alcalde, especially if the fiesta was at his actual house, the idea that the house that received Santiago and San Felipe would be a wachibal, or private shrine for some other image, and that another image would be seated at the table in a custodial position, seems to be an innovation. This innovation is described in detail and analyzed in chapter 5, since it is a very interesting case of agency and of a strategy evolving to deal with the current economic context of the cult.

In 1976 the cofradía of Santiago operated within a highly bureaucratic organization, with oversight and recruitment of members vested in the auxiliatura, that part of the municipal government that embodied traditional authority, that is, principales serving as a board of directors or trustees, while most management functions were delegated to local aldea alcaldes and to the síndico segundo. But two bureaucracies—the municipal government and the local Catholic Church directorate—were in contention to control the images of the saints and the system and goals of collective worship. Two mass organizations, Costumbristas and Catechists, engaged in a polarized and polarizing contest to control the cult of Santiago. The cofradía might have been retained as a group of men charged with sponsoring the patron saint's festival and performing expensive calendrical ceremonies year-round, the traditional model. Or it might have become a group of men dedicated to organizing a mass to honor Saint James, eventually eliminating the calendrical costumbre and probably the cult of the little image on horseback and his sidekick San Felipe, since there is a separate, modern image of Santiago without the conquistador or *mata moros* attributes used by the reform Catholic community.

While it might be imagined that the Costumbristas would strongly support the traditional model, it must be recognized that in the earlier bureaucratic system most of the cofrades were appointed year by year and many resisted or resented the time constraints and costs of this service and feared the visibility and need to act publicly and the exposure to sometimes dangerous spirits (the nawales of images and the souls of the ancestors). So while elimination of the cofradías would weaken the collective expression of their faction's ideology, as individuals many would gain from dissolution of the cofradía system. And as about half the community was involved in Catholic Action in the mid-1970s, there was not monolithic opposition from Costumbristas to having their ideological enemies provide their fair share of the service in the cult.

Thus the strategy of Catholic Action in the late 1970s and on into the 1980s was to replace retiring cofrades with orthodox Catholics who would gradually let the costumbre go. This was facilitated also by the fact that Catholic Action made significant advances in many rural aldeas during the 1950s and 1960s, so that there were an increasing number of principales in Momostenango, men who had passed through service as alcaldes in the hamlets, who were not Costumbristas, and who would name Catholics to the positions. It was also the case that the relatively conservative Italian priest who headed the parish in the 1970s and on into the 1980s was strongly committed to theological reform and to battling paganism. This strategy might have effectively eliminated the cofradía of Santiago before 1990, but it was forestalled. One reason for the forestalling was a strategic response to the Catholic agenda on the part of a relatively small group of very motivated leaders of the traditionalist faction. The adult son of a retired sindico segundo from Barrio Santa Isabel reported it this way:

> About twenty-six to thirty years ago [that would mean between 1975 and 1979] there was a strategy of infiltration by Catholic Action. Then, during the violence when don Alfredo [pseudonym for an important Momostecan Ladino] was appointed to govern Momostenango as intendente, don Alfredo put an end to the appointing of cofrades by alcaldes in the hamlets. This meant that only volunteers staffed the cofradías, but a new priest further weakened them by taking all the alms given during the fiestas for the saints, and even donations given by families for private visits of the images of the saints to their houses. With no way to offset the expenses no one could afford to volunteer. So

in about 1979 my father and two other leaders from Barrio Santa Isabel, but from different families, decided to start an hermandad to celebrate the fiesta. The hermandad constructed a house for its vigil with the images of Santiago and San Felipe here in Santa Isabel, and each year it took the images in two processions around town on July 30 and 31, on the thirtieth in the principal streets and on the thirty-first from the calvario to the church.

This transculturation strategy (Cook and Offit 2008) then substituted a new religious organization inspired by Ladino hermandades for the cofradía as a way to ensure that all the processions and vigils with the little colonial images continued. It also provided a chuchkajaw to continue the offerings and invocations at the Patrón's altars that had been covered by the diputado in the cofradía in the 1970s. While on one hand this strategy represents a clear case of what Waldemar Smith labels the "administered" strategy for responding to economic problems in supporting the festivals of the saints, a strategy of creating a permanent fundraising body as in Ladino hermandades rather than nominating annual sponsors to bear most of the burdens as in the traditional system (Smith 1977:6), it also had the advantage for the Costumbristas of providing a body that insured the continuance of the costumbres in a venue outside of the direct authority of the parish priest.

A second factor also mitigated the effectiveness of the Catholic campaign against paganism. As explained in chapter 1, the Catholics were largely neutralized as political actors during the political violence of the 1980s, and social action in Momostenango ceased to have the form of a dualistic struggle between Costumbristas and Catholics. During the 1980s a third group, Evangelical Protestants and Pentecostals, emerged, which ended up representing 30–50 percent of the population in Momostenango, and a new movement of Maya pride and cultural activism, with religious dimensions, was added in the 1990s. Thus, by the year 2000 or so the rise of a movement of cultural activism and the changes in Guatemala's legal codes that protected the indigenous religion had given protection to the traditions of the cult of Santiago.

By the late 1990s, though, the hermandad for Santiago had lost its original leaders and had not been able to replace them. When the owner of the chapel house died it was donated to the Catholic Church in a bequest instigated by the parish priest and thus was lost as the center for Costumbrista action. At this time several Costumbrista hermandades de bandas arose to raise money for bands that perform during the fiesta, and they organized a new, private cofradía for Santiago that would insure the continuation of the costumbre.

Cofradía members are recruited by the hermandad rather than by the princi-pales, and its leaders lack the legal authority to compel participation. The cofradía now functions in a voluntaristic and privatized system rather than the official bureaucracy that organized the cofradías thirty years ago. The images and silver cofradía insignia are still the property of the church, so processions and vigils that require the presence of the images of Santiago and San Felipe still require permission from the parish priest. As a condition of this permission the priest still requires that all donations revert to the church. Nevertheless, with the last several priests supporting a moderate incultura-tion theology there is now a less-contentious relationship than there formerly was between Costumbristas and the Church. The new cultural activist group is developing its relationship with the traditionalists, a topic explored in the discussion of agency in Santiago's cult in chapter 5.

Santiago's cofradía in Momostenango, then, shows a system under con-tinuing stress but also suggests that there might be sufficient resources and motivations to keep a reduced complex of the cofradías of ongoing impor-tance to the traditionalists going indefinitely. The pattern in Momostenango of dropping in recent years to a core of about eight cofradías is replicated in Patzun and Tecpan (Fischer 2001) and perhaps throughout the highlands. This seems to represent a balance point in terms of what can be afforded and what is needed to perpetuate psychologically and culturally salient relation-ships between a traditional community and their truly important supernatu-ral allies: protectors of the community, fertility gods, owners of nature, and personifiers of maize and lords of the dead. The charter, the ritual, and the sacra have not changed appreciably in thirty years. The mode of organization and the system of funding have changed. Both reflect increasing voluntarism and privatization as bureaucracy and traditional authority have collapsed.

An exploration of agency via a case study in chapter 5 will focus on strate-gies and experiments that are emerging in response to these problematic areas. First, though, we consider the Monkeys Dance (chapter 3), in which organizational matters are pretty constant so far but there have been substan-tial changes in performance, and the disfraces, where we can observe the birth of a new cultural performance that helps to define the issues and com-plexities of seeking to understand Maya tradition in a very pluralized, new kind of village, with indigenous actors seeking simultaneously to retain tra-ditions and to stake a claim to a Maya modernity.

CHAPTER THREE

The Monkeys Dance

Adjusting the Performance

THE FIELDWORK

A description and interpretation of the mid-twentieth-century Monkeys Dance was a key ingredient in Cook's analysis of *axis mundi* symbolism and myths of regeneration within twentieth-century Momostecan culture (Cook 2000:107–18). That account was based entirely on interviews, as the Monkeys Dance was not performed during Cook's residency in Momostenango in 1975 and 1976. The opportunity to observe and document the dance with photos and video in 2006, and to do so with the help and literal blessing of don Pedro, the autor and chuchkajaw of the dance, a son of the 1970s-period dance sponsor who had been Cook's source on the dance, was a timely and much-anticipated culmination of delayed ethnographic gratification. The new work on the Monkeys Dance in 2006 through 2009 has largely confirmed the description from the 1970s but has added considerable richness to the information, including extensive photographic and video documentation, some of which has been presented on the Foundation for the Advancement of Mesoamerican Studies (FAMSI) website.[1]

Cook and Offit participated in offerings and ritual prior to the dance as minor sponsors in 2006 and had many conversations and formal interviews with dancers and dance sponsors in 2006 and 2007. Following the murder of don Pedro in October 2007 we participated by invitation in the practice pole felling and raising at the new sponsor's house in February 2008. Cook returned to Momostenango to observe the dance a second time, including the felling of the dance pole and the closing ceremony at Santiago's well in July 2008. The dance has accommodated to changing circumstances over the past thirty years. The team responded successfully to a series of crises in 2007 and 2008, surmounting what seemed like daunting challenges following don Pedro's murder, a case study revealing how culture and agency interact within Momostecan tradition and expressive culture that is explored in chapter 5.

Older dance sponsors report that Ixbatz ancestors first brought the Monkeys Dance to Jutacaj in Aldea Xequemeya, the staging ground for the dance performed in Momostenango. There are differences of opinion about whether it was Jose Ixbatz—who first emigrated to Rakana in Jutacaj from Pasuk, Los Cipreses—or the brothers Eugenio and Diego Ixbatz who actually introduced the dance and the marimba that accompanies it. In the second or third generation from the start of the dance, Bartolo Ixbatz served as autor (sponsor) and chuchkajaw (diviner/priest) for the dance and also played the marimba. The dance remained in Jutacaj for a time, with Samuel Ixcoy serving as autor after don Bartolo. Sometime around 1960 Agostino Raxc'oy became autor and chuchkajaw and the dance rehearsals were then moved to Xequemeya center, but the marimba remained in the Ixbatz family and was played by don Venancio, the current marimbista, who has held this position for over fifty years. Sponsorship of the dance was passed from Celestino Raxc'oy to his son Pedro between 1982 and 1984, and don Pedro remained as autor and also served as chuchkajaw, except for one year when he was suffering from a serious illness, through the performance of 2006. Following the tragic murder of don Pedro in October 2007 the sponsorship of the dance and the role of chuchkajaw returned to the Ixbatzes, with Mauricio Ixbatz serving as autor and Anselmo Ixbatz returning to the role of chuchkajaw, a role he had taken briefly during don Pedro's illness. If each autor served for about twenty years, this suggests that the dance came to the aldea of Xequemeya in about 1908 and that it might have come with Ixbatzes from Los Cipreses, so it may have been performed elsewhere in Momostenango from an earlier period. The dance combines the Deer Dance, which is well known and performed in many highland towns (Paret-Limardo, 1963; Mace 1970; Cook 2000:110–12; Hutcheson 2003:366–498), with the tightrope performances of animal impersonators—a jaguar (*tigre* or *balam*), a mountain lion (*león* or *coj*), and two monkeys (*mono*, or *c'oy* in K'iche', literally spider monkeys).

In 2005 autor Pedro Raxc'oy agreed to permit Cook and Offit to document the dance within its religious context by serving as minor sponsors or collaborators in producing the dance. He noted that several other foreigners had completed studies in recent years, but the dancers had not benefited. We agreed to participate honorably and to complete our part of the agreement, making the religious offerings and providing the financial help expected of a sponsor of the dance and later providing the dancers with copies of the videos. Under this arrangement we both participated actively in the costumbre and made a video in 2006. We returned with copies of the video for the dancers in 2007. At the invitation of the dancers we also returned after don Pedro's death in October 2007 and participated in the raising of the practice pole at don Mauricio's (the new sponsor's) house in February 2008, where we learned that a copy of our video had been broadcast in Guatemala on channel 4 and that subsequently copies of the video have been available for sale in Momostenango. We had failed to think about the implications of distributing the video as we did, and though the dance team seems to understand that this was not our intention and has forgiven us for our naïveté, we regret the fact that profits from sale of the video are not compensating the dancers or helping to support the dance.

We again participated as collaborators, covering some of the costs for the marimba and some of the food costs of the dancers during the two weeks of the performance, in 2008 and continue to do so through the present day. Here we describe what we have learned through the generous cooperation of the team of dancers and the elders who sponsor the dance, perform its rituals, and seek to keep its tradition, so that a broader community can appreciate its cultural context and religious meaning.

The dance may persist with new meanings as new generations of performers and ritualists seek to retain the tradition of its outward forms, motivated by civic or ethnic pride but with new and more variable religious or spiritual perspectives. The dance is adapting as material conditions lead even those who are dedicated to the meanings explicated decades ago to accept some changes for economic and technical reasons. Thus some observations about changes since the 1970s are included in the following description of the dance as we encountered it in 2006–2008.

THE DANCE TEAM

This dance is not for the fainthearted nor for those who are not committed to the endeavor, or as Momostecans put it, "of one heart." The dangerous tests (*pruebas*) on the rope, sixty feet in the air above the plaza, are accomplished only by those with strong faith and a need to experience and repeatedly confirm personal power derived from direct contact with the supernatural. This is as true today as it was thirty years ago, though many dancers today add their attachment to Momostecan tradition as a reason for dancing, a reason that would not have been cited in these terms in the 1970s, a time when for most Momostecans the local tradition was simply their way of life and not one among many. The reason to dance then was to please Patrón Santiago, thus acquiring his protection, and similarly to please the dead. This is still true.

The team was and is a typical Native American medicine society, the performance complete with clowning, physical ordeals, and the search for personal power conferred by spirits, to which young men are called by sickness, by dreams, and by a desire for excitement and supernatural protection as well as by family connections and social pressure.[2] The dancers are initiands of different grades according to their ranks, and the chuchkajaw is their master.

The team ideally is composed of nine members represented by the nine sherds, or *tejas*, on which copal and candles are burned in ceremonies of cutting and erecting the pole and during the dances and practices. There are two tigres, two leónes, and four monkeys, divided into first and second teams with half performing on any given day, and a spiritual guide and protector, the chuchkajaw of the dance, a priest shaman of aj mesa rank, a rank that is necessary since the offerings are made at powerful and exclusive mesa altars. In 2006 the chuchkajaw, don Pedro, was also the principal sponsor (autor or *autor primero*), while in 2008 these roles were separated. The chuchkajaw must be able to hear the animal spirits calling inside the earth at C'oy Abaj (Spider Monkey Stone) to perform his duties. A little león, a little tigre, and little monkeys—young boys, usually the sons of dancers—also participate in costumed clowning on the dance ground, but they are not involved in the ordeals or rituals. They are likely recruits as monkeys when they reach the age of sixteen.

Ideally, sponsors and dancers promise a novena, nine performances, with the dance performed every other year, a commitment to a minimum of sixteen years of service, moving from entry as a monkey through service as a león and tigre. But some dancers do not promise or do not complete the novena, and each potential dancer decides in any given performance year whether or not to dance that year according to his financial standing, health, and dreams as well as social pressures. The youngest dancer was sixteen and the oldest thirty-two in 2006. Most men in their twenties and thirties now work outside of Momostenango and lack the time to participate in all of the preparatory ceremonies and practice sessions.

A commitment to bring out the dance in the following year is made before the patron saint in November by the dance sponsors; once made the commitment is not lightly broken as Santiago is demanding and dangerous (delicado). To field a team in a given year the first autor needs to recruit in August at the end of a nondancing fiesta in order to have the new team organized and promised by November. Recruitment is based on trust in the power of the dance priest (chuchkajaw) and on family connections and enculturation; thus most dancers come from the adjoining hamlets of Xequemeya and Jutacaj and have had fathers, uncles, and brothers who have danced. For example, don Pedro, the first autor in 2006, who also served as the chuchkajaw, was himself a dancer for many years. His father was first autor and dance priest in the 1970s. Don Pedro's eldest son is experiencing social pressure to take on sponsorship within the next few years, and one of Pedro's grown sons, about seventeen years of age, danced as a monkey in 2006 while his youngest son danced as a little león. After don Pedro's tragic death an older son danced as one of the leónes in 2008.

Production and Performance

Because of the need to practice for two days each month from January through July, in addition to the thirty-six-plus days of costumbre, many of which involve trips to altars on distant mountains and require revolving in-turn dancer participation, only those with flexible time can serve as dancers. Dancing worked well in a community of farmers and weavers who controlled their time and stayed in Momostenango. It does not fit long periods of work in the capital or even in the United States. The *marimbista* cannot recruit and train a replacement, so there is a good chance that the dance music will die with him. The recording of the dance music made with FAMSI support in 2007 may turn out to be useful for performers in the future, but the electroni-cally amplified bands playing adjacent to the dance ground make the marimba inaudible during most of the actual performances anyway.

The Monkeys Dance is a "dance" within a dance, a collection of pranks and clowning skits on the ground and dangerous acrobatic tricks on a rope suspended above the dance ground, performed by a tigre, a león, and two monkeys on any given day, in the midst of what would otherwise be a typical highland Maya Deer Dance.[3] The Deer Dance and Monkeys Dance compo-nents, though part of a single dance in Momostecan worldview, are separated here. Only the tigres, leónes, and monkeys participate directly in the costum-bre at the mountain altars, only they select and cut the dance pole and per-form its ceremonies, and only they are full-fledged participants in a medicine society and its ordeals. The public performances occur over a two-week period, from July 21 through August 4 of alternate years, and include four ele-ments performed in order: the entry, the erection of the dance pole, the dance itself, and the taking down of the pole and closing ceremonies. However, this performance is embedded in nine months of offerings and ceremonies and follows six months of monthly rehearsals. Even during the public dancing phase there are dawn ceremonies and a private performance at the cofradía house. The following description of the performance in 2006 is based on participant observation between July 18 and August 2. The principal ritual symbols (Turner 1977) are here described and interpreted through native exegesis and cultural context based on the authors' knowledge.

Announcing the Dance

The dance sponsor visited the image of Santiago in church, as prescribed by custom, on November 2, 2005, to announce his intention to dance the following July. This began the nine-month period of costumbre, which continues until the dancing is finished and the dancers' potsherds have been delivered to the altar called the Water of Santiago (Puja'l Santiago, or Sacramento) on the west side of the Paclom on August 4 of the following year. This periodicity employs the K'iche' model for religious initiation, as in the nine-month apprenticeship from one 8 Batz ceremony to the next and in delivery of a sherd to the initiating altar when a new diviner is received by the altar.

Erecting the Practice Pole

On January 22, 2005, the dance team cut down a fifty-foot-tall pine tree in the hamlet of Xequemeya and then erected it at the sponsor's house. A specific version of this event that occurred in nearby Jutacaj in 2008, but with a number of atypical wrinkles, is presented in chapter 5. When the practice pole is erected at the sponsor's house each dancer is given, by the dance autor, the large ceramic sherd on which he will make offerings related to erecting the practice pole on several occasions—at all rehearsals and then later when felling and erecting the dance pole in the plaza and while dancing. The practice pole is used for rehearsals once each month from January through June and then for a final, two-day dress rehearsal in July. It is then felled and chopped into pieces, which are used as wedges or shims when the dance pole is erected in front of the church.

Visiting External Mundos and Saints

Between the announcement of the dance in November of the preceding year and the visit to the six altars (referred to as *mundos*, or holy worlds) within Momostenango that occurs by custom on July 18, and occurred on that date in 2006, to clear the road before the last two rehearsals and the formal entry of the dancers into town, dancers and their chuchkajaw visit mountain altars and miraculous saints that define a traditional K'iche' cosmogram centered on Momostenango. These visits are pilgrimages for the dancers and require expensive offerings that must be carried to the offering sites during long and physically difficult journeys. The visits define a topography of powers external to Momostenango, including distant mundos and miraculous saints, and also define the borders of the sacred topography of Momostenango by visiting the four cardinal points. The mundos visited on July 18 then continue this process that was started outside and involve the penetration of Momostenango by the team of pilgrims whose personal powers have been awakened and fortified by the visits to the external power centers. The purpose of this costumbre is to defend the dancers. The ceremonies occur according to a complex schedule that links two sets of *visitas*, a Maya calendar set and a Christian calendar set.

Maya Calendar Set

Don Pedro reported that visits to the mountains are always scheduled on good days in the Maya calendar, according to signs read by the chuchkajaw of the dance, and take place on days numbered one (*ujunubal*) and eight

PLACE	DANCER
Quilaja	Tigre (The two jaguars)
Tamangu	León (The two lions)
Socop	Primero Mono* (Two first monkeys)
Pipil	Segundo Mono* (The second monkeys)
Minas	All Dancers
Volcán de Santa María	All Dancers

Offerings are made at each visit by dance sponsors (autors) and dancers. The following list would be required for a dance sponsor. A dancer would do this much in some cases where an unusual need for protection or atonement exists, but would ordinarily offer less.

OFFERINGS: 18 doz *copales*, 200 wax candles of the size sold at 5Q per bunch, 300 tallow candles, 2 lbs sugar, 2 lbs chocolate, 2 bunches *ocote* (resin soaked pine splint fire starters), ½ lb. incense, ½ lb. *ajonjolín* (sesame seeds), 100 colored candles, and 13 candles de 50.

CHRISTIAN CALENDAR SET

On specific dates in the Christian calendar visits are made to miraculous images by all the dancers.

1/15	**Esquipulas**: Visit Cristo (the black Christ), the cave, Cruz Milagro (the miraculous cross) and Compadre Abaj (A chuch qajaw turned to stone for having sex with his comadre)
2/28	**Chiantla (María Candelaria)**: Visit the Virgin in the church and the altar called Minas Porobal (Mine Burning Place).
1st Fri lent	**Ayutla (Tres Caidos)**: Candles in church, there is no porobal.
2nd Fri lent	**Chajul (another Virgin Candelaria)**: Visit Andrés (mesa y silla) and Oxlajuj cruz (13 cross) de Jesus Nazareno.

Figure 3.1 Typical itinerary, offerings, and dates for costumbre.

(*wajxaquibal*). The mountains are visited in the following order, and for each visit there is mandatory participation for specific dancers. The first four are the mountains at the cardinal points that figure in the Momostecan yearbearer cult, visited in the sequence east (Quilaja), south (Tamancu), west (Socop), and north (Pipil). Minas is a cave near Huehuetenango and Santa María is the huge volcano that guards the pass to the coast south of Quetzaltenango.

Visiting the Local Mundos: July 18, 2006

On the Road

On July 18, 2006, the chuchkajaw, the two tigres and two leónes, and three of the four monkeys, accompanied by two anthropologists who were being inducted as dance sponsors, left the plaza in Momostenango at about 4:00 a.m. in a light drizzle to make prescribed offerings at six a mundos for protection of the dancers and sponsors. The four mountain altars—Puerto Joyam (the door Joyam), Pa Sanyep' (at the sand), K'ak' Ja (red house), and Pa Xetun (at under the drum, or at under the maguey)—paralleled the current road on its east side, running north from the high ridge (*cumbre*) between Momostenango and San Francisco El Alto down into town. We then visited the cemetery east of the town center and finished at the Spider Monkey Rock (C'oy Abaj), an altar located in a fissure in a cliff face above the baths northeast of the town center on the road to Xequemeya.

The drive to Puerto Joyam, on a steep mountain road with lots of switch-backs, took place in heavy fog in the darkness well before dawn, in a pickup with one headlight and a worn-out windshield wiper. To the anthropological observer seated in the pickup cab and the white-knuckled driver with his face pressed to the windshield, this clearly marked the journey as the dangerous-passage phase of an ordeal. We arrived at Puerto Joyam, elevation about nine thousand feet, with about an hour to go before sunrise in a moderate wind and very cold rain. Traveling from altar to altar is itself, then, a meaningful unit within the ritual structure, that is, a ritual symbol in its own right, as part of an initiatory ordeal involving physical danger, privation, and exhaustion.

Sweeping the Altar

Every altar is always swept before lighting a fire, which provides one of the terms used for an altar, a *mesabal*, or swept place. The sweeping purifies the altar, removing any vestiges of the offerings or attached sentiments, requests, or complaints from the ceremonies of previous users of the altar. In the case of Puerto Joyam in 2006 the sweeping was accomplished by breaking off leafy branches from bushes near the altar and sweeping briskly in the light of a flashlight and in a cold and steady rain. Invocations do not begin until the altar has been properly swept.

Blessing the Costumes

Costumes are usually rented from San Cristobal Totonicapan, though a few are now available for rent through the agency INTERVIDA at the municipal offices in Momostenango. The masks (and the crowns worn by leónes and tigres) are venerated and are thought to have powers because they have been worn by other dancers and have been blessed at shrines over some time. When the altar has been cleaned the masks are set atop the bundled costumes and placed on the rocks and potsherds that constitute the altar or on the ground flanking the altar and its fire. Two tigre, two león, and two monkey masks are honored, sometimes with the tigres together on one side and the leónes on the other and sometimes with a león and tigre together on each side. Always there is a monkey on each side and always the masks are in rank order and symmetrically arranged, establishing two teams of masks, as there are two teams of dancers.

Invocations

As soon as the masks have been placed the chuchkajaw begins invocations in K'iche', occasionally interrupted by Catholic chants and songs, which continue throughout the ceremony. In 2006 the invocations, which are invitations to the named powers to come and be present at the ceremony to

Figure 3.2 Dance team with masks and crowns on costume bundles at Pa Sanyep'.

accept the offerings, began in the rain and dark well before sunrise. God, Jesus, Mary, Santiago, San Felipe, and the angels San Gabriel and San Rafael were called, then mountains (or their altars), called *mundos*, each addressed as table and chair (*mesa* and *silla*). Then the sequence was repeated but with a sense of urgency. "Placement at the feet of the powers comes now, the mercy comes now, the word comes now, the speech comes now, right now the day, right now the hour, right now the day." This invocation continued for several more minutes, during which time the fire was being laid. The powers were all called again and then, following a formulaic invitation to the day and the hour, emphasis shifted to ancestral figures, the *nantat*, called with increasing urgency as three little crosses of resin-soaked pine (*ocote*) were laid in a circle of sugar on three crosses drawn with sugar in the fireplace. This culminated in a dramatic moment just before the fire was lit with the invocation of the deceased father of the chuchkajaw, Celestino Raxc'oy Vicente, the man who served, until his death, as the preceding chuchkajaw and first autor of the dance.

The Fire

Still in the darkness of the end of night the fire was started at Puerto Joyam when the chuchkajaw lit a single bunch of candles lying amid the three sugar and ocote crosses arrayed within a circle of sugar in the fireplace. Then copal was fed into the small fire, marked by another invocation of the day and the hour, followed by our mother/father (*ka nantat*)—that is, the ancestors—and the mundo. During the first few moments of the new fire the theme of ancestors was continued. Then the chuchkajaw offered copal, their sacrifice (*tojba'l*) to the souls of the deceased members of the named patrilineages of dancers (as in *que tojba'l común Barrera*). The chuchkajaw asked for health for the dancers and rest for the deceased ancestors and continued to invoke ancestral and familial powers. Then rattling was heard in the darkness as several dancers prepared to sweep a trail around the perimeter of the altar. Fire is the central ritual symbol in the traditional religion, which the Momostecans call burning (*poronel*) when speaking K'iche'. It is the only way to call the powers, since the invocations are invitations to a feast and the fire provides sustenance, consuming wax candles and incense for the saints and angels; copal, candy, and liquor for the mundos; and tallow candles for the dead. Beyond this, though, it is a medium of communication.

Periodically during the invocations specific requests for protection, health, rest, or a clear road are made. And there are also crucial transition points, especially at the end of an individual's blessing at the fire. If the fire burns brightly and consumes the offerings, and especially if the flames grow suddenly and swirl clockwise, this is a sign that the offering is acceptable and all is well. If the fire smokes or sputters and dies down even when it is stirred, this is a sign that there is a problem with the offering or the requests or with the preparation of the client. In the case of the first offering made for Cook at Puerto Joyam, the fire nearly died when damp rosemary sprigs used for purification were tossed in and would not revive after stirring. This prompted the chuchkajaw to demand to know the cause of the problem, but none was obvious. When Offit's ceremony began the fire flared up and burned with cheerful crackling. Don Pedro's response was that we would try again at Pa Sanyep'. Had that fire failed to accept the offering it seems that some major penance and additional costumbre would have been needed, or perhaps the project would have collapsed at that point. Fortunately the problem did not recur.

Sweeping the Trail and Activating the Masks

At Joyam the final events before sunrise were the sweeping of a circular trail around the central ritual precinct and the donning of masks by the dancers. The latter was not done in any structured way and seemed to be entirely according to the volition of the individuals involved. In the liminal period between darkness and dawn the newly blessed and activated masks were donned, and dancers entered into the character of the beings they would embody in the dance. Tentatively at first and then with more confidence and authority, they became monkeys, though only briefly. While it is not possible to know what the dancers were feeling, they report that if the ceremonies are

Figure 3.3 An early phase of the fire at Pa Sanyep'. Offerings at this point include sugar, three ocote crosses, dozens of copal nodules, chocolate wafers, grains of incense, and a single bunch of tallow candles, the tallow indicating that this is the phase of the offering destined for the souls of the dead.

Figure 3.4 At C'oy Abaj a dancer feels the power of the león.

working they feel the strength or force of the animals when they wear the masks. This is a sign for them and for the chuchkajaw that the invocations and offerings and all the costumbre of the dance over the past eight months leading up to this moment have been effective. At Puerto Joyam as the sweeping of the trail concluded it was time to begin blessing the dancers. The sky was pearl gray and the mist-softened pine forest was visible in cold gray light.

The Circle Run and the Blessing of the Dancers

The dancers were called by the chuchkajaw to be blessed, in rank order, starting with the first tigre. Each dancer brought a single bunch of wax candles and a packet of one dozen copal nodules. The dancer is a penitent asking forgiveness and acceptance, and he kneels. The candles were placed on each dancer's heard while the chuchkajaw prayed for his safety. Then the dancer kissed the candles three times and the chuchkajaw fed them into the fire. The dancer opened his dozen packets of copal one at a time, handing each to the chuchkajaw, who fed the nodules into the fire. The chuchkajaw kept up a continuous invocation of saints, angels, mundos, and the dead during the entire proceeding, requesting health and protection for the dancer and his family and rest for his deceased relatives. When the offerings were completed the dancer crossed himself and leaned over to kiss the earth. Then the participating sponsors, the two anthropologists, were blessed, following the same pattern but with many more offerings, as noted in the list at the beginning of this account. Then the dancers were called back in rank order for purification. Each penitent knelt again and the chuchkajaw sprinkled scented water on a foot-long sprig of rosemary and gently whipped and then brushed each dancer, beginning with the body, then doing the arms, and ending with the legs, brushing away from the body toward the extremities with a motion like that of an agent with a security wand in an airport. The chuchkajaw also cleansed himself in this way at Pa Sanyep' before cleansing the dancers.

During this phase, while each dancer was making his individual offerings, the team, arrayed in rank order, ran around the altar, circling the penitent and his priest nine times in a counterclockwise direction and then nine times clockwise. Sometimes they sprinted and sometimes they jogged, with the pace set by the highest-ranking dancer in the group. Occasionally they raced and the order of the running was lost for a while. Two had rattles and two had short, braided leather quirts, and so there was a constant rattling and snapping, and the runners also whistled loudly while running. If someone falls it is considered a bad sign, a sign that they have not completed their individual vows to remain sexually pure or that they have reservations and are of two hearts. The second monkey, the youngest in the group, fell several times. This resulted in some bantering and good-natured light whipping with the quirts and did not really seem to be taken very seriously by anyone. These were high-spirited teenage boys and young men, and whenever possible they had fun. There was constant joking and teasing within the group.

Later don Pedro addressed our questions about the running and whistling with the following remarks:

Question: In the photo at Pa Sanyep' they are running around in a circle. What does this mean?

Figure 3.5 At Pa Sanyep', while the first tigre, kneeling, interrupts his blessing to answer his cell phone, the dancers, led by the second tigre, begin the second phase of the run, nine clockwise circuits.

This means that they are being overcome by the nawales of the animals. For this they run, to give strength to their feet, because it is thus Whiiihihihi. . . . And to see one that falls, he needs a whipping because it will be like this whenever [i.e., to fall here means also to fall from the rope]. Here one sees when there is failure, one falls there and the failure [will be] sustained. If not [i.e., to prevent this], then we go to arrange the road, yes, then for this it is a sign.

Question: And when they whistle—is this the sound of a hawk? [In the cemetery a hawk had flown over the dancers and given a piercing whistle. They had all responded in kind and became quite excited by the sign.]

The situation is that for them, it is a feeling like being an animal. . . . This is invisible. Invisible as they are, it is felt by them, though invisible it is real. They have no fear. This is why we put it [the offerings and invocations], we send it to you, and I know it has no worth if you are not protected.

The Farewell

All of the ceremonies except for the visit to C'oy Abaj ended similarly. The group knelt in a semicircle with the chuchkajaw either in the center facing the altar or anchoring the left wing so that the group was arrayed in rank order to his right. The closing involved singing of Catholic litanies in Spanish and asking for forgiveness. The second tigre, who served as the cantor or reader (aj bi'x), sometimes read an accompanying text from the missal while the chuchkajaw invoked the powers. The dying fire was stirred several times with a stick to be sure that the entire offering was consumed. At the end of the offerings at each altar, except for C'oy Abaj, where it was physically impossible, all the participants crossed themselves three times and bent over as a group to kiss the earth.

Invoking the Dead at the Cemetery

The ceremony at the cemetery, like that at C'oy Abaj, was unique in some respects. It was restricted to an opening ceremony in which the fire was started with invocations, a collective offering, and a closing. It lasted for only fifteen minutes. The team had planned to make the offering on the steps in front of the calvario, but a new sign had been posted there forbidding burning. The calvario, a whitewashed chapel where Costumbristas visit the souls of their deceased family members, is the home of the image of the entombed Christ (called Corpus), which is understood by traditionalists to be the lord of the dead. It is where the souls of the dead are propitiated on the Day of the Dead and on days Aj Pu (Cook 2000:159–67). The chuchkajaw led the group to the ossuary near the middle of the cemetery, a small building with a domed roof and a single, high window. Whenever bones are removed from a tomb to allow for a new burial or are encountered while digging a grave or maintaining the cemetery, they are placed within this structure through the window. It is a good place to encounter and propitiate the common souls of the dead and can stand in for the calvario, which has this same function.

Calling the Animal Spirits at C'oy Abaj

A fissure with a ledge below it on a cliff face at least one hundred feet above the baths, which are located in a deep and wide ravine southeast of the town center, is the location of an altar that belongs exclusively to the dance team. A dancer once fasted, prayed, and cried at this altar and slept there for the forty nights of costumbre. An earth spirit invited him into the cave hidden within the cliff and provided him with a wonderful, old-fashioned dance costume. There are reports that monkeys are seen here in the years when the dance is to be brought out. There is only a narrow ledge in front of the altar, and it is just possible for the entire team to fit on the ledge. Here a collective offering is made, and the chuchkajaw calls on the mundo to release the animals so that the dancers will have their courage and skill when performing on the rope. As at other altars, some of the dancers here wear the masks and crowns for brief periods of time, and some may feel the courage of the animals. In 2006 the first león, greatly encouraged by the costumbre, climbed onto a little promontory of stone above the dance team, where he whistled and made the hand-blowing and expansive arm gestures indicating the presence of the

Figure 3.6 The team flanks the chuchkajaw on the burning ground in front of the ossuary.

fearlessness that comes with the power of the animals. The ceremony at C'oy Abaj is followed by the *cruzada* at the autor's house at midnight, a final consecration of the masks and the practice dance pole before the first dress rehearsals take place the following afternoon.

Rehearsal at the Autor's House, July 19 and 20, 2006

Invocations and Offerings at the Dance Pole

The dance pole was cut and erected at the sponsor's house on January 22, 2005, and the first practice session was then held there, with another each month through June. The seventh and eighth rehearsals are the only dress rehearsals and were held, as is customary, on July 19 and 20, with one of the two teams practicing each day. After lunch the costumed dancers from team one of the Deer Dance and the Monkeys Dance began clowning around on the practice dance ground. While this was happening the marimba was set up and tuned while members of the other team fastened the dance rope to the top of the pole and tied a guyline from the pole to a tree in the opposite direction from the dance rope in order to steady the pole and be sure that the dance rope could be pulled tight. A slack rope swings too much, making it dangerous and very hard to do the tricks. The nine tejas representing the chuchkajaw and the dancers had been placed in a line from the base of the pole to the

Figure 3.7 The dance team on the ledge at C'oy Abaj. Though it is not clear in this picture, the ledge drops vertically to a streambed in the bottom of a ravine, about one hundred feet below.

anchor during the cruzada the night before, and candles and copal were placed in each and burned to consecrate the dance ground. Now the tejas were moved and arranged in a circle around the base of the dance pole. The chuchkajaw and his assistant lit offerings on the tejas, and the chuchkajaw invoked the powers and asked for the safety of the dancers. Following the invocation the chuchkajaw danced briefly in front of the marimba and at the base of the pole, carrying a smoking censer.

This is a time of light-hearted clowning by the costumed dancers with a small audience of their relatives and neighbors of the dance sponsor. The Deer Dance couple, Pedro and Catalina, and the dancers called *segales*, representing Spaniards, chased the monkeys, león, and tigre, trying to whip them and shooting them with their wooden pistols. The Monkeys Dance animals wrestled each other, tried to abduct Catalina, and captured eight- or ten-year-old boys from among the spectators, wrestling them to the ground and piling on them, "licking" their faces, and tying their shoelaces together. Some dancers were hung-over on the first day from the cruzada of the night before, the chuchkajaw was noticeably drunk, and the second tigre, who did not have to dance on this first day, was sleeping on the floor in front of the house altar, where he had passed out.

Stretching the Rope

When the blessing of the pole was finished the team stretched the rope as tightly as they could by heaving on the end of it while a couple of team members wrapped it around the anchor stake and cinched it there between heaves. When it was as tight as they could make it, it was tied off. During the rehearsal on July 19 the guyline broke during the stretching of the rope and there was no good way to repair it, so the rehearsal continued with a wobbly pole and slack rope. The performing dancers later complained, and the chuchkajaw was blamed for not having performed an adequate ceremony. On the second day, with a new guyline, the pole and rope were tight and confidence in the chuchkajaw was restored.

Ascending the Pole

The tigre performed first, followed by the león and then the two monkeys, the male monkey with two back flaps hanging from his belt going first, followed by the female monkey with a single flap. Each dancer in turn climbed the pole after the preceding dancer had finished his performance. The pole was about fifteen meters tall and had a sequence of short wooden ladders lashed to it so it could be climbed. The practice pole always has a fork at the top that can be used to guide a rope so that a team on the ground can raise the ladders in order for lashing. The ascent took each performer several minutes, for visibility is very poor through the mask, basically allowing only one eye to see out at any given time, and the dancer periodically feels the force or power of the animal and gestures, rattles, and whistles while climbing.

The Pole-Top Signs

When a performer reaches the pole top he demonstrates the fearlessness of the animal he is portraying. Minimally this means that he will show signs like whistling and arm extension gestures when he reaches the top, or he will rest his abdomen on the pole top and spread his arms and legs so that he is balanced on a point about the size of a teacup fifty feet in the air. Those who have really acquired the power of the animals may kick their legs and wave their arms or do the whistling, rattling, and arm extension gestures while balanced on the pole top. They may also shake the pole violently, demonstrating courage and animal impetuosity.

Figure 3.8 A tigre and a león feel the force of the animals and respond with arm gestures, rattling, and whistling.

Figure 3.9 A león balances on the pole top, rattles, and whistles.

The Tests on the Rope

After performing on the pole top the dancer transitions to the rope. This appears to be one of the more dangerous times, and most dancers seem to move slowly and with considerable care, though some performers will shake the rope during the transition, especially if it seems to be slack. This demonstrates their strength and courage and shows the other dancers and the chuchkajaw, who is straddling the rope where it is anchored on the ground, that the rope is loose. If the rope is loose enough a violent shaking or swinging of the rope at the pole top can nearly topple the chuchkajaw, who is quite likely somewhat inebriated and will fall easily.

The tests on the rope usually begin with some leg-hooked spins (*vueltas*), first in one direction and then in the other. After sliding down the rope for ten or twenty feet the performer hangs upside down by his legs while swinging his torso, sometimes violently. Regaining his position atop the rope, he slides down a bit more and attempts another trick, perhaps hanging under the rope by both hands or holding the rope under one arm while his body swings free and he makes running motions. The most difficult and dangerous trick, which is not attempted by all, appears to be holding the rope between the legs in an upright, straddling position and then releasing the handhold on the rope and extending the arms in a horizontal position. The best dancers may then regain their hold on the rope and begin spinning rapidly in the straddle position with the rope between their legs.

Dancers report that they do not have names in K'iche' nor in Spanish for the specific tricks. These tricks are called pruebas (Spanish for proofs, or tests), and again a corresponding K'iche' term seems to be lacking. They are

Figure 3.10 On the first day, a leg-hooked spin (vuelta) when the rope is dangerously slack.

Figure 3.11 On the second day, a leg-hooked spin on a good, tight rope.

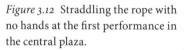

Figure 3.12 Straddling the rope with no hands at the first performance in the central plaza.

tests because they are interpreted as proofs of individual spiritual powers conferred by the forty days of sexual abstinence beginning on the holy day Espiritu Santo and by the many offerings and invocations that have been made to repel evil influences and to call up the power of the animals to make the dancers fearless. One dancer made the following brief report, which here has been combined from two different interviews:

> A pair of dancers [e.g., the first and second tigres, who dance on alter-nate days] watch out for each other. When one is on the rope, the other is watching out for him. Both must avoid sex, and the behavior of one can affect the other or even the whole group. There is an obligation to go in turns, because otherwise it is exhausting, but sometimes, if one is not prepared, it is better not to go. Sometimes there is only one tigre or one león, and then you must do it all. . . . I dropped from the rope one time. Everything was fine and I had completed several tests, but I had misbehaved with a woman during the costumbre. I was hanging from the rope and suddenly I relived the scene with the woman. I became frightened and lost my strength and fell. The power of the animals is given by the costumbre and we feel it as fearlessness.

The Landing

As the "animals" near the ground they come within reach of the quirts of the Deer Dance performers, who are dancing and clowning under the rope. At this time Pedro and Catalina will begin whipping an animal, who may respond defensively by rapid spinning, which drives the tormentors back out of range. Upon reaching the ground the performer hugs the chuchkajaw and then rejoins the dancers under the rope. After the last performance the danc-ers may run around the chuchkajaw several times.

Figure 3.13 A male monkey (see the two flaps on the left) demonstrates the normal rope-top position used for moving down the rope. Note the rattle attached by a loop to his right wrist.

Delivering the Flowers, July 21, 2006

The Palacio

The municipal authorities must issue a permit (*acta*) for the dance and to allow the removal of a tree from the cemetery and are also relied upon to provide a truck for hauling the pole into the plaza and a team of officials to oversee the removal of the tree from the cemetery and its safe passage through town to the plaza. On July 21, in mid-morning, the dancers in costume marched into town from C'oy Abaj, where they had performed a dawn ceremony. Accompanied by the marimba, they brought a bouquet to the mayor and first councilman (*sindico primero*), who were awaiting them in the mayor's office.[4] The marimba played in the waiting area outside of the mayor's office and the animals danced while the dance sponsors entered the office with the bouquet. The staffs of office of the municipal officials were displayed on the desktop between the dance sponsors and the town officials while the

Figure 3.14 Dancers circle the chuchkajaw, in position on the rope anchor stake at the end of a rehearsal.

sindico gave the dancers some instructions about selecting, transporting, and erecting the pole and they thanked the officials for their support.

The Church

A second bouquet is then presented to the priest or to the sacristan as his representative in the church, either at the main altar or to the left of the altar where Santiago and San Felipe are kept. This is again a symbol of subordination in that the dancers are requesting permission to erect a pole on church property and to use the church building as their staging area. They must also request permission to enter the north tower on the façade to measure its altitude with a rope, to station a crew there while erecting the pole, and to use the tower for ascent while dancing.

Erecting the Pole, July 21 and 22

Selecting and Measuring the Tree

After the morning Deer Dance and following lunch on July 21 a rope was lowered from the roof of the north façade tower in front of the church and marked with a knot to measure the desired height of the pole. A pole any taller than this height (plus two meters in the ground) is too long to maneuver through a tight corner on the road from the cemetery to the plaza. A very tall and straight pine tree located on flat ground on the southeastern margin of the less-utilized upper part of the cemetery was chosen. It was the first monkey's job to climb it with the measuring rope looped around his waist. This was a dangerous and impressive feat without climbing equipment and took about ten minutes. The climber remained in the top of the tree and used the measuring rope to haul up a machete to trim the tree. Branches, some the size of small trees, fell on a turkey coop belonging to a family that lived nearby. The owners used a bucket of grain to encourage the turkeys to roost elsewhere. The coop and some corn plants were damaged, and the autor of the dance offered compensation to the family, but since the dancers were acting on behalf of the community and serving Santiago, the owners did not desire any compensation. The measuring rope was used to haul up the thick, braided rope (laso) used in the dance, which was tied firmly near the top of the tree to be used to help fell the tree. The climber descended on this rope, making the dancers laugh by doing a few spins on the rope (vueltas) just before he reached the ground. The first tigre then offered his shoulders as a stand for the second tigre, who tied the rope off on the trunk of the tree far enough above the ground to prevent anyone from easily loosening it and using it to climb the tree overnight to steal the rope. The dance team planned to return in the morning with first light to fell the tree.

Felling the Tree

With the first and second tigres and the monkey who climbed and trimmed the tree manning axes and the dance team and other volunteers on the rope the tree was brought down in the cemetery at about 7:00 a.m. Amazingly, though it dropped into an area with numerous graves it did not land directly on any and none of the concrete crosses marking the graves were damaged. Clearly the costumbre was working. Officials from the town government, many of them sucking lollipops, arrived carrying their staffs of office with handkerchiefs so that their hands did not directly touch the sacred staffs; they were there to oversee the rolling and turning of the tree trunk in the cemetery and the removal and replacement of crosses marking graves that were in the way.

Offerings and the Tejas Complex

When the tree had been felled, trimmed, and rolled and maneuvered until it was out of the actively used part of the cemetery, the chuchkajaw and dancers placed the nine tejas along the tree trunk in rank order. Then, when offerings were burning in the tejas and with the town officials looking on, they first walked and then ran around the tree trunk, striking the areas between the tejas with their whips. It is said that this ensures that the *palo* is cooperative during the journey to the plaza. Then they walked the length of the tree trunk, stepping over the tejas. If a teja is bumped and falls, it is a sign that the costumbre of the person who is responsible is not as it should be. When the walking of the tree was completed the dancers used tight loops in their quirts to lift the tejas, still holding burning wax and incense, and carried them to the tree stump, where they were arranged as an offering to the felled tree.

Transporting the Pole to the Plaza

In moving the trimmed tree trunk from the place where it fell to the paved road, the team, augmented by an even larger number of volunteers, strengthened by marimba music, and overseen by the municipal officials, was directed by the second dance sponsor, don Juan. They skidded the tree trunk out of the cemetery using rollers and levers as needed to cross uneven ground, often to the "one–two–three" prompts of don Juan. This was very difficult work, as the heavy butt of the gigantic pole frequently plowed into graves or small, natural ridges and had to be levered into a new position. Don Juan's shouted directions became increasingly hoarse but remained strong all day. The municipal government provided a dump truck to haul the pole for the mile or so from the upper cemetery to the plaza. There was a difficult passage where a right-angle turn had to be made at the intersection below the Paclom hill and a block above the municipal palace and park. Here the pole was a little too long and wedged against the curb, but with levers it was lifted up on the sidewalk and just barely made the turn. Upon arrival at the plaza the pole was again skidded by manual labor through the market stalls to a cleared area in front of the church. Here the socket at the northern corner of the façade in which the butt of the pole is seated had been reopened while most of the team was working in the cemetery.

The pole was aligned with the hole and the team and officials established a roped-off area surrounding the pole and the hole. A crowd began to gather along the ropes to observe the ceremony of the tejas and then the erection of the pole. During this period it is bad luck if a dog crosses the roped area, and volunteers with whips were stationed in strategic locations to try to discourage canine trespassers. Since there are many dogs and the sacred precinct is on their normal thoroughfare between the plaza and the covered market, this is a difficult task. Several dogs managed to cross the sacred precinct in spite of the vigilance of the guards, and the ongoing battle of wits and tests of agility entertained the crowd during slow times in the proceedings while sometimes horrifying the dog-loving gringo observers.

The Hole

In 2006 the offering for the pole was placed in the hole by the chuchkajaw of the dance, don Pedro. He created a quadripartite field using about two

Figure 3.15 Offerings are placed along the tree trunk.

hundred copal nodules and then surrounded it with ninety-seven small wax candles and one large candle in the east. In commenting on a picture of the prepared hole don Pedro said,

> The tree [pole] is alive. You know that all things are alive? Then for this reason it must be overcome so that it doesn't offer harm to the dancers. Then when it is thrown down, when it is here in the plaza, we offer the secret of the hole. We put three hundred candles, one hundred candles [i.e., two hundred copal nodules and about one hundred candles]; more

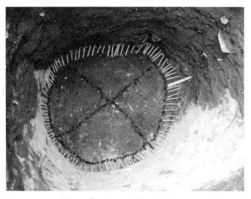

Figure 3.16 The offering, with the large candle in the east and the quadripartite world of the four mountains indicated by an X of copal; that is, the four directions are read between the lines. This model of the center is designed to center the pole.

Figure 3.17 A log keeps the base of the pole out of the hole until the pole reaches an angle of about forty-five degrees. Then the chock is removed by hammering with the back side of an axe, and the pole slides into place against the butt plate for the final stage of erection.

than this will not increase the effect. So then, in the picture there is the center, this is what receives the pole so that it will not strike the church. You see the cross, because it is Quilaja, Tamancu, Socop, and Pipil, the four cardinal points.

Question: And the big candle, what is that?

Ah, that is the protection, that it be received, that the pole does not strike the church. This is the center, and it is the king that is the fat one. The invisibles that are walking, that is this one. There is a commander, as in the nation there is a president, one who commands.

Offerings and the Tejas Complex

The placing of offerings on the pole and whipping of the pole that took place in the cemetery were repeated in the plaza. Again each member of the team placed his teja on the pole and made an offering of wax candles and copal. Again the whipping and walking and running of the pole, a process that has a diagnostic purpose in identifying anyone whose personal commitment is lagging. They can be whipped by the dance team and counseled and scolded by the chuchkajaw and may make additional offerings to request forgiveness. It is far better to handle this now then to have someone fall from the rope because of poor spiritual preparation. The first whipping in the cemetery was to domesticate the tree/pole so that it could be carried from the cemetery to the plaza. This second round of offerings and whippings is so that it will allow itself to be erected for the dance.

Figure 3.18 The pole is erected by the dance team and many volunteers using scissor jacks. As it is raised the jacks are slid down the trunk, with the short ones being removed in turn and replaced by longer jacks at the high end.

Erecting the Pole

After the ceremony of the tejas ends at about noon, the rest of the day is devoted to erecting the pole. This is done with the help of a large crew of volunteers, with as many as eighty men involved during the peak period when there are four or more active braces under the pole. Long poles are arranged in pairs of graduated lengths and lashed together near their tips so that they work as scissors. The first prop is a sturdy, five-foot-tall T that is fitted under the sixty-five-foot-long pole about twenty feet from its tip. Then the lashed scissor poles are fit under the pole, one pair at a time. The leader calls out "one–two–three," and on "three" the work teams pull the scissors together, raising the pole. As the pole is raised the scissors are moved slowly toward the base as the taller ones are fit into place out near the tip. Six such pairs are used, and as the pole is raised the shorter ones are dropped out and chopped into pieces, which are used later to shim or wedge the pole in place as it begins

Figure 3.19 Whipping the pole in the plaza.

Figure 3.20 Walking and whipping the pole.

to seat itself in the hole. There is considerable danger since the dance pole could easily tip over to either side as it begins to reach angles above forty-five degrees. If it falls it could kill or injure workers below. The final moment when the pole stands up and slowly seats itself, leaning gently against the front of the church, is a moment of considerable triumph and demonstrates the power of men, properly prepared with the right attitudes and the right magic and guided by tradition and their intelligence, to dominate nature.

Dancing in the Plaza, July 23, Morning

The Deer Dance

The chuchkajaw and the monkey dancers perform costumbre every day at sunrise at C'oy Abaj. They arrive in town in costume at about 9:00 a.m. and prepare to dance. In 2006 we observed and documented the dance for its first two complete performances in the plaza. Both days the dancing started at about 10:00 a.m. and the rope was stretched across the dance ground at about noon, with the four animal impersonators each taking about ten minutes to descend. The entire dance would be finished in the early afternoon, well before the afternoon rains began. The Dance of the Mexicanos was performed for the entire afternoon on the other side of the plaza, often in the rain, as was the Dance of the Conquista when this dance was brought out again in 2008.

The Deer Dance, within which the monkeys team performs as clowns before their acrobatics on the rope end the dance, has changed dramatically in recent years. In the 1970s the dance told the story of an old couple, Pedro Botón and his wife, Catalina. They had a strained relationship and lacked domestic tranquility, as manifested in stylized bickering and in a little skit in which their dogs attacked don Pedro, but they controlled the magic for hunting deer. They were commissioned by a group of Spaniards to hunt the deer and visited the four corners of the dance ground, concluding a successful hunt. At that time there was a script for the dance, owned by a dance master who taught the characters their lines. The basics of this older performance are outlined elsewhere (Cook 2000:110–12).

Today the dance continues to portray the traditional characters—the old couple, a group of Spaniards, two dogs, and, at least in theory, four deer, though in 2006 and again in 2008 there were only three—all in expensive rented costumes. However, the dance master died several years ago, and at one time or another we were informed that the script was lost or that it was no longer used because, according to don Pedro, the plaza is now so noisy that there would be no point in reciting the lines anyway since nobody could hear them. This is certainly true, as even the marimba music is often drowned out by the lively salsa played by professional, nationally known bands (e.g., Los Terremotos Conejos, or The Earthquake Rabbits) in front of the church, literally a yard away from the dance ground, with vocalists, keyboards, horns, guitars, and drums amplified over two or four refrigerator-sized speakers.

As it is performed today the dance focuses on the deer, who, from time to time, dance up and down and around the dance ground with a graceful skipping, prancing step and lots of turns and bobs and swirls. The rest of the time the action, in which the aloof deer take no part, is a conflict pitting the couple

Figure 3.21 The dance used to have four deer, two male and two female, but in 2006 there were three.

Figure 3.22 Don Pedro dances. Notice his cane. Two segales, Catalina, and a dog are in the background.

and their allies the segales against the tigre, león, and monkeys, who do not figure as characters in the official Deer Dance. The animals seek to molest or abduct Catalina and wrestle with the segales and don Pedro, while Pedro, Catalina, and the segales pursue the animals and whip them with their quirts.

These animals are no respecters of persons or conventions. They drag children out of the crowd, wrestle them to the ground, and tie their shoelaces together. Sometimes they get into real fights with protective parents. On one occasion an angry mother drove them off of her crying son with a long wooden stave. They make fun of tourists. One may pose for a picture while

Figure 3.23 A deer prepares to dance diagonally across the dance ground while the marimba plays.

Figure 3.24 The tigre and the león molest Catalina.

Figure 3.25 The "female" monkey with a rattle.

Figure 3.26 The "female" monkey with a baby on its back.

another gets behind the photographer and trips him or her. They climb on vehicles. In short, they do not behave like well-socialized humans, a trait that is shared by the animals they portray but also by other nature personifiers depicted in K'iche' dances, as in the case of the *grasejos* (*tzulab*) dancers halting a cofradía procession of María Concepción and using their whips to lift her skirts (see Cook 2000:171–82 for the tzulab).

Stretching the Rope

After Pedro, Catalina, and the deer have all had a chance to dance their solos around the dance ground and there has been some time for clowning, an hour or two into the dance, at about noon, the rope is stretched across the dance ground and anchored on the opposite side of the plaza. The chuchka-jaw takes his place straddling the rope. Then, while the clowning and nonnar-rative dancing continue below, the tigre, the león, and the two monkeys each in turn ascend the church tower to the roof of the church and then begin their tests on the rope.

The Tests on the Rope

The tests in the plaza are exactly the same as those described above at the rehearsals and so are not described here. However, the stakes are higher, as the pole is five meters taller, the ground below is concrete pavement, and there is an audience of hundreds. It is important to recognize that for the dancers

Figure 3.27 A monkey and a león molest a youth dragged from the audience.

Figure 3.28 As in other K'iche' dances, children portray *chiquito* versions of some key characters. In this case, as at the rehearsals, sons of the leónes and tigres clown as chiquitos. Their participation is not considered delicado, and they do not have to follow any special rules, nor is costumbre performed on their behalf, as the costumbre performed for their fathers should protect the entire family.

there are supernatural dangers in addition to punishment for inadequate preparation. Enemies in the crowds below use sorcery to seek to make the dancers fall, and envious observers may cause damage through the evil eye, so larger crowds also represent a greater supernatural danger. In 2008 a león reported a close call when an aere, a spirit wind, possibly sent by an enemy, blew into his mask, causing his eyes to water so that he couldn't see. He credited the power of the mask he wore with the fact that the tears dried immediately, so that his vision cleared and he safely completed his performance.

The Whipping of the Animals and Returning to Earth

During the wrestling and clowning prior to the acrobatics on the rope and at the end of each performance on the rope as the animal comes within reach of dancers on the ground, Pedro and Catalina whip them with their quirts (*chicotes*). The symbolism of the dance pole and the whipping of the pole as explained above pit humans against a recalcitrant and dangerous natural world and are fraught with imagery of sexual conflict; this same symbolism is repeated again in the whipping of the animals.

Here is don Pedro's take on this conflict and the role of the whip in the dance:

> Well, Pedro Botón is her husband, and the tigres want to violate Catalina. The tigre wants to take his woman. But as it is, well, his [Pedro's] politics is his pistol, and this one is his favorite one to beat. And this is also true of Catalina. It is for this that they give it [the tigre] shit, these people. This tigre, this león, because they molest a lot, this is why they do this.

Figure 3.29 The rope is anchored in the plaza.

It is like, they want to fuck [*chingar*], it is like their desire is to screw [*joder*], and so this is why it is done this way.

Question: Is this just in the story, because, well, do animals wish to have our women?

No, it is not to violate them, but they do want to carry them off to eat them.

This classic culture-versus-nature oppositional structure appears to be the central theme of the dance as it is now produced. The opposition is mediated by costumbre, both by the offerings understood as payments to nature deities (mundos) and also by the knowledge, the *secretos*, left by the primeros that provides their descendants with the power both to control nature (as in raising the pole) and to internalize and use the powers or spirits of the animals to enhance individual courage and personal strength. The opposition is an active cosmic principal within K'iche' cosmology. Humans and wild animals remain locked in conflict throughout the performance, and there is neither resolution nor a clear winner within its current, simplified narrative structure. The possession-like imbuing with animal potency and courage, though, does free the affected dancers from conventional restraints and, temporarily, from the power of their enemies and the evil eye. This suggests that the conflict is resolved in them and, for a while, within the liminal period marked by repeated respectful human visits to the altars and appropriate payments to the nawales who own them and dispense their powers.

Figure 3.30 Catalina whips the tigre while don Pedro and an attentive crowd look on.

The return to earth, and eventually the return to unmediated human existence, is a return to conflict and to the slings and arrows of outrageous fortune. The tests are now over for today, though, and they have been passed. A relieved tigre or león or monkey embraces a relieved chuchkajaw, grateful that during this short time of extreme and public vulnerability and danger the malice and evil power of one's enemies has been forestalled and the supernatural dangers of the walk of life, of the balancing act of life in which one is sustained by physical strength, courage, and adherence to custom, has been enacted again with a satisfactory resolution.

Visiting Patrón Santiago, July 23, Afternoon

At the end of the dance on the first day the entire dance team embarked in several pickups for the house of the alcalde of Santiago's cofradía for lunch, followed by a procession from the house to the hermandad chapel, as described in chapter 2.

Dance at the Ermita

When the dance team arrived at the cofradía house each dancer in turn knelt before the image of Santiago and his companion, San Felipe, displayed on the altar table in the front room and was blessed by the deputy of the cofradía. Then a lunch of rice with chicken and black beans and tamalitos was served in a back room. After this the marimba played in the courtyard and each of the deer did a few turns around the courtyard while the other dancers stood in little groups and kept time with their rattles. Unlike the street dances, there was no clowning in this performance. Following the dance the team took its place in the procession, and to the sounds of strings of firecrackers and the firing of bombas in a billowing cloud of white, sulfurous smoke the procession left the cofradía house for its procession to the hermandad chapel.

Ending the Dance

The dancing continues every day until August 3. Cook witnessed and participated in the termination events in August 2008. The last dance occurred on Sunday, August 3. The plan was to bring down the pole at about five in the evening, but there were still large crowds in the plaza and a mass in the church, so a decision was made to wait until the mass was over and the crowd dispersed before felling the tree for a second time. At eight, in a light rain, the Monkeys Dance team began to remove the shims that held the pole upright and, using the laso, which had been reattached near the top, and two additional guidelines to steer the pole into a safe vector away from the church steps, attempted to pull it into a lean that would allow it to be chopped down safely. It hung up for a while against the light post at the northwestern corner of the church steps. A significant group of spectators was watching and a film crew was attempting to record the process, but none of the spectators offered to help on the ropes, so it was touch and go, a powerful reminder that this undertaking is not guaranteed and that disaster is possible at any time. With the energetic leadership of the two tigres the team and a dozen or so volunteers finally freed the pole from the light post in a shower of sparks. It was then chopped down and chopped into pieces by the team, some stripped to the waist and steaming in the cold rain. The team was invited into a local

Figure 3.31 A segal and two deer prepare to dance in the courtyard.

Figure 3.32 In this south-facing view the dance pole leans against the northern turret on the façade of the Catholic church with the rope stretched across the plaza to the west. A tigre dancer is beginning a routine of tricks hanging above the plaza.

cantina then for beers by the chuchkajaw and the autor, and there was a period of exhausted and grateful rest and reminiscing.

At about seven in the morning most of the team accompanied the chuchkajaw to the well of Santiago, a concrete cistern located near the base of the Paclom overlooking the stream valley to its east. The tejas that had been used in all the ceremonies for two weeks were placed carefully in a neat stack behind a small tree on the edge of the cistern by the highest-ranking dancer who was present, since the first tigre had to open his store and could not attend. While the chuchkajaw offered copal, candles, and prayers of thanksgiving at the altar on the edge of the cistern, the other dancers sat on the curb across the street from the altar reading a newspaper and playing with a digital camera belonging to one of three Baylor University students who had been invited to come and observe the ceremony, until they were called up for a group blessing and farewell. In his final interview in July 2007 don Pedro provided a very succinct description of the entire dance:

> After we throw it [the pole] down we bring it here [the plaza] and make a ceremony here in the *plazuela.* Then we begin to raise it. After it is raised we celebrate. After the celebration we begin the tests [*a probar*]. Then, after a total of fifteen days, we put out all the ceremony [*apogar,* as in blowing out a candle] at Pipil [the altar on the eastern mountain] and then with Patrón Santiago Apostól. And more, when we end this, to close the ceremony, thank God, the mundo, the invisibles at C'oy Abaj. Secondly, we go to give thanks at the ujuyubal of Patrón Santiago Apostól [his hilltop altar at Paclom in the center of town], thankful that we have now lowered the pole. Third, we go to the house [of the dance sponsor] to close the silla, the mesa [to close the mesa altar] and to explain [at the mesa altar and at the altar table in the sponsor's house] that we have now ended the devotions. Fourth, we give thanks at Uja'l Santiago [the well of Santiago, where a spring is located on the west base of Paclom] to return the tejas there at El Sacramento [i.e., at the cistern that captures the spring water], there we go to deliver them. It ends thus after these following days. We do the farewell [*despedida*] and each returns to his house.

Variations on a K'iche' Hero Myth

The total performative complex of the Monkeys Dance is a pilgrimage. It is a trip to the other world, enacted as a complex of magical and divinatory encounters with the patron saint, earth spirits, and primeros (souls of the dead dancers) and mediated by abstinence and by compulsive ritual offering cycles. In the life-risking ordeals of selecting, measuring, and cutting the pole; erecting the pole; scaling the cliffs at C'oy Abaj; and performing on the rope, the dancers acquire power that is tested and proved repeatedly during their journey together through months of preparations and performances.

In visiting the mundos, the altars, the dancers invoke the powers of a complex hierarchy of saints, angels, and earth spirits; the holy days; and the souls of the dead dancers and of their own ancestors, often one and the same. They seek signs of the acceptance of their gifts of burnt offerings, prayer, and dancing, while in the process reifying a traditional, imagined Momostenango, defining its borders (the four sacred mountains), and making correct entry by visiting six mundos on a path that parallels the entry road from Puerto Joyam in the cold bunchgrass and pine highland on the southern border to the dance altar at C'oy Abaj. At every stop the animal spirits belonging to the earth itself are called to possess and empower the dancers. Thus an imagined Momostenango, an image largely fixed in tradition, is delimited and given renewed substance and meaning in the dance rituals. Momostenango is changing dramatically, but so far its reification in this dance's ritual, and at least situationally in the minds of the participants, is not.

The Monkeys Dance initiatory complex is an enactment of the hero myth (Campbell 1949), a sojourn in the other world where adversaries are encountered and defeated, marked for many dancers, as for Campbell's hero, by encounters with the archetypal female generative principle (Campbell's marriage to the goddess) and male authority principle (atonement with the father).[5] The dancers spend sixty days in the other world, a liminal period mediated by sexual abstinence and constant costumbre. One dancer reported that "the costumbre appears to me in my dreams as a beautiful woman and asks me to forsake my wife and to go away with her," and of course for sixty days the successful initiand has forsaken his wife and all other human sexual partners. Santiago is also encountered in dreams as a demanding patriarchal figure who requires service and to whom an accepted promise to dance, or a renewed promise following a lapse, represents a Momostecan hero's version of the atonement with the male god, a symbolic father. At the same time, many dancers begin as young men and dance at least in part out of obligation to their father and grandfathers, taking their prescribed places, as in American military families, becoming vessels for the wills and values of their ancestors, another kind of atonement.

In the waking world during these sixty days the dancers are engaged in a constant struggle with personified malevolent forces (witches, envious enemies with the evil eye) as well as their own too-human tendency to lack conviction or courage at a critical moment or to be seduced and to lose their sexual purity. The tejas with offerings at the base of the dance pole and the constant prayer of the chuchkajaw sitting on the rope where it is anchored in the plaza are their guardians. There are constant signs of personal power or of dangerous lapses in the favor of the mundos and the ancestors: fires that won't accept offerings; potsherds holding candles and copal that drop from the fallen dance pole when stepped over during an important ceremony in the cemetery or in the plaza; a dance pole that stubbornly refuses to be erected; a sudden, paralyzing fear of heights or vertigo at a critical moment climbing the cliffs above C'oy Abaj or surmounting the dance pole and looking down on the crowds; and in the worst cases, not just bad burns from the rope during turns on it but a fall of fifty feet to bond-snapping and life-ending concrete pavement. Thus the powers invoked by the dancers and their chuchkajaw communicate with their children and their servants, the dancers.

In 2006 a monkey who had taken on the dangerous job of climbing and trimming the hundred-foot-tall pine tree in the cemetery and had done so fearlessly and with great panache could not understand why his two children were sick that night with high fevers since he clearly had the mundos and Santiago on his side. Ambivalence of the sort engendered in this dancer, or in the first tigre who refused to dance for unknown personal reasons that same year, has always been present in dance teams and cofradías and helps to explain attrition. But those who are successful in both costumbre and dancing are initiands returning on August 4 from a sojourn in the other world; they return with the boons of personal power and protection for themselves and their families for the ensuing year and with the gift of Santiago's patronage for another year for the entire community.

In the highland Maya world today, though, the hero myth is also enacted in a new but increasingly salient version by trips to El Norte.[6] The mundos have long been imagined as gringos, and so a visit to Gringolandia in search of a boon (money is sometimes called in Momostecan K'iche' language U sakil Tiox, the light of God) and of patronage is also a hero's quest. The passage is extremely dangerous, and not just in the border crossing: on a Mexican train, a Momostecan passenger reports he awoke in the morning to find a severed head on the seat next to him. The sojourner to the fields, restaurants, and construction sites of Gringolandia is welcomed home as a hero, an initiand, a veteran, a Bodhisattva who may now, as a coyote, guide others in the passage. Jennifer Burrel (2005:15) describes the appearance of the migrant hero returning home and participating in the fiesta in Todos Santos, dressed in his new American finery, even sporting an American flag cape. Thus new identities are being negotiated and community is being reenvisioned in Maya village cultures.

In the context of the Monkeys Dance, paradoxically the two hero myths are conjoined in ways that threaten, will ultimately change, and might strengthen the local tradition. In the midst of the first July practice session in 2006 at the dance autor's house he received a call on his cell phone from a dancer who was not dancing that year because he was working in the United States. He remembered that it was a day of costumbre and practice and wanted to check in and visit with the dance team. Thus the two liminal worlds of Gringolandia and the sacred space beneath the dance rope were, for a short time, linked together, becoming one as arenas for mythical heroism and *communitas*. With modern technology the hero/initiand may now call home and so, though some emigrants still disappear without a trace and many clients visit day keepers to ask about their husbands or sons missing in El Norte, the hero visiting the other world no longer has to rely exclusively on the Popol Wuj system of the planting of magical divinatory maize in the floor of the house. The eldest son of the dance autor in 2006, who may still eventually take his turn as autor of the dance, was planning to work in construction in Virginia in 2007. Though the opportunity fell through, some brave young men will hopefully return with enough money to make their sponsorships possible in future years. And if not, another magical threshold, a Western Union office, though it is plagued by computer problems, has opened in Momostenango.

Production in the Transnational Post-Peasant Context

Unlike the cofradía of Santiago presented in chapter 2, the Dance of the Monkeys has never been integrated into the bureaucratized authority system established during the liberal period, even though local history suggests that it was first performed in Aldea Jutacaj sometime between 1870 and 1900, at about the time that the caudillo Teodoro Cifuentes was reconstructing Momostenango as a Guatemalan pueblo. Furthermore, as an all-volunteer entity operating from one of the aldeas that was most resistant to Catholic Action it was largely immune to the political struggles of the middle twentieth century. There was no attempt by agents of Catholic Action, fully engaged with Costumbristas in the epic struggle to remove or preserve paganism in the church and its cofradías, to oppose this little, closed medicine society operating in the boondocks and providing such entertainment to the larger community.

Since the 1970s the Monkeys Dance proper has not really changed at all. The simplification of performance noted above, related to the death of the maestro and loss of the script and to the noise in the plaza that makes the reciting of line pointless and makes it impossible at time to hear the marimba music that accompanies the dance, has eliminated the acting-out of the story of the Deer Dance to which the Monkeys Dance in Momostenango has become assimilated. The monkeys, though, seemingly continue as before. The dance, the overall Dance of the Deer, Tigers, Lions, and Monkeys as it is sometimes called, or the monkeys component specifically, as described above, represents an important resource available to local residents and to any interested postcommunities to use in constructing Momostecan and indigenous identities and in utilizing the festival as a nostalgic and therapeutic performance space, as explained in chapter 1. Though there has been some difficulty in filling the entire roster of dancers recently and it would be presumptuous to predict that the dance has a secure future, it is not clear whether the transnationalized economic context is working against it or in its favor. Remittances and the continued interest of emigrants in keeping an imagined Momostenango alive work in its favor, while the absence of young men who are away working presents serious problems. These issues are explored in more detail in connection with the motivations and strategies of the dancers and the sponsors, especially as these came to light in the rapid reorganization that occurred when don Pedro was murdered. This discussion is continued in connection with Momostecan agency and tradition in chapter 5, after investigating the implications of a new cultural performance that is now central to the meaning of the festival, the convite, or disfraces, presented in chapter 4.

CHAPTER FOUR

Foreign Characters

Visualizing Identity in the Guatemalan
Highlands in the Twenty-First Century

BY RHONDA TAUBE

When most scholars discuss highland Maya dances of Guatemala, they are probably referring to the well-known dances, *danzas tradicionales*, or "traditional" dances performed at various holidays and festivals throughout the year, such as the Dance of the Conquest, the Deer Dance, or the Dance of the Mexicanos. The dances have captured the attention of academics, tourists, and locals alike for good reason, as they provide insight into and function as an analytical tool for understanding the complexities of Maya culture and religion. Recently, however, numerous indigenous people from the western highlands have developed another form of dance that has gained in popularity. The Guatemalans refer to these two types of dances as convites, "masquerades" or invitation dances, and disfraces, "disguises." The convites and disfraces, like the danzas tradicionales, appear during the annual festival dedicated to the community's patron saint. The dances feature nonindigenous, untraditional, and pop-culture characters seen on North American mass media outlets, such as horror film creatures Freddie Kruger, Alien, and Predator (figures 4.1–4.2) and Mexican movie star Cantinflas (figure 4.3), as well as a host of children's cartoon characters (figure 4.4). Figures from contemporary politics such as Osama bin Laden, Saddam Hussein, Hillary Clinton, and Barack Obama are also seen (figure 4.5).

Figure 4.1 Freddie Kruger, Momostenango, 2004.

Figure 4.2 Alien vs. Predator, Momostenango, 2005.

Figure 4.3 The Mexican movie star Cantinflas, Momostenango, 2005.

Figure 4.4 Rugrat behind Freddie Kruger, Momostenango, 2004.

Figure 4.5 Barack Obama, Momostenango, 2009.

Anthropologists often lament the disfraces or else ignore them altogether, otherwise interpreting them as antithetical to cultural authenticity (Howes 1996:2).[1] Nevertheless, the dances not only relate to recent Maya history and are expressive of local cultural logic but also represent Guatemalan identity politics and provide insight into indigenous-Ladino relations as well as the effects of neoliberalism and transnationalism on Maya communities (Fischer 1999). Identity construction in the western highlands is a dynamic, plural process involving not only the influx of foreign elements but also shifting agendas that reflect changes in national policies. This chapter explores the convites and disfraces of the K'iche' Maya community of Momostenango and views them as a social field indicative of the contemporary sociopolitical situation in Guatemala, one that provides a platform for the K'iche' to negotiate, redistribute, and validate local knowledge and power.

Unlike the traditional dances, the indigenous convites are based on a form previously developed within the population of the Ladinos, the Guatemalan dominant culture. The Ladino convites borrow the form of Maya dance, yet instead of retaining the same primary function of public performance, the Ladinos have imbued their dances with a superficial entertainment value, meant to highlight wealth within the community.[2] I analyze the Maya disfraces and Ladino convites as a means of distinguishing differing perspectives regarding the construction of a national, ethnic cultural identity. In other words, in the dances one can clearly see the different processes each group uses for negotiating the viability of their role in the social, economic, and political spheres of Guatemala today. Festival theatrical dance is a platform for entertainment, but it also expresses values and provides symbols to use in identity construction, linking national identities to patterns of consumption of North American mass media.

In discussing how the act of consumption creates consumer meaning, Grant McCracken notes, "One of the most important ways in which cultural categories are substantiated is through the material objects of a culture. . . . [Objects are] created according to the blueprint of culture" (1988:74). In other words, local goods function as cultural markers that provide the framework for perception and make social interaction possible (Howes 1996:2). David Howes (1996:2) parallels this concept with Jean Baudrillard's "system of objects" (2001:13), a social assemblage with a coherent set of meanings that always say something about their users. However, Howes also goes on to consider what the situation is that occurs in cross-cultural consumption. "For when goods cross borders, then the culture they 'substantiate' is no longer the culture in which they circulate" (1996:2). In today's world it is common for goods to travel and to cross national borders, destabilizing the concepts of code, markers, and intended system of objects. Recently, the logic by which different societies receive these goods has been understood as a transformation in order to communicate local values that are accorded by their destination culture (Howes 1996:5; Thomas 1991). This is not a particularly novel concept, but it is useful for understanding how goods are often changed in harmony with resident standards and ideals (Howes 1996:5).

In discussing the phenomenon of cross-cultural consumption, Howes (1996:5) uses the term *creolization* to refer to the inflow of foreign goods, their reception, and local domestication. Developed as a sociolinguistic theory during the 1970s, creolization refers to the point when a simplified contact language becomes a fully developed primary native language, articulating the global versus the local. In terms of cross-cultural consumption, creolization emphasizes the creativity of the consumer and highlights how consumers contextualize goods by inserting them into particular social relationships (Howes 1996:5–6). Other scholars employ the term *mestizaje* to refer to the unique combinations born out of a blending of the global with the local. Yet as García Canclini (1995:11) notes, mestizaje, a term borrowed from biological models, often implies—intentionally or not—a mixing of races. García Canclini prefers the term *hybridity*, as it includes forms of hybridization that extend beyond the racial and religious to include various types of social and ethnic intermixing. However, one aspect of receiving and domesticating foreign goods and services that creolization, mestizaje, and hybridity all bypass are the processes that take place during this act of cultural translation.

In "Translation and Discursive Identity," Clem Robyns (1994) discusses the problems that arise when translating texts from one language or culture to another. However, much of what he discusses is apt for an understanding not only of the transformation goods undergo when moving from one culture to another but also of cultural concepts and practices. Robyns (1994:405) argues that confrontation with the nonidentical and the act of highlighting difference with others are tactics groups use to denote themselves as groups. Stuart Hall (1997:21–22) writes about a similar notion in his discussion of what it means to be "English" and how the English create their identity against the backdrop of the "Other." Hall states, "Identity is always . . . a structured representation which only achieves its positive through the narrow eye of the negative" (21). People who feel they fit in with or link themselves to a particular culture do so because they rely partially on a shared set of norms. However, the awareness of such a common system is achievable only through the confrontation with its absence, according to Robyns (1994:406–8) and Hall (1997), as seen in other cultures. Individuals always negotiate their own identity against difference. Therefore, the forces that produce cultural self-definition involve continuous contact between cultures. Moreover, those relations are generally devoid of parity; instead, they form an intricate network of relationships created by the superposition of political, economic, scientific, and cultural associations.

Robyns goes on to suggest that the asymmetrical nature of intercultural relations is directly linked to imbalanced power relations, involving an ideological aspect of identity construction. In other words, in establishing its identity through cultural practices a group conceptualizes, replicates, and even challenges social interests and power relations. The self-conception of a common cultural practice or identity implies that there is also an attempt to preserve this identity, and hence the culture. For the K'iche' Maya of the western highlands, public dance-dramas sanctify specific locations and make them community places that lie at the core of one's identity. The act of dancing forms a part of the sense of belonging to a community of like-minded people. It creates an "us" who can be distinguished from "them," in essence saying, "we do this." These sacred places form a reservoir of meaning that people can draw upon to tell stories about and thereby define who they are.

LADINO CONVITES

According to Pedro Roberto Rodas (pers. comm., August 3, 2006), proprietor of the convite costume shop in Totonicapán, Guatemala, contemporary dances in the highlands, such as the disfraces and convites, began among the Ladino community approximately sixty years ago as a reflection of indigenous feria performances and dances. In Guatemala, *Ladino* refers to either a person of Hispanic descent or of mixed blood or a Maya who has chosen to live as an acculturated Westerner. As Charles Hale (1999:298) notes, in Guatemala the term *Ladino* covers a great heterogeneity and generally refers to anyone who is "not Indian." In other words, anyone who is Ladino identifies with European culture and heritage (Hale 1999:299). Guatemalans always use the terms *Ladino* and *Maya* or *indígena* in contrast to each other. The terms also denote one's placement on the "scale of civilization," marking degrees of education as well as social and economic advantage (Little-Siebold 2001:182). As Carol A. Smith notes, "Class in Guatemala is inextricably bound up with constructions of race and blood." (1995:733). Many in the dominant culture regard the Maya as obsolete, defined by their commitment to traditional culture and lack of ability to combine this tradition with technology (Nelson 1996:298–99). As Diane M. Nelson (1996:300) notes, the Maya who are transnational, become technologically savvy, learn to read, live in cities, and do intellectual work are appropriated by and automatically become "Ladinos," indicating this is not a "racial" divide as much as one of cultural identification.

Although the ruling elite in Guatemala is composed of Ladino families, most Ladinos are middle-class, salaried workers and low-end bureaucrats (C. Smith 1995:734). One indicates his or her Ladino status through Western-style dress, speaking only Spanish, employment away from the milpa, and wage labor outside of the community. Many Guatemalans have made a distinction between these two groups, conceptualizing Ladinos as part of mass or urban culture while the Maya represent folk or rural, traditional society. The indigenous-versus-Ladino ethnic division has traditionally underpinned the social order of Guatemala; more specifically, it congealed indigenous identity as defined by characteristics that are distinct from those of Spaniards and people of European descent (Annis 1987:17).

In spite of the fact that Ladinos and indigenous K'iche' have coexisted in highland communities such as San Miguel Totonicapán since the eighteenth century, it is the Ladino population that is identified with "modernity" (Zamora 2003:i). The Ladino community equates modernity in this regard with progress, while tradition is viewed as backward and ignorant. Ladino convites may have developed as a reflection of Maya festival dances, however, as Marcelo Zamora Mejía (2003) suggests, Ladinos in the western highlands, especially in predominantly indigenous areas, employ convites dances as a means of both elevating themselves above and distinguishing themselves from traditional Maya society and culture. Zamora suggests this is another form of Ladino response that has developed since the middle of the twentieth century to an elite, commercial K'iche' that causes Ladinos to question the validity of the modernity with which they have traditionally associated themselves. Today many K'iche' are breaking out of the mold of romanticized, traditional rural dwellers and are asserting their rights to have access to a modern lifestyle and its conveniences. They constitute the rising group of urbane, city-dwelling Maya.[3]

Recently the new urban indigenous have been achieving the same levels of success and modernity as Ladinos: for example, the same level of education, dress, language, and economic power. Zamora (2003) argues that the Ladino community that resides in San Miguel Totonicapán has been rearticulating their supposed modernity, which they represent in a local dance called the Convite Navideño.[4]

A convite is a comic parade in which all the participants wear disguises and masks. It passes through the streets to invite neighbors to the local festivities. Ángel Pérez Quiroa of San Miguel Totonicapán founded the Convite Navideño in 1946 (Espinoza 2006). According to his son, Miguel Pérez Rivera, Pérez Quiroa was concerned at the lack of participation within the community and the low level of happiness at Christmastime. He was the first Ladino to use costumes of animals and movie stars to bring people out of their homes in unity and celebration (Espinoza 2006).

In this particular community the Ladinos no longer constitute an elite hegemony but through their discourses and social practices incorporate elements of global culture and mass media in order to redefine their identity. According to Zamora (2003), the Ladinos want to be different from the indigenous populations, who they define as traditional. In this way, Zamora suggests, the convite should be seen as a project of modernity; the Ladinos intend to distance themselves from the indigenous populations and to construct a tradition that permits them to address the hegemony that they used to monopolize, including government administration, economics, and social life.

One manner in which the Ladino community distinguished themselves through the convites was to prohibit indigenous participation. The Ladino convites were and still are managed and organized according to strict rules that govern the membership and conduct of the contributing dancers (Pedro Roberto Rodas, pers. comm., August 3, 2006). Male couples intending to dance must belong to a society that arranges group rehearsals and submits applications en masse to the cabildo, the local municipal government, for performance eligibility. About a year before the festival, the dancers begin to meet in secret and select who their dance partners are going to be. At this time they also begin to formulate a design for their masquerade, which they next present to the costume shop. In addition, the dancers who are not going to perform must request permission to be absent. Otherwise they are subject to a fine and may lose the right to dance in the future (Zamora 2003:57). Likewise, dancers must participate in all organized performances throughout the year.

A second way that Ladinos employ the convites to highlight difference is through an emphasis on their unique access to North American mass media. Through the convites, Ladinos attempt to highlight their transnational status through their knowledge of such characters as Shrek, Santa Claus, and even Scooby Doo. They are the members of the community who can afford to buy cameras, DVDs, iPods, and cable television. They are part of the global "flow" connecting disparate regions to media images, standards of living, and discourses of human rights founded in the United States (Appadurai 2001:6). In addition, appearing side by side with the cartoon characters are masked dancers performing as the *borracho*, the drunken indigenous man who

Figure 4.6 Gandalf the Grey from *Lord of the Rings*, Momostenango, 2005.

signifies the backwardness, uncultivated quality, and ignorance of the K'iche' population (Zamora 2003:117). The sadness associated with the indigenous K'iche' character is the antithesis of the cheerful entertainment provided by the animated creatures, drawing another line of distinction between the two groups. The costumes the dancers select connect them to the world outside of the pueblo.[5] Gandalf the Gray from *Lord of the Rings*, Yoda from *Star Wars*, Sulley Monster from *Monsters, Inc.*, Stuart Little, and a host of additional cartoon characters, both current and vintage, appear in recognizable form (figure 4.6). Although they defy North American notions of incorporation, they symbolize an insider status to their audience and function as a sign indicating knowledge beyond the immediate community.

Guatemala's recent connection to global society began under ominous conditions. During the most violent phase of civil war it suffered pariah status; then the international community became involved in peace negotiations, bringing delegates from numerous countries to Central America.[6] MINUGUA, the United Nations Verification Mission in Guatemala, is still visible today.[7] Established in 1997 to verify and ensure the cease-fire between the government and the URNG (Unidad Revolucionaria Nacional Guatemalteca) and initially created for only a three-month period, it continued its institution-building activities in support of peace until December of 2004. Guatemala entered the peace process at same time that the world was transitioning into a global-market economy and nations were crossing borders through economic ties (Jonas 2000:218). This paved the way for the inroads of neoliberalism: the rise of policies concerning privatization of state-owned enterprises, deregulation, the lifting of trade barriers, an almost exclusive focus on export to the world market, a harsh critique and dismantling of internal markets, and a dismantling of welfare institutions or state-supported social programs.[8] All of these elements were efforts to attract investment by foreign capital (Jonas 2000:219). As Guatemala attempts to maintain its participation in global economics and attract foreign investors, one technique the Ladino community employs to demonstrate its awareness of international affairs is through public performances and dance.[9]

The use of dance as a Ladino medium of expression is at once an appropriation of an indigenous cultural form and a mimicry of Maya sacred public space and tradition. As noted by several authors (Bricker 1981; Krystal 2001; Zamora 2003), public dance for the Maya has also functioned as a site of indigenous cultural resistance in the face of numerous threats over the years. Ladino dances bypass these concepts, reducing public performance to a stage for ethnic competition. On the surface, Ladinos embrace the new social equality the K'iche' have experienced since the civil war; they still see it as a novelty, as new contrasts with old (Hale 1999:299). Much of this animosity is fueled by Ladino concerns over "la violencia," the violence of the civil war; they still feel the presence of the insurrection by the indigenous populations and are concerned that civil strife may happen again (Hale 1999:300).

INDIGENOUS CONVITES: THE DISFRACES OF MOMOSTENANGO

My first trip to Momostenango was with my husband, Karl, during the summer of 2003, shortly before the much-contested presidential election featuring the infamous candidate and former dictator Efraín Rios Montt, "El General." As we drove up the winding mountain roads blanketed with pine trees, I was struck by the overwhelming number of trunks painted with the blue-and-white FRG, the acronym for the Frente Republicano Guatemalteco, the Guatemalan Republican Front, Rios Montt's ultrarightist political party. He headed the military dictatorship of 1982–1983 and presided over the worst phase of the scorched-earth counterinsurgency/genocidal war program.[10] I felt general trepidation venturing into the western Maya highlands for the first time, as this was an area greatly affected by the consequences of the civil war. Unlike other communities in the region, Momostenango was relatively unharmed during these trying and violent times owing to its allegiance to the president and long-standing commitment to the conservative government (Huxley 1939; B. Tedlock 1982; Carmack 1995). Recent events in the capital added to the already-mounting concern I was experiencing, as only a week prior we were bystanders at the latest and one of the most aggressive political demonstrations in Guatemala's recent years, rumored to have been instigated by none other than El General himself, "El jueves negro," or "Black Thursday."

The path leading to the town center (*cabecera*) is spotted with bright pink-, yellow-, and turquoise-painted buildings supporting signs and banners that display the names *Sol* or *Gallo*, depending on the owner's beer of preference. Turning a street corner we spot the procession of alcaldes, or town elders, and *regidores*, or aldermen, the diputados bearing the effigy of Patrón Santiago (figure 4.7). The chuchaxeles, women in this highest-ranked position, follow closely behind. The small, pale-faced, black-bearded equestrian image representing the saint bears a sword in his upraised right hand. San Felipe, a lesser-known scribal saint, accompanies Santiago on his excursion and functions as his secretary, as Santiago cannot read or write and some say he speaks only K'iche' and thus requires a Spanish-speaking translator (Cook 2000:77).

The pious support the elaborately decorated red, green, and gold palanquin that holds the effigy of the two saints on their shoulders and ambulate through the cobblestone streets accompanied by a small band of musicians who play horned instruments, drums, wooden flutes, and the marimba. Other devotees carry ornate staffs indicating their status in the cofradía, the men's association. The perfume-like smoke of copal incense billows out from the hands of other faithful who swing *incensarios* directly before Santiago's path. This is one of the days when the saint leaves his home in the church and seeks out his followers in their realm, a reversal of the proscribed rituals and personal venerations that

Figure 4.7 The procession of the altar of Santiago through the streets of Momostenango, 2005.

Figure 4.8 Mexicanos precede the procession, Momostenango, 2006.

normally take place between the worshippers and Santiago in the privacy of his church or of his *ermita*, a small chapel that houses the saint when visiting a barrio or aldea. Here today he is in public, available to all.

Preceding the solemn procession is a group of costumed dancers and performers, some dressed as Mexicanos (figure 4.8), represented as mariachis, holdovers from an earlier time that function today as sacred symbols of power (Manuel Jaminez Tambriz, pers. comm., August 9, 2004). Other dancers are costumed, while still more sport attire representing various animals of the wild, including monkeys, lions, and jaguars. These characters interact with one another in a completely different manner: they antagonize, chase, and whip each other for their lascivious behavior. They spill over into the group of onlookers, instigating humorous reactions and soliciting amused and mirthful responses from the children (figure 4.9).

They form an integral part of the festivities, as they are the dancers who tell the story of the Xajooj Kej, the Danza del Venado, or Deer Dance. Through music, distinct gestures, arranged poses and *pasitas*, or steps, they enact the tale of the hunter who respectfully entreats the Lord of the Animals and successfully pursues his prey. Many suggest this dance has its origins in the pre-Columbian past (Janssens and van Akkeren 2003), possibly a performance reserved exclusively for elite or royal members of society.

Ironically, within the Maya community public dance-dramas exhibit the tenacity of Maya culture and, at the same time, its flexibility. Dances and performances that have their origin in pre-Hispanic culture easily mix with Spanish liturgical theater, combining native forms of worship with Catholic

Figure 4.9 The monos y tigres (monkeys and tigers) capture young boys and tie their shoes together, Momostenango, 2008.

saint's days. The marimba, the sacred instrument of the community performance, has its origins in Africa, a byproduct of slave culture (Navarrete
Pellicer 2005:70–74). However, because of their years within native organization, choreography, design, and instrumentation, most scholars consider
them indigenous in nature. The Maya have customized these dances and
modified their execution over time, with local and culturally determined
preferences highlighted. The first time many North Americans and
Europeans, including myself, experience the dances in an indigenous community, we feel dismayed at the lack of narrative cohesion and organization
expressed. My initial reaction, after standing around for forty-five minutes,
was, "When are they going to start?" I was surprised to find out I had been
watching the dance that entire time. This is because, regardless of the hybrid
nature of the dances' origins, the Maya produce them to conform to their
own tastes and criteria.

We run through the streets following the mobile pageant around the four
sides of the cabecera, eventually returning to the parque central, or central
park, the main plaza and vital hub of activity. The crowds are teeming, packed
so tight it is hard to move. Karl looks back at me over his shoulder to make
sure I am still there and spots me in spite of the half-dozen people who have
wedged their way between us. We reach the main courtyard where the dancers will arrive, and much to our astonishment, another, completely different,
type of performance is taking place.

At five feet five I tower over most Maya, yet during my first experience with
the disfraces I strained to stand on tiptoe just to catch a glimpse of the scene
that was about to unfold. The music began and immediately I was surprised.
This was not the q'ojom, or marimba, that I had come to expect but rather the
blasting sound of contemporary cumbia. Indeed, I recognized the song as a
popular hit off the radio. The dancers appeared and the crowd, which surrounded me on all sides, surged forward to watch the spectacle. However,
these dancers were unexpected; they did not sport the garb of the milpa farming campesino who bears the heavy weight of choreographic history. Rather,
these were members of the community wearing costumes impersonating key
players in North American and global politics. I recognized someone clad in
a mask of Arnold Schwarzenegger, but on second glance saw there were actually two Arnolds. In fact, there were dancing, paired duplicates of all the costumed characters. Similar to the traditional masquerades, some of the
performers appeared to wear masks that local artisans made. Others resem-
bled rubber Halloween visors or even the attire of an amusement park cari-
cature. The dancers did not carry incense, they did not circumambulate
around the community to the four sacred directions, and their movements

did not relate a narrative. They performed a couple's line dance, side by side, two of a kind.

During my first extended stay in Momostenango during June, July, and August 2005, a local indigenous family hosted me. Eligio and Apolonia, my hosts, lived across the street from Pa' Sabal, the sacred and ancient Maya altar discussed by Barbara Tedlock as the site of 8 Batz ceremonies (1982). My first time in their house, I could not help but notice the extremely large *Blue's Clues* cartoon character heads hanging from their rafters. Because of my interest in them, they obligingly took them down from the ceiling and donned the complete costume in order to perform on my behalf. Having seen the disfraces dances the previous two summers, I was under the false assumption that they were part of an anti-Catholic movement to undermine the traditional dances, such as the Mexicanos or Danza del Venado, that run concurrently. However, Eligio is a guía espiritual, "spiritual guide," or Maya *sacerdote*, or priest (figure 4.10).

He practices the cultural activist version of indigenous religion, which includes some Catholic imagery and ideas. His training and beliefs are specific to a newly institutionalized and officially antisyncretic, or purified, Maya spirituality. He is a practicing spiritual guide and performed a ceremony for the success of my research. Moreover, he regularly participates in the disfraces dances rather than in the traditional dances. He, his father, and his older brother have performed for years as a variety of different characters. The cartoon that I knew as *Blue's Clues* they referred to as Chuch Panador,

Figure 4.10 Eligio performs a Maya ceremony at the sacred site of Pa' Sabal, Momostenango, July 2005.

"Baker Dog," indicating the loss of translation. For Eligio's family, the baker dog was a comical character reflecting their understanding of our common dog biscuits. In a land where most people often cannot afford to buy baked goods, the idea of "cookies" for dogs represents the wealth and overindulgence of the United States.

The characters that appear during the disfraces combine a Guatemalan fascination with popular culture with an indigenous flair for the imaginative that extends beyond the Ladino convites. In recent years (2003–2009) I have seen such noteworthy real-life figures as Fidel Castro and Che Guevara (figure 4.11). Ace Freeley from the rock band Kiss (figure 4.12) and, as previously

Figure 4.11 Fidel Castro and Che Guevara, Momostenango, 2006.

Figure 4.12 Ace Freeley from the rock band Kiss, Momostenango, 2006.

mentioned, Hillary Clinton, Arnold Schwarzenegger, Osama bin Laden, Guatemalan president Álvaro Colóm (figure 4.13), and Harry Potter (figure 4.14) have all danced. In addition, the fright creatures from *Alien vs. Predator* and Freddie Kruger from *A Nightmare on Elm Street* have appeared in the disfraces. Cartoon characters, a popular favorite among the Ladino dances, do not appear with as much frequency in Momostenango, although I have seen characters from *Rugrats* and *Blue's Clues* perform. The Momostecos prefer a variety of hybrid creatures and figures from locally known proverbs. For example, Niño Perdido, the Stray Child, is a street urchin who has no shoes to wear or bread to eat because his parents spend all their money on alcohol. Although meant to be humorous, it is an indication of a Guatemalan reality. Some characters are based on well-known types, such as gladiators and ninjas. The costumes the dancers appear in have an inimitable and distinct appearance, unlike any representation I have ever before seen. Other unique characters include Las Espias de las Mentes Siniestras, "the Spies of a Sinister Mind" (figure 4.15), and Las Chicas de las Estrellas, "Star Girls." They are the invention of the dancers who wear the costume or the "author" of the dance, a dance master who choreographs the moves and coaches the group. Although these characters are complete fabrications, the K'iche' dancers and dance masters refer to them and all the recognizable figures as *dioses y reyes*, "gods and kings," indicating their supernatural quality. Some of them are real kings and old local heroes from other towns. One featured and recurring character

Figure 4.13 Álvaro Colóm, president of Guatemala.

Figure 4.14 Harry Potter.

from the past is El Rey de Maiz, "the Maize King," a contemporary adaptation of pre-Hispanic characters, as distant and imaginary to the K'iche' today as many of the cartoon characters.

As a formalized institution, the Ladino convite societies in the western highlands easily regulate and limit their membership. That is, this was true until approximately ten years ago, when Maya dancers began to form their own convite groups, generally referred to as *grupos de disfraz*, "groups of dis-guises." Coincidentally—or not—this was the approximate time of the sign-ing of the 1996 Oslo Peace Accord, a significant document that ensured a cease-fire agreement and provided the greatest degree of hope for reconcilia-tion between the Ladino and indigenous communities in Guatemala. It was also the final document signed that officially ended the thirty-year Guatemalan civil war. On the surface, this end to civil strife may have opened the doors for new dances in indigenous communities; although not directly related, it provided the sustenance for new opportunities among the K'iche'. Despite the fact that Momostenango has maintained a conservative way of life, the popularity of the disfraces dances indicates a growing interest in things of the world, particularly North America (Hutcheson 2003).

The K'iche' version of the convites combines the Ladino fascination with the mass media and characters from the United States with a local cultural logic inherent in Maya dance. The dancers follow many of the same rules that formalize the Ladino societies of performers. They select their partners in private, maintaining as much secrecy as possible; they practice together for

Figure 4.15 Las Espias de las Mentes Siniestras (the Spies of the Sinister Mind), Momostenango, 2006.

eight to nine months before the dances; they put considerable contemplation and thought into the design of their costumes; and they pay a substantial sum for the privilege of participating. The disfraces societies perform on special days during the festival of Patrón Santiago. I have seen many community dances in the highlands before, but never have I experienced such a packed plaza as during the disfraces.

The analysis of the Ladino versus the Maya convites lies in a comparison of the types of discourses created through these public performances; in other words, in what ways are the dances constructing a conversation about the United States and modernity? What are the different interpretive frameworks and what are the narratives that make up these conflicting historical geographies of the imagination (Davenport 1997)? The Ladino dances very markedly represent a place and space enabling participation in the global marketplace (Appadurai 2001). The bodies of the dancers themselves play out the connection of the convites to commerce, as they perform for a set price before the wealthy families' homes and businesses. In almost all cases the dance costumes represent characters and products from North America— Ronald McDonald, Santa Claus, Shrek—generating a discourse about the production, distribution, and consumption of goods. The convites characters primarily connect to children's movies, cartoon characters, and stuffed animals, one of the United States's foremost playgrounds of consumerism, representing a commonly held concept of the United States as a place of financial *imaginaire*. Moreover, the creatures are all directed toward the attention of youth, juvenile in subject matter, creating a subtext that the *bailes convites*, and by extension the danzas tradicionales that they are modeled after, are childish or child's play.

For the Maya, the dialogue created by the dances and costumes centers on a socially constructed geography that is consistent with indigenous conceptions of space, a site of geographical imagination, a dream world that has shifted to "simulacra" in mass culture yet retains social logic and meaning. The constructed geography represents an abstract conception of place, a mythical United States only slightly related to the geographic location. This is the new Tollan. For the Aztec Empire at the time of Spanish contact Tollan was a collective vision of a previous, remote, and superior space, a mythical place with a glorious, abundant, and creative past (Carrasco et. al. 2000). Garrett Cook likens the Momostecans' conception of Spain in the colonial and postcolonial era to pre-Hispanic constructions of Tollan as a "distant city from which ultimate authority and its local symbols . . . emanated. Spain is the Tulan [*sic*] of the post-conquest mythology" (2000:23). More recently, the emphasis on the Spain of Cook's description has transferred into and is projected onto the United States as an imagined geography and source of definitive influence and power. One visual example Cook (2000:127, fig. 4.6) provides includes an image of the Dance of the Conquest performed in 1976 featuring a Spanish flag with a small American flag and peace sign sewn above the caption "Captain Alvarado C.A." Today the Maya access and process this space through the Internet, migration, and employment, yet it is still full of supernatural, otherworldly, and underworld characters. As Cook notes (this volume, chapter 3), many stories of trips to the United States read like tales of heroic mythology. Tollan, Spain, and the United States are places where anything is possible and the disfraces dancers represent denizens of this magical-religious realm.

That the disfraces characters assume a magical and mysterious aspect in Momostenango indicates the participants' belief that their contribution in the dance is an act of penitence and faith and a public display of their piety, underscoring a fundamentally Maya worldview (Juan Tzoc Lajpop, pers. comm., July 31, 2006). As a demonstration of their devotion and commitment to God, the dancers perform costumbre, or religious customs, two days before the dances in front of the altar to Santiago. They ask the spirits for health, luck, and success in the dance (Juan Tzoc Lajpop, pers. comm., July 31, 2006). Moreover, before the dances begin the performers salute the four directions and acknowledge the presence of the spirits. These expressions connect the disfraces to the community's traditional public performances; although the two types of dancers physically perform in separate plazas, they compete with one another temporally, as the two run concurrently.

The K'iche' disfraces are a reflection of the Ladino convites, which themselves are a reflection of Maya ritual public performance. However, K'iche' disfraces are more closely related to indigenous cultural logic; ritual performance and theatrical dance have long functioned as an open site for critically reconstituting social practices in Maya history. This takes place through public commentary, articulated through public dances and performances, that distinguishes proper choices one must make in response to a rapidly changing local environment (Bricker 1981; B. Tedlock 1982; Krystal 2001). Ritual clowning has long been a component of Maya dance and the disfraces may well be a new face of this type of event (Bricker 1973; K. Taube 1989).

This is not to suggest that the disfraces are fundamentally similar to the traditional dances of Momostenango. Aside from the obvious differences of the costumes and characters, the disfraces are a competition of sorts. They are a "competition of egos," as the community recognizes individuals for their dancing skills. One highlight of the disfraces, borrowed from the Ladino convites, is when the dancers reveal their identity (figure 4.16).[11]

The viewers and dancers consider this the most exciting part of the dance, the crescendo of the event, when, after dancing all day long, the performers remove their masks. This is such a significant aspect of the event that fireworks accompany the dancers' disclosure, followed by a dance in the town hall that is open to the public. In addition, the dancers perform all day to contemporary cumbia, not the traditional marimba. This emphasis on new music accompanies the prominence of new costumes; they must change every year and are part of the attraction. Unlike the traditional dances, disfraces performers do not dance in the same costumes as their fathers or grandfathers. Moreover, both sexes may partake. In fact, in the summer of 2006 in Momostenango one of the pairs participating was female. In the summer of 2007 a group of women danced *convites femininas*, "women's convites," for the very first time in Momostenango. Groups of women dancers have been performing in Santa Cruz de Quiche for about fifteen years. The emphasis among the viewers is not on joining in or involving themselves but on taking in the visuals; thus it is not a true communal event but one that distinguishes and glorifies individuals for their unique abilities.

The Ladino response to the K'iche' disfraces is primarily derision.[12] There is an overt attitude of superiority and separation that emerges when discussing the indigenous disfraces with Ladinos, one that is internalized by some indigenous people as well. Flavio Pérez Zárate, a local Momostecan from a wealthy and influential urban indigenous family, referred to his family as "civilizado," or acculturated and sophisticated Maya (Garrett Cook, pers.

Figure 4.16 The most exciting moment is when the disfraces dancers reveal their identities.

comm., January 6, 2009). He falls into Carmack's (1995:264) category of petite bourgeoisie, an affluent, middle-class indigenous citizen. Zárate wrote disparagingly of the indigenous disfraces in the local publication *Qab' Antajik, Nuestra Identidad,* "our identity," a Spanish-K'iche' bilingual venue that appeals primarily to K'iche' speakers:

> El convite "Ladino" era una armonización de ritmo, orden y preocupaba mucho lo plástico para que la presentación final mostrara creatividad en lo bello y en la forma de danzar buscando ser refinado al máximo posible. Y el convite Indígena? Su enfoque trágico caminaba sobre el riesgo de la ridiculización de diferentes personajes y actors . . . provocaban malestar . . . era grotesca. (When the Ladinos dance the convite, they display harmony, rhythm, order, and a concern to demonstrate creativity and beauty in a dance that is as refined as possible. . . . The indigenous convite? It is a tragedy risking ridiculousness of different characters and actors . . . and is bothersome . . . it is grotesque; Zárate 2006:4–5, translation by the author.)

The motive behind Zárate's article is unclear, but it brings attention to the fluidity of identity construction, with its variables depending on social context. His desire to dissociate himself from the indigenous devotional practices of the disfraces is, however, very clear. Is he trying to align himself with a Ladino perspective in order to bolster his already comfortable position in Momostenango? In a national context Zárate himself may fall under the category of Ladino, but what effect will his article have in his hometown? Is he hoping to capitalize on a Ladino dialogue and confrontation as a strategy of accruing more globalized cultural capital?

The Ladinos want to highlight their international status, yet the Maya are the true transnationals. Because there have been no tax reforms in Guatemala to finance social goals and no peace dividend in the form of land or jobs, the only choice of many Guatemalans is the transnational solution (Jonas 2000:225). This involves migrating to the United States and sending back remittances. Guatemala's working and indigenous populations are transnationalized on an unprecedented scale (IOM Guatemala 2003a, 2003b, 2004; Jonas 2000:225), largely as a result of racism, civil strife, and the violence they endured during the years of the civil war.[13] "The Guatemalan diaspora (primarily in the United States, but also in Europe) played a central role in determining what stance the international community would take in relation to Guatemala's peace negotiations. The fact that the Guatemalan diaspora was so largely made up of victims of army brutality delegitimated the army and indirectly helped the URNG win the international diplomacy wars" (Jonas 2000:225–26). These events brought international attention to Guatemala and transnationalized human rights (Jonas 2000: 226). Because of the very nature of the relationship the Ladinos have with the indigenous population, the indigenous possess the global connections that the Ladinos desperately want.

In their attempts to capture traditional society, many anthropologists regard the customary expressions of indigenous culture as endangered, on the verge of extinction (Annis 1987; Hawkins 1984). Other theorists see the introduction of mass media as an incursion of information technology from an external and foreign center of production, one so strange and unrelated as to be considered incongruous to and even to undermine the conventional Maya community.[14] While it is true that the production and dissemination of telecommunications lie far outside the immediate indigenous town, their introduction to the region has not caused values and identities to disappear by acculturating North American sensibilities. No one viewing the disfraces dances would confuse them with any level of corporate culture or Western characteristics. Rather, the spread of mass media to the indigenous areas of the Guatemalan highlands has spawned a new brand and opportunity for identity construction, one that is creative and viable, reviving traditions with new forms of self-representation and enhancing cultural mobility.

Many scholars, such as Max Horkheimer and Theodor Adorno, have written about the negative effects of mass media and globalization. I would argue that the disfraces are a response to globalization and the dances strengthen values and identity rather than erode them. According to Jesus-Martin Barbero, assimilating popular culture in Latin America is a means of ensuring continued existence: "The popular classes assimilate what is available and recycle it for their physical and cultural survival" (1993:19). The dancers are continuing a practice and process that began with the arrival of the first Europeans, adopting new or foreign forms and maintaining native meaning.

As Garrett Cook (pers. comm., 2009) notes, the citizens of Momostenango have created contradictory yet at the same time viable options for public performance and expressive culture that share the same immediate terrain. Both forms of dance, the traditional-indigenous and the disfraces, exist within a largely conventional and mostly impoverished proletarian segment of society. However, they represent two coexisting imaginaries, one that is traditional-indigenous and one that is bourgeoisie. The traditional-indigenous dance performances reenact versions of the past and, at least in their expressive culture, seek "reconstruction and renewal of an ancestral world and of a world that is closely linked to Momostecan sacred geography and local precedent" (Cook, pers. comm., 2009). The disfraces, on the other hand, while still sharing some of underlying Maya cultural logic of religious celebration, nonetheless elide the local by focusing instead on the present and future through the evocation of North American mass media. The indigenous-traditional dances seek to resurrect and maintain the local Maya world of their ancestors, while the disfraces attempt to incorporate and emulate the enigmatic and often elusive other world of "Gringolandia" into immediate local space and imagination. Through the disfraces, the people of Momostenango have created one avenue for maintaining the past at the same time as they demonstrate that they are clearly rooted in the present.

CHAPTER FIVE

The Dynamics of Contemporary Maya Religious Tradition

Agency and Structure in Selected Case Studies

tilizing three case studies, this chapter explores the actions of key participants in the reproduction of festival expressive culture as they respond to the changing social and economic context of the festival and seek to further their agendas. It seeks to identify the conceptual models guiding their work, finding that some derive from Momostecan and Maya tradition while others have external origins but may nevertheless be used, at least in part, to pursue traditional goals. Religious entrepreneurism functioning within the sector of the cult of Santiago is motivated by the desire for money and local recognition as well as a profound commitment to the supernatural patron and to at least some traditional local values. The case studies show how individuals, in pursuing specific goals and strategies, are both reproducing and transforming the institutions that make up the cult of the patron saint and the religious indigenous expressive culture of the festival.

CASE 1: A CRISIS IN THE PRODUCTION OF THE MONKEYS DANCE IS SUCCESSFULLY RESOLVED THROUGH TRADITIONAL RESPONSES

In chapter 3 we described our involvement with the team that produces and performs the Monkeys Dance. As a result of our collaboration as minor sponsors, our production of the video in 2006, and our return for follow-up interviews in the summer of 2007 we had become well known to the dancers and sponsors and had developed personal relationships and mutual trust with several. When don Pedro, the main sponsor and the ritualist for the dance, was murdered in October 2007 we were called and informed (see Offit and Cook 2010; see also Smith and Offit 2010 to contextualize the wave of violence of which Pedro's murder is an example). The murder took place just a month before the November deadline for promising the dance in 2008 and left the team of dancers and the other sponsors without leadership. Furthermore, the dancers were having disturbing dreams and did not know whether the murder was an indication that the protective power of the dance had failed or whether the unexpected, violent death was a sign that the dance should not be performed. As one put it in an interview about a year after Pedro's death, "They were saying about this dance when Pedro died, 'Goodbye, monkeys.' Thus they spoke, but it was not what happened."

In December we learned that a new sponsor and a new ritualist had been named, that most of the dancers would return, and that the first practice session had been scheduled at the new sponsor's house in February. We were invited to attend and participate. When we arrived in Momostenango we visited the cross marking the location of Pedro's murder and his grave with one of his sons and one of his best friends, who had also served as his cosponsor in the dance for about twenty years. This gave us the opportunity to learn a little more about the murder and the responses of the interested parties to this threat to the dance. Then we spent two days with the dancers and helped erect the practice pole.

December 2007: New Leadership for the Dance

During his life don Pedro had sought to recruit and train not just dancers but also a chuchkajaw for the dance. Here are the words of don Anselmo, who succeeded him as chuchkajaw in 2007:

> I didn't wish to get involved in the dance [when I was a young man]. It was for the patrón [and so very delicado and demanding]. The poles were planted according to [the costumbre of] my grandfather. There was the word of the chuchkajaw, and the candles he planted in the earth.
>
> I did rocketry for nine years. I was chuchkajaw for a group of rocketeers. And there was a group called the hermandad del banda, those who provided the band for the patrón's fiesta. I stayed with them collaborating, but the patrón came to me. And the dancers, the monkeys

and the tigre and león, arrived. They took me by the arms. [In a dream?] Yes. Then I went to pay my fine to the patrón and at the Maya altar I paid my fine to the grandfathers and to the chuchkajaws that had died, that this devotion would not fall on me, because I could not afford it. This takes money. To be the autor or the chuchkajaw carries [the obligation to pay] money. It [the offering] sufficed for three or four months. Then they came to me again in a dream. Two tigres or, as it was, monkeys and leóns: "Stay you immediately, as the autor, and as the chuchkajaw, because don Pedro is going to die."

"No."

"Yes, but we will go with you." Then I had to find out what the vara would say. What is this? It is from my grandfather and the patrón, who want me to do this work, for thus it was answered in my dream. I was trying to get by with other devotions, but the patrón wanted the dance. So first I collaborated with don Pedro, I made my contribution, I told him in January that I would collaborate. For us Q 100 is a lot of money. We were with don Pedro for twelve or fifteen years. But Pedro said, "Don't just collaborate, come with me and you will be the chuchkajaw too. I am chuchkajaw, and so if I die, you will do me the favor [of continuing the costumbre]." So in this he would be first chuchkajaw and I would be second. So that the pole is lifted, so it doesn't fall, and so the young men don't fall. So for this don Pedro made the costumbre, and I made the secondary costumbre. In all this we served together.

So then don Pedro became ill with diabetes. It was not the year to bring out the dance, but I was at the ermita, I don't remember why I had gone, and I ran into don Pedro. We went to a cantina and there he told me, "You will remain as chuchkajaw because I am dying." He had been to the doctor and they told him they could not cure him.

"You are the chuchkajaw," he told me, and don Tino was autor. [His father, Celestino?] No, his son, Celestino Abram. "So you are going to remain as chuchkajaw."

But I sensed that he would not die. I sensed that the sickness did not suffice. Then I asked of my holy days that he not die. So then I told Pedro that I sensed that he would not die. So it was July 23, the fiesta had started, and I told don Pedro that on this same day he should visit the patrón in the ermita. "You bring your candles, and you say that within the year you will bring out the dance. Make a promise to do it and you won't die." So we went to the ermita and promised to bring out the dance within the year. The next day the sickness stopped.

[And when did this happen? Was this, say, twelve years ago?]

No, it was eight years ago [1999 or 2000]. Yes, eight years ago when this touched him, but we were working together for years before this.

So these devotions with the patrón. This is all because it had been done earlier by my ancestors. If they had not done it, it would not have fallen on me.

[Ah, this is in the blood, in the seed?]

Yes, it is the seed, it is the seed. I am the great-grandson of Diego Ixbatz and so it has seized me; I have another brother, but he was not grabbed, he was not called. Who knows why it is?

All of this meant that when don Pedro was murdered in 2007 he had left a trained successor to replace him in the office of chuchkajaw. But don Anselmo is a poor man and lacks the resources to serve as an autor. He was already serving as diputado of Santiago's cofradía in 2007 and truly preferred not to take on the additional responsibility of performing all the costumbre of the Monkeys Dance. In any case, it would not be his decision, since one could volunteer or resist but only the vara, questioned appropriately in a collective divination on a propitious day, could name and confirm the autor and the chuchkajaw of the dance.

In response to the question of how he and don Mauricio became chuchkajaw and autor, don Anselmo provided the following account.

After the death of don Pedro all the boys [the dancers] were asking about how the devotion would continue. Sometimes they said that don Tino should take over, or another of Pedro's sons, for he has many, they are numerous. But as of now, none have any money.

After we buried don Pedro I went to my house with my wife. The dancers accompanied me to my house. I have my little store and I sell beer. So in a little while don Mauricio arrives accompanied by don Antonio, who also followed don Pedro. They order beers. "Now that Pedro has died we are [left] with Herrera," they say. [I.e., they recognize that Juan Herrera, Pedro's closest collaborator and the man who directs the cutting, transporting, and raising of the dance pole, is now de facto leader and possibly will become the autor.]

"We need to discover who will be the autor and chuchkajaw. We don't ask you to get mixed up in this [i.e., in nominating people] but just to help discover if the patrón says it can [continue, because then] it can, and if not, then no."

This is not a game, it's hard work. The don says, "We have to find out who is his worker."

"Okay, then you don't want it this way?" [I.e., with don Juan as autor, or perhaps waiting for don Juan to call a meeting.] And don Mauricio tells me, "No, I am only trying to get things moving."

Well, then, all this has its owner, it is so powerful that it is frightening. They tell me that it can be done, that the group can visit don Juan. So I am thinking, well, darn it all, guys. What are they thinking [or what do they know?] that they [think they] can intrude in this way [with] nothing more attended to? [I.e., place don Juan as autor, or get mixed up in it themselves as outsiders, without preparatory costumbre and divination.]

So don Mauricio and don Antonio went with the boys, and they met with the two tigres, and then they went together to meet with don Juan.

"Then, now we will do this dance. Don Pedro has died, well then, we have to make the dance [without him] this year. Don Mauricio and don Antonio are with us," the boys told don Juan.

Don Juan replied, "Okay, but you need to find a chuchkajaw. Someone to ask permission and to ask who should be the autor. And you need to find a day, one of the Kiej days, to select the chuchkajaw, to select the autor. You have to go to one who has this power. Go do this with don Anselmo."

So okay, I was here [in his consulting room behind the barber shop on the town square] one Sunday [the big market day when many clients come to see him]. The two tigres came in.

"Please, sir, we have come to you to request the favor of costumbre at the four points."

"Do you know when it should be done? To raise the question to discover the answer with the vara?" [As we learned later, there was some contention about the day of Kiej that was selected, one with a low number, indicating less power. Here don Anselmo distances himself from this decision.]

"The fifteenth of December of 2007, when the next day Kiej falls, the day 4 Kiej."

"So did don Mauricio meet with you?"

"He arrived."

"And who advised you to contact me?"

"Don Juan Herrera."

"Ah good, don Juan. He is respectable and he walked with don Pedro too." Okay, so I consulted the Maya calendar to find four days for the four costumbres (at the cardinal points) to prepare for the meeting, the election, to identify the autor. To ask the patrón for this favor. To serve a lunch and to serve the spirits of this day Kiej. Then to deliver the answer on the table [he thumps the table with his forefinger as he says this], who is the autor, and who is the chuchkajaw, and what are we to do for this dance?

So I did the costumbre. When the day Kiej arrived the four costumbres had been completed, and I went with the group to find the answers to our questions. We had the meeting at the house of don Pedro Ixc'oy at La Cruz [a paraje in Aldea Xequemeya]. I arrived and I discovered that I was the only one [with a vara prepared to do the divination]. So then don Mauricio was ready to do this, and we cast the seeds for him and it was approved. And as don Pedro had been both autor and chuchkajaw we asked if don Mauricio should do both, and the answer was no. Four times we asked and it was always no. So then we asked about the others. The autor was set but not the chuchkajaw. All of them were the same, not one was accepted. So then it was suggested that I might serve. I said no, not unless someone else is here who can examine me. There was another who could ask, Antonio Ixcoy, but he had not brought his vara. Don Juan Herrera is also a chuchkajaw. He could do it the four times. So I lent him my vara.

I have two. One is for chuchkajaw working Toj, 7 Tzi, 8 Batz, 9 Eh. This is the first one that one delivers. Now of the mesas, the greatest is Kan. I am charged with responsibilities at many Maya altars, I have 8 Kan, 11 Kan, 12 Kan, 13 Kan. [These are his responsibilities as diputado of Santiago's cofradía.] I have like ten altars, all mesas.

I gave one [vara] to don Juan Herrera so he could examine me. [I.e., sort and count the seeds in a traditional divining ceremony.] He did it two, three, four until five times. I don't have time as I am also diputado of the cofradía and chuchkajaw of the hermandad de la banda, so I told them that I could not do it. But as don Juan said [here he again thumps the table while speaking], "The vara commands." So thus it was that with the death of don Pedro it fell on me, December fifteenth of 2007.

On December 15, 2007, two months after the murder of don Pedro, the dance team's leadership had been reconstituted, and there was still time to erect a practice pole at the house of the new sponsor and to begin the series of visits and offerings at sacred places described in chapter 3. In addition to Mauricio, the new autor, and Anselmo, the chuchkajaw, there were several other older and experienced collaborators, led by don Juan Herrera and including don Pedro's sons, in position to help cover the costs and to provide technical advice about felling the trees used for poles and erecting them, first at the autor's house in February and later in the plaza in July. There was, however, still some residual anxiety among the younger men who had planned on dancing. Perhaps some still worried that Pedro's death was a sign, and all were unsure of the untried new author. Many believed that Mauricio wished to serve as both autor and chuchkajaw. One dancer said, "Anselmo's divination indicated that Mauricio bought the position of autor, and he wants to straddle the rope [serve as chuchkajaw]." He was too assertive and overt in his desire to take Pedro's place. Though his clan, the Ixbatzes, had a long association with the dance, he was an outsider who had not danced himself and who had never performed the costumbre for the dance. Because he was both a distant relative of don Anselmo and a carrier of the Ixbatz surname, his nomination as autor moved the dance back to its earlier place among the Ixbatzes. For Pedro Raxc'oy's sons and relatives, two of whom were dancers and at least one of whom had been groomed to take on the authorship, the naming of Mauricio was seen to shift control of the dance from Xequemeya center back to the aldea Jutacaj, where it had originated. It was also a consolidation of all three of the publicly recognized positions of leadership, the autor, the chuchkajaw, and the marimba player, in a single patrilineage that had controlled the dance once before and a transference of the dance out of the Raxc'oy family, where the positions of autor and chuchkajaw had resided for two generations. The familial politics of all this were generally downplayed or denied by everyone involved, but when the autorship of Mauricio became problematic in February, the marimba player, who is Mauricio's neighbor and paternal uncle and who was quite intoxicated at the time, repeated over and over, "the autor is Mauricio Ixbatz, the autor is Mauricio Ixbatz," always with an emphasis on the surname. These issues were, however, of little moment for the dancers, with the possible exception of the two who were Pedro's sons.

Since Anselmo had served as chuchkajaw of the dance for one year some time ago when Pedro was seriously ill and had been groomed by Pedro to assume the position, since he had made traditionally appropriate and socially acceptable demonstrations of resistance to assuming the position, and since he had already played a prominent role in the cult of the patron saint, he was known and trusted. The dancers were reasonably comfortable with him as their protector and guide. The entire team would, however, be tested again in February.

February 2008: The Practice Pole

The tree designated to become the practice pole was located near the bottom of a small ravine, part of new sponsor (autor) don Mauricio's property in Recana, and it was beautiful. Roughly eighteen meters tall and perfectly straight, it was the type of tree that is still ubiquitous in this part of highland Guatemala and gives the region its lush beauty. The dancers raced down the steep ravine to take turns with the huge double-bladed axe, mocking each other's technique and boasting about their own as they trimmed its branches. They had relished the excitement of chopping it down at sunrise but also realized the enormity of what the tree meant, as they had slept under it the previous night and made burnt offerings to it as a means of paying homage to what would become the focal point of their fears and anxieties during the practice season.

It was time for lunch and the tree was still firmly lodged in the ravine, resisting the initial attempts to drag it up to the edge of the milpa. Six older women appeared with beans and *chuchitos* (small corn tamales) to feed the assembled crowd of dancers and neighbors who came to help out on this propitious day. Don Pedro's name was invoked frequently at lunch, as it had been throughout all of the dance preparations, and his spirit seemed to hover over the gathered.

It was a magical scene, scented with pine, as the dancers and don Mauricio returned from lunch and walked the tree trunk, whipping the tree with small, braided leather quirts, attempting to break its resistance so it could be pulled out of the ravine, while the two oldest men played the "Rey Quiche" on marimba and cane flute. With the assembled spectators cheering them on, the men began walking the fallen tree in rank order, until about midway through their journey, when don Mauricio, a fifty-seven-year-old tavern owner, slipped off the tree and fell six feet to the steeply sloping ground below. The others laughed and continued upward, but when don Mauricio did not quickly get up, the dancers looked at his fallen body and one, Felipe, called out, "Don Mauricio, it is broken!" The others jumped down and gathered more closely. Don Mauricio's left ankle and foot were hanging by a shred of skin and tendon at a ninety-degree angle to his left leg, the jagged ends of his fibula and tibia exposed for all to see. Don Mauricio stared out at the group with a dazed expression, clearly the victim of shock. One of the dancers immediately grabbed his leg and reset it, just as don Mauricio's wife and family arrived from their nearby house. He was then quickly carried to the shade of a clump of avocado trees on the edge of the milpa, wrapped in a blanket, and given rum to ease his suffering. As his kinfolk gathered round him, the other dance sponsors and dancers formed a tight circle slightly away from the stricken leader and his family, collected all the money from everyone present to help with the hospital bill, and then engaged in a solemn discussion about such an ill portent at the start of the first year of don Pedro's dance after his murder.

This was not the first bad omen that haunted a member of the dance team. Tomás, a charismatic leader and one of the tigres, who served as the missal reader during all costumbre, the man who was called upon when work was most difficult, said there were numerous ill portents before don Pedro's death. Two of the dancers from the previous dance year had embraced women while wearing their costumes and were not invited back. As mentioned earlier, a popular television channel (Channel 4) had obtained a pirated copy of a video made by the two anthropologists and had broadcast it on national television without consent, bringing the dancers undesired notoriety for obscene language and unruly behavior. And then there were the dreams that haunted Tomás.

Tomás's dreams began in July 2007, just after the *coheteria*, or festival of fireworks, that was sponsored by don Pedro on alternating years with the Monkeys Dance. The dreams were dark ones, and they indicated that the dancers were in peril. Tomás has not received the spiritual call to become a diviner, and therefore he went to don Pedro, the most spiritually gifted man he knew, to interpret the dream for him. They discussed his dreams on three different occasions, and Pedro's interpretation was always the same, that the dream foretold that death was coming and that the victim, in Pedro's words, "will be one of us." Pedro's subsequent murder had both validated the dream and alleviated Tomás's fears, as death had claimed its victim. But when don Mauricio fell, fears emerged anew that the dance itself was in peril and that the dancers were tempting the fates and possibly incurring don Pedro's wrath by trying to carry on the dance.

Gathered in a tight circle, the six participating dancers, two remaining autors, two anthropologist/collaborators, and chuchkajaw were now forced to consider the meaning of don Mauricio's fall and to decide if the dance should continue. On the edge of the milpa, the future of the most famous and revered of Momostenango's traditional dances, one with an unbroken chain of sponsors and performances going back at least six generations in Aldea Xequemeya, was at stake, and the ghost of the murdered don Pedro was everywhere.

All those present knew how the answers to their fearful questions were to be discerned. We repaired to a dark room in don Mauricio's compound and began a two-hour process of discussion and divination that would provide the answers. At the front of the room was don Mauricio 's altar, covered in spent candles, coins, pre-Colombian artifacts, and a photo of Momostenango's patron saint, Santiago, accompanied by his secretary and companion, San Felipe. Next to the photo were placed thirteen bundles of copal incense wrapped in corn husks, and four red votive candles were lit. A smaller table was placed in front of the altar, where the chuchkajaw, don Anselmo, placed a small table covering of traditional handwoven cloth and his bag of divinatory seeds (seeds of the tzité tree; see B. Tedlock 1982 for a detailed description). Don Anselmo was seated at this table, while all others were given seats surrounding him, and after a brief invocatory Maya prayer and a Hail Mary said by the group, the process began.

The dominant elder and cosponsor, don Juan Herrera, argued that the primary matter was to define the questions that were to be asked by don Anselmo of the powers that ordained how the sorting and counting of the seeds would unfold. It was quickly concluded that answers were needed to the following questions: Why had don Mauricio fallen? Should the dance proceed? And if it were to proceed, should the same practice pole be used? Don Anselmo then set to work, methodically mixing the seeds and laying little piles of four seeds in rows and columns, always noting the remainder, one to four, in the final pile. As don Anselmo read the permutations of the seeds and listened to his blood for signs, those assembled began to offer their own explanations for what had occurred and how best to proceed, often with several talking at once.

Two camps quickly emerged. Tomás and two others feared that the dance had been cursed, a result of don Pedro's murder, the sins of previous dancers, and the result of poor calendrical design of the events by the planners, holding the first reunion of the dancers on a day that was insufficiently powerful. They believed that it was best for the safety of all to refrain from dancing this year. In addition, the dance was now without a primary sponsor, as don Mauricio would probably be unable to pay the prohibitive costs of sponsoring the dance, an outlay of Q 25,000–30,000, money that would be needed for medical bills. Then a messenger entered the room to report another ill omen. The pickup truck transporting don Mauricio to the hospital had gone into a ditch, though thankfully there were no injuries.

The second camp was led by Bernabé and Felipe. Like Tomás, both were veteran dancers with important roles, yet unlike Tomás, both had been married for years and had children who also participated in the dance as little leónes and monkeys. They suspected that the blame for don Mauricio's injury lay with him, and that it was likely a result of his being bewitched or punished for an act unrelated to the dance. Don Mauricio was partly to blame because he had not made his initial burnt offerings with all of the other dancers, as is usually done, but on his own. While expressing tremendous admiration for don Mauricio and for all that he had done, they said that he was not the man to lead them, and they must find another sponsor and continue the dance.

Rather propitiously at this point, don Anselmo stopped the divination and indicated that the seeds had told him that don Mauricio's fall had been his own fault, the result of a curse put on him by a rival, and his accident was not sent by don Pedro nor a result of the ancestors' displeasure with the dancers. He further indicated that the dance should proceed but that a different tree had to be chosen, with the bad tree cut up for firewood. Mauricio could continue as sponsor if he confessed and paid his fine. The group briefly discussed the findings, which were strongly endorsed by the influential don Pedro Torres, who, as an initiated diviner himself, the senior collaborator, the director of the cutting and erecting of the pole, and a close friend of the murdered don Pedro, had considerable authority. All proceeded outside to select another tree.

In the end, another palo was selected, this one on level ground and with easy access to don Mauricio's milpa. It was felled, hauled to a spot near don Mauricio's house, which required the removal of a mature avocado tree that was in the way, and erected with the use of a series of scissor-jacks of lashed, rough-hewn poles. Offerings were made and drink and food were distributed, all in accordance with past tradition. Yet the band that arrived to play music all night was discharged, since the wife and family of don Mauricio were in a state of mourning about his injury and the financial ruin that it might portend. There was sadness in the air as the dancers and sponsors reminisced about don Pedro, spoke in hushed tones about don Mauricio, and speculated about how they would manage to find a dancer to take on the role of the missing monkey and, more importantly, a well-heeled elder willing to accept the burden of becoming the sponsor should Mauricio withdraw. Tomás accepted the authority of the divination but still seemed anxious about all of the ill omens that had befallen the group and the general state of "spiritual insecurity." Though he remained uncertain about dancing in February and was receiving some pressure from his new bride to withdraw, he had made a promise to dance, and he did ultimately dance the role of first tigre during the festival in July.

Tomás's concerns about ill omens were only confirmed when Zelote, the colorful first monkey who was now one of the veteran dancers of the group, resigned from the dance in April, creating a second vacancy, and then was murdered in June 2008 in the nearby municipio of Santa Lucia. The dancers were stunned, but as he had broken his promise to dance, his death could be attributed to punishment from Patrón Santiago and so supported the dancers' beliefs about the power of their saint and of the dance. In July the dance went on, albeit with only one additional new recruit, and so still with only seven of the usual eight roles filled and with a sponsor who was home from the hospital but walking with a crutch.

July 2008: The Performance

The only noticeable difference between the dance in 2008 and the performance in 2006 described in chapter 3 was that, at the request of the dancers, the anthropologists had returned to Momostenango with a four-foot-by-two-foot poster of don Pedro to honor and celebrate his sponsorship of the dance. The first tigre and Garrett Cook mounted the poster on a thin plywood backing and covered it with clear plastic, and the dance team hung it from the roof over the marimba stand on the western edge of the dance ground. It was displayed for two days, and then, out of respect for the current autor and the new chuchkajaw, it was removed and kept in the room behind the barbershop where the dancers would meet to disrobe after the performance.

Though it could not be observed directly by the audience, there were also two vacancies among the animal impersonators who did tricks on the rope. One monkey had not returned at all and had been replaced by a new recruit, one of the sons of don Pedro. Another had dropped out in April, as explained above, only to be murdered shortly later, and had been replaced at the last minute by one of the sons of don Juan. The son of don Juan had lived most of his life in Guatemala City, did not speak K'iche', and though welcomed by the other dancers, was teased about his lack of fluency in the native language. He had tripped several times, had spilled his offerings during some of the ceremonies prior to the start of the festival, and had confessed to having had sex during a period of required abstinence. Even though he paid his fine, the chuchkajaw believed that the rope was too dangerous for him in this first year, so he was not allowed to perform during either the practice sessions or the public performances in Momostenango. He paid his share for the rental of a costume and usually dressed in costume to perform on the ground, but he would have to make a quick switch with the other female monkey, who took his place on the rope in the rotation of alternate days of dancing. It is expected that a counterpart will cover for his partner on any day or days when a dancer is not physically or emotionally up to the challenge, and this forms a very intense emotional bond between those who share a costume, but a shortage in the roster that requires dancing or especially tricks on the rope every day without a break is very demanding and dangerous and is a major sacrifice by the performer.

The pole was selected in the cemetery on the southern slope of a ridge and had to be raised up to the top and then hauled through an area with many graves to the road along the northern side. It was very hard work, but it went smoothly and there were no bad signs during the felling, hauling, or erecting of the pole.

The dancers may have been a bit more nervous than usual while performing, since, though they were convinced by the divination and by the lack of additional bad signs during the practice sessions and the felling and raising of the dance pole in the plaza that the dance itself was not cursed, the dance's magic had seemingly failed to protect don Pedro and don Mauricio. Dancing places one in a perilous situation, hanging from a rope sixty feet above the plaza in full view of any enemies in the crowd below who might have the evil eye or who might be seeking to raise an attacking evil spirit. Still, only one dancer reported an attack. The first león reported that he just started his first performance on the rope above the plaza when he felt a wind suddenly blow into his mask, an aere, or spirit-wind. It made his eyes water, and he could not see clearly for a moment. Then, just as suddenly, it stopped, his vision cleared, and he went on with the performance. He suspected that this attack might have come from the ghost of the recently murdered dancer, with whom he had had a strained relationship since, though they had the closeness and mutual regard of a pair sharing a costume, the other dancer had wanted to take his place as first león and had suffered from envy before he resigned. In any case, though, as he explained it, the power of the mask had protected him.

Tradition, Agency, and Cultural Reproduction

Momostecan tradition, which has been designed to deal with predictable adversity within a society where sudden deaths have never been particularly uncommon, was followed closely in the rapid reorganization of the leadership of this dance team. Within a community of believers confronting novel circumstances, divination provides a means for discussing matters and possibly reaching consensus during the process without forming clear-cut factions. With or without consensus or the emergence of nascent factions, it provides authoritative decisions that produce a significant reduction in anxiety and yield effective collective responses.

In this case there was no need for any significant innovation in behavior nor restructuring of the institution in order to make things work. This was true and will remain true so long as there is a directorate of older and experienced retired dancers and properly initiated ritualists to oversee the dance and to organize collectively when needed. Ordinarily the dance sponsor is responsible for recruiting dancers and for raising the funds needed to keep the dance going and is its public face, but if he is working effectively and if the group is to have a future, he is never really alone. Instead, he functions as the public face for a larger group, much as the alcalde of an aldea traditionally represented a group of generally invisible principales. He is also responsible for identifying and apprenticing younger men, often from among his sons, who can be trained to assume the position when he is ready to retire or when he dies.

A dance team, however, is very different from a traditional cofradía or the visible authorities in an aldea in that it is and has been voluntary. But in the traditional value system of local K'iche' culture the sponsor and chuchkajaw should seek to resist service when it is seemingly thrust upon them, as don Anselmo did, even though it was clear to everyone that he was actually interested in and willing to accept the position. Don Mauricio, then, was a bit suspect as an outsider to the group who suddenly began acting to organize the group in its time of crisis and who made it clear that he was interested in a leadership position. As the position of autor is very expensive and no one else was really ready to take it on, it was his even if he sought it a bit too openly, but it was also his with some reservations and a wait-and-see attitude reflected in the idea that he bought the position or that his fall was a sign that he should not have been autor. The splitting of the chuchkajaw role from that of autor after two generations in which they had been conjoined also reflected this ambivalence about a candidate who was perhaps too eager to accept the responsibility. The autor enables the dance to continue, but it is the chuchkajaw who both directs and protects the dancers, so for them it is far more important to gauge the character and the spiritual power of the chuchkajaw and to have someone in that role in whom they have confidence.

During the nineteenth-century expansion and reorganization of the cofradías within a centralized and bureaucratized administrative structure with compulsory service, the dance teams were allowed to remain decentralized and voluntary. Thus they seem to have retained more of the feeling and social structure of the pre-Hispanic chinamit or *calpul*, a locally based community that was organized around both collectively shared labor on a corporate estate and collective participation in the cult of a tutelary deity image maintained by a leading patrilineage. The chinamit served as the model for decentralized cofradías during the colonial period (Hill and Monaghan 1987; Fox and Cook 1996; Cook 2000:29–33). This older Maya form of community organization survived the nineteenth- and early twentieth-century imposition of bureaucratized and centralized cofradía organization in local cults of privately owned saint's images, called *wachibalab*, and so would have been available as a model within the local culture for construction of the dance teams.[1]

Whether or not the dance's organization derives from this native model for community, the Monkeys Dance was able to respond to sudden adversity effectively and to retain its traditional twentieth-century form, even within a new and in many respects unsupportive post-peasant social and neoliberal economic context. This is because it has long had a flexible and voluntary form of social organization and so has not been affected adversely by the increasingly factionalized and marginalized traditional authority structure of principales and auxiliatura. It also has been successful at reproducing itself because don Pedro was careful to identify and train potential successors for his role as chuchkajaw (Anselmo) and as autor (his sons, particularly don Tino). Had Mauricio not come forward, then don Tino probably would have served as autor as a result of social pressure, but he was glad to have a reprieve for financial reasons. Still, he is waiting in the wings, so to speak, in the event that Mauricio cannot continue, as is don Juan Herrera, who truly does not want to be autor but likely would accept if the role was thrust upon him by social pressure and divination.

Finally, the dance has been successful in retaining much of its structure and meaning because it has adapted effectively to attrition, for example, in eliminating the acting out of the script of the Deer Dance, justified by the noise in the plaza, even though the real reason may be the loss of the dance script or of a maestro for training the dancers. Since the dance script has been abandoned in favor of clowning and impromptu skits, the traditional marimba music is less important and the dance can probably continue with the same meanings for the performers even as the performance loses and changes much of its content. The real challenge for the dance in the future is that of recruiting young men to assume the roles of the animals. The younger generation may be less inclined to hold traditional animistic beliefs, though that is unclear. In addition to the Costumbristas there is a pool of recent converts to cultural activist Maya religion, some of whom might be willing to serve as dancers, though that pool in Momostenango may involve more women than men and generally lacks the seemingly critical family connections to ancestral and recent dancers.

The current crop of dancers, seven in total since they are short one monkey, are well versed in the requirements of the dance. Of the seven, six have close family members who were dancers themselves at some point, all recall being fascinated by the dance since their earliest days, and all of them are proud to have taken up the cargo to be a dancer, yet they all also point out that they never truly understood the tremendous sacrifice that being a dancer entails. While all dancers fear the ultimate sacrifice that some give for the dance, namely injury or death from a fall, it is the commitments of time and money that make the dance such a heavy burden for all involved. All devote thirty-five days to the dance: fourteen days of performing the dance during the annual fiesta and between ten and fifteen days performing costumbre at various sacred places in the K'iche' region outside of Momostenango, as well as various days for meetings, practices, and costumbre performed locally. In addition, each dancer contributes nearly $800 for the right to participate, including rental of their costume ($200–$250) and mask ($50), a fee for food and drink ($150), and religious offerings ($300), plus transportation costs and fines levied by the group for failure to perform any of their functions adequately. The financial sacrifice accounts for an estimated 20–40 percent of their annual income, not to mention the opportunity cost (see Offit and Cook 2010 for a full accounting).

Felipe, whose father danced in the Mexicanos Dance, has always wanted to dance. Mateo's father died when he was only three, but his grandfather was at one time part of both the Dance of the Conquest and the Mexicanos Dance, and Tomás's father was a participant as well. Don Pedro inherited the autorship from his father, and don Juan's father was an active member of dance teams in the distant past. Yet current dancers differ radically from their progenitors in one significant regard: their progenitors were farmers and artisans fully vested in the local economy. They were "hombres de maiz" in the words of Miguel Angel Asturias, and the milpa provided their food, at least some of their money, and their identity.

The 2006 dance team included an assistant to truck drivers based in Guatemala City, two street vendors who live and work largely in Guatemala City, one itinerant vendor who has a biweekly route between Guatemala City, Quetzaltenango, and the border region of Huehuetenango, two young men who live and sell various goods on the streets of the coastal city of Escuintla, and a tuk-tuk driver who lives in Totonicapán. As noted earlier, during one practice session in 2006 don Pedro received a call on his cell phone from a dancer on furlough working in posthurricane construction in Florida who knew it was a day of costumbre and wanted to wish everyone well. While many of these men maintain small homes on ancestral land around Momostenango and some work small subsistence plots with the aid of family members, only Tomás truly resides in Momostenango, and he is no milpero but instead runs a small, rented store selling dry goods and food on the central square.

The main problem for cultural reproduction is that represented by Juanito in 2008. His father, don Juan, owns land and a house in Xequemeya, the community of origin for the dance, and is an important dance collaborator and possible future candidate for autor or chuchkajaw. Juanito, though, has lived all his life in the capital, working in his father's business and visiting Momostenango at festival times. He does not speak K'iche' and cannot be present for all the practices and preparatory rituals. With young men leaving Momostenango to go to high school and even pursue higher education, or more commonly to work in the informal urban and international labor sectors, the dance has to adjust. It is encountering serious challenges to reproduction at a time when it may be an increasingly important symbol of local tradition and both Momostecan and Maya identity.

CASE 2: A CULTURAL ACTIVIST SEEKING LEADERSHIP IN THE CULT OF SANTIAGO SPONSORS A NEGLECTED FIESTA

The Events

For about the past twenty years, on the night of July 23 there has been an observance honoring Patrón Santiago and San Felipe in a chapel originally constructed in 1986 by the Committee for Construction of the Ermita of the Patron on donated land in Barrio Santa Isabel. Cook and Offit witnessed the chapel events together in 2006 while making a video record of the Monkeys Dance, having accompanied Santiago and San Felipe and the Monkeys Dance team in the procession from the cofradía house to the chapel after lunch on July 23. Cook visited the vigil at the hermandad chapel again for several hours in 2007, and then Cook and some Baylor students were invited, by a new sponsor, to participate in producing and decorating for a newly designed festival in 2008 and 2009. This building and its relationship to the cult of Santiago had interested Cook and Offit for several years, and its history was finally revealed through interviews with a member of the original committee in 2009. This history and the features of social organization that it reveals are critical for providing context for the agency of contemporary actors as they reproduce and construct the festival.

The committee's officers in 1986 were the most influential Costumbristas living in the town center and included two ex–sindico segundos.[2] The chapel was intended to serve as the location for the annual cofradía festival, which prior to that time in the late nineteenth- and twentieth-century system of festival sponsorship had been sponsored by the alcalde of the cofradía and usually took place in a rented house. The committee intended that the new ermita would allow the cofrades to save money and would insure that the processions each year could be planned with a regular destination.

The initial committee leadership was formed among the leaders of a preexisting hermandad for Santiago that had been organized among Costumbristas, including some acculturated Maya leaders from the town center, in 1965. From the 1950s through the 1970s there was a constant concern among Costumbrista leaders that Catholic strategies to remove paganism from the church would result in a weakening of the important costumbre performed for Santiago and in the lessening of their power and influence in town. The hermandad was formed in part to serve as an independent, parallel entity that might take over cofradía functions if the cofradía were disbanded or taken over by Catholic activists and in part to consolidate and give tangible expression to the strength of the urban/acculturated–indigenous/rural Costumbrista alliance. It was probably the first indigenous organization in town to utilize the strategy of having a large membership pay regular dues to underwrite fiesta costs rather than the system of rotating sponsorships found in the cofradías. Waldemar Smith (1977:6), borrowing from Ladino religious brotherhoods, named this strategy the "appended strategy." Though it was earlier known as the indigenous hermandad for Santiago, and up through the 1970s it sponsored its own procession with the colonial image of Santiago, paralleling but separate from the cofradía procession, it evolved into an organization that is today called the hermandad de bandas. One of its official missions is to raise money to cover the costs of the bands used in the cofradía processions with Santiago and San Felipe during the annual festival.

The cofradía itself, though, is a much-changed institution, and the hermandad's functions have come to include the oversight and recruitment of the cofrades of Santiago. A separate hermandad exists for Holy Week, with apparently similar functions related to the cofradías of Corpus, Capitagua and Santa Cruz, and Santa Bárbara, the latter responsible for the image of San Simón. This role of oversight of the cofradías by hermandades developed between the 1980s and today as the traditional and official authority structure was increasingly diminished in scale and power and as privatization of the national and local economies was instituted through neoliberal reforms. It has several related motives.

A succession of Catholic priests since the 1950s had worked to enhance church control over the cofradías—for example, through control of visitas and elimination of beverage and offering sales. Combined with increasing restiveness by distant aldeas, and especially by resistance to cofradía service in those aldeas that had large numbers of Catholic activists and where cacique families had converted, this meant that the cofradía system was under considerable pressure by the 1970s (Cook 2000:27–49; see also chapter 2). Two definitive developments occurred in the 1980s. First, the priest decreed that all alms and donations given to Santiago during the festival were to go to the church and not to the cofradía. Second, a Ladino municipal alcalde—appointed by the military during the height of the violence in the 1980s and closely allied with the Costumbrista and acculturated Indian faction—eliminated involuntary service in the cofradías in order to focus the communities' stressed resources on service to the town through the auxiliatura. This meant that the principales were no longer responsible for appointing cofrades and that the sindico segundo was no longer responsible for oversight and control of the cofradías. Suddenly cofradía service was completely voluntary, and the shared church and government oversight and control no longer existed.[3] The Catholic priest was now the sole governing authority.

Costumbre versus activist Catholic polarization had declined during the 1980s and 1990s as Guatemala was reorganized by violence, which included persecution of Catholic activists, and by the emergence of a new economy that encouraged privatization and as local religious pluralism exploded through the development of numerous Pentecostal and Evangelical Protestant churches. By the midnineties a sect of cultural activists desiring to purify and revitalize a distinctively Maya religion, as described in chapters 1 and 2, had also become prominent players in the local religious pluralism of highland villages. Two indigenous Catholic priests were sent to Momostenango in succession in the early twenty-first century. They sought to inculcate a new enculturation theology aimed at accepting some nondoctrinally crucial Costumbrista religious trappings in order to bring more Costumbristas into the church. The church, then, while not exactly supportive of costumbre, took a long view and so seemed to be willing to coexist with the local syncretized cult of the patron saint for a time, so long as the Costumbristas were willing to participate in mass and to include formal and official Catholicism, including a leadership role for the parish priest, in the more public manifestations of their religion.

With this background established, it is time to return to consideration of the festival itself to understand how the indigenous traditions in the cult of the patron saint have responded to these developments through the strategic behavior of key actors. The festival on July 23 that had been sponsored by the cofradía in the 1970s at what had been the hermandad chapel has been retained, as Costumbristas are always reluctant to drop observances or rituals that have become integral to their cult. However, it is no longer followed by the entrance of a new alcalde and cofrades on the following morning at an induction ceremony in the municipal cathedral (Cook 2000:83). As part of the reorganization of the cofradía its new alcalde, who has been appointed by the elders in the hermandad with an open term, has begun sponsoring his own fiesta for Santiago and San Felipe at his house on July 22, a festival with expensive bands and food and drink for all attendees, including the dance teams (Monkeys, Mexicans, and Conquest) that is allegedly costing well over Q 10,000. With minimal support from the hermandad and from the diputado, who is a poor man, the alcalde is obliged to cover this cost.

During the early twenty-first century, then, the new festival at the alcalde's house, an intentional return to the earlier, prehermandad ermita format, had created a vacuum in sponsorship of the more public vigil and festival on July 23, the traditional time for the cofradía festival that had been moved to the hermandad chapel in the late twentieth century. Thus in 2006 and 2007 we witnessed a very simple and by Momostecan standards a dispirited (*triste*) event in the hermandad chapel. The procession's brass band, paid for by the hermandad de bandas, had delivered Santiago to the chapel and quickly departed, leaving no music at the chapel. Santiago and San Felipe were placed on the altar table and then were greeted by a twenty-minute prayer session in a chapel space that was about one-third full, with some invocations in K'iche' and some prayers in Spanish accompanied by several chanted or sung litanies, all led by the diputado of the cofradía. The chapel was not decorated; the only illumination came from candles on the floor and, for a short time, from wan, gray late-afternoon light entering through four barred windows on the north and south just below the roofline. No food was served, and small parties just came and went all night to offer candles and seek personal blessings. Some brought gifts of scarves, towels, or boots to present to the image. At midnight the alcalde and the diputado changed the images' outfits behind a screen of Momostecan blankets. Thus in Momostecan usage the events at the hermandad chapel in 2006 and 2007 would best be characterized as a visita or vigil but not a fiesta, and the overall feeling was triste.

Things were different in 2008 and 2009. A local man in his thirties, called don Eligio in this account, was the leading Momostecan member of a mainly female regional association of cultural activist Maya calendar priests (sacerdotes Mayas, also called *aj q'ijab*, or day keepers), called the Nine Thread (Belejeb Batz) Council of Diviners.[4] For reasons that remain somewhat unclear but are explored below, don Eligio had become increasingly interested in contributing to the local cult of the saints. In 2007 he attended the festival and, with his wife and children, donated a pair of boots to the image. In making this donation he became acquainted with the alcalde and diputado of the cofradía, since only they could actually place the boots on the image's feet. In his conversations with these officials and participation in the vigil he learned that nobody was sponsoring this part of the festival. Thus don Eligio realized that he could honor Santiago, enhance his supernatural patronage, and further his public visibility as a supporter of Santiago if he took over this poor, neglected festival. In 2008 he enlisted the help of several women from Quetzaltenango who were members of the Nine Thread Council and of two Baylor students who were looking for an ethnographic project to sweep the chapel and cover the floor with donated pine boughs. He enlisted his dad, an electrician, to restore power to the fluorescent bulbs in the chapel, he hired a marimba band, and he arranged to have sufficient tamales and atole to feed a crowd of three hundred people. He also arranged to have a woman who was a trained Catholic lay leader come from Totonicapán to lead a complete rosary to open the festival after Santiago and San Felipe were installed on the altar.

In 2009 the festival followed the same general pattern, with enhanced decorations, since don Eligio had received a donation of about twenty dozen roses in addition to the pine boughs. Basket-shaped containers hot glued to the walls each displayed a spray of roses, and rose petals were scattered over the pine boughs on the floor. Instead of the rosary, the welcome featured a series of prayers led by the Momostecan parish priest in white vestments and included a homily on the life of Saint James and the importance of works as opposed to words. Don Eligio stood on the priest's right side behind the small, red-draped altar table that sat in front of the images of Santiago and San Felipe on a much larger table covered with Momostecan blankets. Often looking to heaven and raising his hands palms upward, he was a bit glassy-eyed and was clearly inebriated. Several times the padre gently restrained him by placing a hand over his hand as don Eligio tried to become more actively involved in the service. The crowd was large enough that all the food was distributed and don Eligio and doña Tomasina served everyone but did not get to eat. After the crowd was served most left and the normal vigil ensued, but accompanied by music and with some drunks dancing close to the brass band near the entrance.

Since vows are made as novenas in Momostenango, don Eligio will still have to sponsor this festival seven more times. This burden is significant, as he cannot be assured of continued financial assistance from the community and he cannot afford to sponsor without help. In a private conversation right after the festival in 2008 doña Tomasina explained that she was terrified: "Why did he make this vow which now endangers the entire family? It is well known that Santiago is very delicado and will kill the children of those who do not keep their promises."

In fact, within about a month of those comments doña Tomasina was involved in a bus accident on the Pan-American Highway (CA-1) in which the bus rolled into a river and she sustained a concussion and her collarbone was broken. They nearly lost their baby, who was found in the water after a heroic search in the dying light at the end of this terrible day and then suffered from hypothermia, shock, and persistent bowel complications from ingesting polluted water. The latter required hospitalization and several expensive courses of treatment before she was returned to health. Within a traditional Momostecan understanding of service to the saints, this calamity was an appropriate punishment for doña Tomasina's condition of being of two hearts about the vow. Santiago relented and spared the child only after she confessed her sins and paid fines to Santiago, and the extended families also paid much greater fines to the hospital. The enhanced festival in 2009, with roses and the involvement of the priest, combined with additional presents of new boots and towels, was part of the continuing effort to reassure this dangerous saint of the fidelity of this family, as well as another chapter in don Eligio's campaign to achieve a position as a leader of the cult.

The Sponsor of the New Fiesta

Don Eligio is neither poor nor wealthy by local standards, but he cannot afford to sponsor this fiesta with a band and free food for hundreds every year for nine years. Most of his closest relatives are Mormons and do not approve of the idolatry in the festival, so he had to line up significant support from members of the Nine Thread Council and from personal connections in Momostenango. This may become increasingly problematic, as Nine Thread's recent rapid expansion in membership has the form of a pyramid scheme. As new members were recruited they paid their teachers for classes and ceremonies. The group then stopped growing, and so the last recruits never regained their expenses, and active members remain responsible for very expensive ceremonies. After rapid growth both regionally and locally between 2005 and 2007, growth stopped in 2008 and the group suffered retrenchment for the first time in 2009.

Don Eligio is a mediating figure in many ways. His father is a native Momostecan from an acculturated indigenous family and his mother is a mestizo woman from the southern coast who has lived in Momostenango for thirty-plus years and has learned to speak fluent K'iche'. Many of the acculturated families became Adventists and Mormons during the second half of the twentieth century. Don Eligio's parents and the rest of his immediate family are active Mormons, and don Eligio was raised in the Mormon Church. He worked as a truck driver for several years but found himself without direction and suffering from depression. He developed a drinking problem that did not fit his Mormon identity and did not respond to family intercession.

He had several blackouts while driving and finally had an accident that ended his career as a driver. In his search for a cure for his drinking problem and a new life he visited a diviner, who advised him that he was being called by the Holy Earth and needed to undergo an apprenticeship and initiation. At that point, while studying alone based on texts he had purchased, he returned to his city and began offering his services to friends in the capital as both a diviner and a *brujo* (witch). He reported that his practice was quite successful, as he was acquainted with various bars and brothels from his truck-driving days and he found many new clients among the women and men who both worked in and patronized these establishments. After his initial success in the city, he returned to Momostenango in order to serve his home pueblo and learn from the many famous shamans of the region.

He is part of the vanguard within a confused generation that has had to leave Momostenango for work and whose members have often struggled to establish their identity, fitting in neither in Momostenango nor in the larger society. In don Eligio's case the situation is doubly confused by his mixed parentage and his greater than average need for recognition and influence. He is an outsider who, once he separated from the Mormon community, has sought to become a leader through religious entrepreneurism. His initial strategy in the period between the late 1990s and about 2007 was to focus on becoming a recognized *Aj q'ij*, or Maya priest, within the cultural activist revitalized religion that developed in the highlands with the rise of Maya activism following the end of the civil war and the celebration of and resistance to the Columbus quincentennial in 1992. He had a genuine conversion, and his life was renewed by the ceremonies, by his acceptance in this community of believers, by his growing faith, enhanced by his ability to cure his clients. He married a woman from a family of Costumbristas, and as she was active in the indigenous women's movement, he joined her as one of the few male members in Nine Thread. He quickly rose to prominence as the main coordinator of ceremonies at the famous altars in Momostenango for the members of this congregation, most of whom were from Totonicapán and Quetzaltenango.

This group and other, similar activist religious groups had moved toward the creation of a cycle of calendrical Maya ceremonies without Spanish/Catholic admixtures in what C. James Mackenzie (1999, 2005; see also Stewart and Shaw 1994) has called antisyncretism. Thus we are presented with an interesting problem. Why did don Eligio, between 2006 and 2008, apparently abandon the quest for a purified Maya religion that he had championed in our conversations with him in 2006 and take the initial steps toward a position of leadership in the cult of Santiago?

His recognition among the leaders of the syncretized religious observances within the fiesta was enhanced considerably in June and July 2009 when with the autors of two of the traditional dances in the community he opposed the municipal alcalde's attempts to use the swine flu scare to cancel the festival. With expensive legal help and following several visits to the capital to confer with the minister of sports and culture as well as a purported phone conversation with the president of Guatemala, this group prevailed and the mayor reinstated the festival. Garrett Cook joked with don Eligio that the new laminated sheet metal fence around his house created a fortress to protect him from the mayor's followers and also joked that since his extended family now owned a microbus all he would need was a dark jacket and tie and he could run for mayor in the next election. It was clear from his response that don Eligio had actually thought about this possibility but could not imagine how he could finance a political campaign.

Tradition, Agency, and Cultural Reproduction

Don Eligio's strategies in his role as a cultural broker and festival producer suggest that he is engaged in a two-stage process of transforming and preserving indigenous religion. In this pattern individuals with a need for recognition who are suffering from the identity confusion that has grown out of the rapid pluralization of rural Guatemala and Momostenango and who lack firm grounding in and family connections to the local syncretized religion initially develop new identities as practitioners of a more abstract Maya religion. But in practicing in a real place—at the altars in Momostenango—and in becoming familiar with older ritualists who actually embody the local syncretized traditions as well as becoming aware of the growing vacuums in leadership of the public institutions that express Costumbre, they experience a second and less profound but very important conversion. They seek to claim identities as Momostecan religious leaders. In doing so they take on responsibility for the reproduction of the tradition, but they do so with innovative ideas, like setting up recording sessions with traditional musicians and involving women in roles that were previously open only to men, as in the plan, as yet unrealized, of training some women to play the religious chirimía (shawm) music.

Thus there are indications of a process in which an initial phase of Mayanization occurs at both individual and collective levels, followed by a phase of localization/indigenization that seeks to preserve the local traditions but to change or improve them—for example, to provide more active roles for women—and to revitalize them by consciously bringing back features that have been lost in recent years or decades. More on these efforts to reinvigorate the tradition follows in the next case study as well.

Don Eligio realized that there was more opportunity for leadership within the growing vacuum in local Momostecan religious life than in the Maya movement, but especially more opportunity for a cultural broker who is able to effect a joining of the two, to bring some funding and some ritualists and lore from outside into Momostenango to revitalize local tradition while at the same time focusing on that local tradition. This local tradition is ultimately more real or tangible than an abstract theological movement and has a history embodied in a sacred infrastructure, while its ritual cycle is increasingly endangered by attrition in the new economy and the new religious marketplace. It seems likely that the interest shown by foreign anthropologists in the dances and the cofradía and the recording of traditional local music was also an influence.

The challenge for don Eligio, and others like him, is to present and manage an acceptable image within the community of local Costumbristas, where he is something of an outsider and somewhat suspect because of his obvious drive for a leadership position, much as was the case with don Mauricio and the Monkeys described above. But during this time of challenge, when the resources needed to keep the local costumbre of Santiago intact are scarce, he, like Mauricio, has found an opening. As in Mauricio's case, it has turned out to be an opening that, within the framework of Maya beliefs about the supernatural causation of personal calamities, carries a heavy price.

Don Eligio has confessed to us that he is considering the possibility of following don Anselmo as diputado of the cofradía. If this quest is pursued successfully it will place a cultural activist chuchkajaw in one of the most prominent positions in the cult of the patron saint. There is some opposition to and suspicion of don Eligio, for example, frequent comments to the anthropologists by other religious leaders that he is not trustworthy and is a liar or claims that money sent to him to help plant a cross to mark the location where don Pedro was murdered was never delivered and that he has told other aj q'ijab in Momostenango that he has arranged for a delegation to visit the United States. As in the case of don Mauricio in the Monkeys Dance, don Eligio may find it easier to gain a position as sponsor of important cult institutions than one as officiating ritualist. It seems to be a potentially successful but uncertain and expensive strategy to seek to parlay one into the other.

CASE 3: THE CONSTRUCTION OF A NEW SHRINE
FOR THE INDIGENOUS SAINT SAN SIMÓN
DEMONSTRATES HOW RELIGIOUS ENTREPRENEURISM
UTILIZING MAYA PRINCIPLES IS REVITALIZING
THE LOCAL RELIGIOUS TRADITION

The Shrine

As noted above, the alcalde of the cofradía of Santiago has initiated a new festival to honor the images of Santiago and San Felipe. Prior to the traditional festival in the ermita on July 23, the recent evolution of which was described above, he sponsors an all-night festival in his house, a festival that is now known as the cofradía fiesta. For most of the time that they are at this newly designated cofradía house, Santiago and San Felipe rest on a long table in the front room, which has become a shrine. In 2007 this sacred space included a series of powerful relics on the floor and candles offered in front of the altar table, which was decorated with flowers and held glasses of water and plates of tamales for each of two the images. Additionally, on the right end of the table as it is faced by a petitioner there was a small image of San Simon, while seated in a chair at the right end of the table, in a position that is continuous with the seats just inside the door occupied by the custodians of the shrine, there was a life-sized image of San Simon seated in a chair. In 2007 it was dressed in the red-and-white traditional clothing that would have been worn by a Momostecan man during the colonial period and perhaps into the earliest twentieth century.

During a visit and conversation about the altar table and the increasingly shrine-like room, the owner, the alcalde of Santiago, provided the following commentary:

> The big rock on the left comes from Salpachán in Pueblo Viejo. This one, I was burning and it came from the mountain ["cerro," in this context probably referring to the mundo, the power of the altar], pum pum it came [it emerged from the earth suddenly, near the altar]. So then I said, "This is for me." I burned incense and candles and I brought it with me. Now this one, it was in Coban, Chic'oy Mundo. So I was at Chic'oy where there are mountains ["cerros," but again he means altars, or mundos] like this, I was burning there when it emerged. Thus it wanted to say to take it to my altar. This in Chic'oy Mundo.
>
> Question: This appears to be from a volcano, this type of rock . . .
> Yes, it is from Chic'oy Mundo, in Tactic.

Question: In Tactic there is a little mountain with an altar and it has a cross, and there is a Jesu Cristo . . .

But you didn't go down in the cave. That is where I obtained this rock. I was performing the costumbre for Patrón Santiago in the time of the fair [feria]. I do costumbre far away, and I found it. Now this one was in Pipil Abaj. Again I was burning, who knows how the mines work [*minas* may mean any underground caves and tunnels; in this case he was referring to the hidden powers within the earth], but it is from Pipil Abaj, Pipil [the sacred mountain of the north].

Now this one, I got it at, what's it called, Santo Tomas . . . La Reunion.

Question: And these stones are nine?

Yes, but I have others above [i.e., stored in the rafters or attic of his house], including the biggest one. These are for candles [many are doughnut stones with holes in the middle, perhaps designed to hold the butts of standards or as the heads of pre-Hispanic war clubs?] and these were given to me by an old man. His costumbre told him to leave it to me as he was about to die. There are nine of these.

And look here. These are from Las Minas, these two, from Taksin Mundo in Huehuetenango. And this one, look at this, this is original natural stone, not made, this is true. This one is from, it is from, from, . . . Chichicastenango in Pascual Abaj [an altar much visited by Costumbristas on a hill south of downtown Chichicastenango]. I was there burning at Pascual Abaj, there among the trees, and when I finished I heard a sound, whisshhhh. And I wondered what it was, but I finished my ceremony and as I was walking among the trees and who knows how, but I stubbed my toe, and I wondered, "What is this?" and I lifted it forcefully. It was heavy and covered with mud. So, what am I going to do with this? I went to a store there below and bought rum ["guaro," i.e., locally distilled liquor, aguardiente, or burning water]. I bought a large rum and cleaned it up. And there in a store in Chichi the owner said that if I wanted we could sell it to the gringos. "And what will you pay?"

"Q 300."

"No. I am not going to sell it because I found it, it is not made, and when I carried it, it was heavy."

Question: There in Chichi they find these like this, with arms crossed, only they call them *cawiles* . . .

Yes, but they are made. This is not made. How did it appear there? And it was covered in mud. And now when I place its candles before it, I always give it its candles, how it smiles, and this part reddens. It has its meaning [*significado*], its nawal, then. And as I am altar silla, as I am mesa [a priest of the highest and most powerful grade], then I have it here. And then at María Tecún, there at Las Cuchillas there is a mountain [again possibly the altar] at María Tecún where I encountered another. It all has its meaning. For example, from Patrón Santiago, the ancestors left these for me [referring to a collection of old silver coins on his altar table], Mexican pesos and other old pesos, these are relics and this is *mebil*, it is mebil [old coins with the power to attract money to the owner]. This is of the patrón, and I have faith in all of this, and this is my altar.

And there above [attic or rafters] I have other large saints removed because when the santo [Santiago] came I didn't have space. I have things put away because last year when the people came I lost lots of things, the people came and stole them. But now, no. Here on my altar always, always. And these are San Simónes, and here the people come by and see me putting my candles for San Simon [i.e., the door is left open so people can observe the altar].

"Good, come in."

They come in and they can request what they want. They ask for protection or make their offering according to their faith. There are no other Simones in Momos, just little ones in private houses. I am thinking to serve the people because now some go looking. He is free, the person, to come and ask his protection as he desires. This will be a house of visita for people, this is what I am thinking, but I still need to complete a few more things.

The door is open all night and petitioners may come and go, burning candles on the floor in front of the images. A hired band plays dance music all night from its position on the southern side of the house courtyard, reached by passing through the room in which this shrine is located. Alms placed in the saddlebags hanging over the neck of Santiago's horse during visits at the new cofradía house or at private houses visited during processions or placed in a bowl on the litter at any time during the cofradía procession are recovered by the sacristan and go to the church. Thus the alcalde's position as sponsor of the new fiesta, as decorator of the palanquin, and as performer or sponsor of the costumbre for Santiago during the entire year is very expensive, and yet it does not directly generate any income to support the cofradía.[5]

The head of the cofradía, therefore, is now employing a strategy to convert the front room in this cofradía house, which is his privately owned house, into a year-round shrine, specifically a wachibal for the Guatemalan deity San

Simón. San Simón, also called Maximón and sometimes don Pedro, represents an extremely complex and thoroughly syncretized iconographic bundle of meanings. Identified with Judas Iscariot and with Pedro de Alvarado, San Simon is said to be a god for the merchant because he sold Jesus. He is called a traveling agent and is said in Momostenango to walk all around the world and to know all its parts. Usually, at various shrines in Guatemala San Simón is depicted as a Ladino or gringo, seated in a chair with a suit on and with glasses, and he always wears a broad-brimmed hat and frequently is depicted with a cane in his right hand. The hat and the attribute of cigar and cigarette smoking represent traits of the ancient Maya merchant god that have survived in this cult, since both were associated with the image in the middle twentieth century at a time when local Maya ritualists had no archaeology- or epigraphy-based knowledge of ancient Maya religious iconography. Famous images of San Simón in shrines with national and regional visitation are found in San Andrés Itzapa, San Andrés Xecul, Zuníl, and Santiago Atitlán.[6]

In Momostenango an image of San Simón is erected in the plaza during Holy Week (see Cook 2000:145–58 for a detailed description), and like the patron of the unlucky days, or *uayeb*, in the ancient Maya calendar he oversees a time when the altars are closed and the normal supernatural powers are suspended. This representation of San Simón in the plaza in front of the church also combines the symbolism of a Ladino patron or paymaster seated at a table with the symbolism of the mesa altar, since the clothed, and so hidden, body is a cross made of flowering bunchgrass, and the mesa altar is understood to be a table placed in front of a Maya cross. The mountain lords or spirits were imagined to appear as Ladinos and gringos during the latter twentieth century. Thus the usual Ladino/gringo symbolism paradoxically identifies the image as a local mountain spirit and owner of nature, though the dressing of the specific San Simón at the new shrine in Momostecan típica sends a rather different message about indigenization. The cross that represents the body of San Simón during Holy Week is undressed in a hidden location and immolated on Saturday to prepare for the return of Jesus from the underworld with the rising sun on Easter Sunday morning.

The image of San Simón seated at the end of the altar table at this shrine was purchased in Chichicastenango, where it was originally made twenty-five years ago, with nine days of offerings to initiate its power. Its original owner didn't want to make its fiesta any more. He was getting old and had lost his wife, and his son didn't want to take over the responsibility of the San Simón cult with the obligation to provide for a fiesta on October 28. Its new owner brought it to Maya altars to be blessed and to have its power activated, in the same way that the dance costumes and masks are activated as described in chapter 3. When asked how one could tell if such an image had power or if there was a ceremony to activate the power of the image, the new owner said there was a special ceremony. Human bones recovered from the cemetery were placed inside, at the base of the throat or where the top of the sternum would be if the image actually had a human body. "*Muchik bak* it is called, when the bones are placed inside. This helps it to call the nawales. A San Simón can do either good or evil as it is asked." The owner of the shrine made the following additional comments about this San Simón:

> Well, he has his significance on the days Kan and Ix, when he is given his rum [guaro]. Yes, on the chair altar days (altar silla) he gets his fire-water and cigarettes.
>
> Question: So is he then owner of the mesa altar?
>
> Yes, he is owner of the table-chair [mesa silla]. It is true. He is owner of the chair-table [silla mesa], because I had this [i.e., the speaker is initiated as an aj mesa with the obligation to serve the mesa altars], he asked me for it, he demanded it. Yes, this is his meaning. Here in the nighttime when I am here there is always movement on this altar. It makes a noise like this [tapping and drumming on the table with his finger].
>
> Question: And this doesn't frighten you?
>
> No. I pray and place candles here during the night. And others, they do this under a cloth, but I don't, because I don't want to lie. They, well, there are thirteen nawales, thirteen nawales. Then I begin to speak with them. Who can serve and what needs to be given. There are thirteen nawales, thirteen nawales. They are of the silla mesa. This is why I have them, because they are owners of the silla mesa.

This permanent shrine would be occupied each year briefly by Santiago and San Felipe, who as guests of San Simón would attest to his power and prompt a temporary, substantially heightened visitation by the faithful. If successful in attracting local and perhaps regional visitation it, like other San Simón shrines in Guatemala, would provide a steady stream of income through cash offerings donated at the shrine but more importantly through sales of beer, wine, aguardiente, candles, cigarettes, and incense, which could be used to cover the expenses of the cofradía, the alcalde's share of which are estimated at more than Q 25,000 ($3,500) each year. And in this case, as noted in the account above, the figure of San Simón is critical to the owner's development of a professional nawal mesa practice, a form of syncretized Maya spiritism in which powerful spirits are called by a medium to his table at midnight (Saler 1960, 1967) and asked to answer questions or confer blessings on the clients of the table's owner.[7]

This illustrates the way in which the Santiago-centered cult institutions and the people who struggle to carry them into a new century are adapting to the neoliberal economic realities of Guatemala within a Costumbrista conceptual framework.

Agency and Tradition

Don Apolonio turned thirty in 2007, making him exceptionally young to serve as the alcalde of a cofradía, and he had begun in that service two years earlier, at age twenty-eight. His youth causes some tension between him and the diputado, a sixty-year-old ritualist who has been involved in the cult of Santiago for decades and who is highly respected among the Costumbristas who maintain Santiago's cult. The alcalde complains that the diputado feels compelled to remind him about the costumbre even though they each are responsible for making offerings on different days, and he resents this lack of confidence in him, especially since besides doing about half of the rituals he also pays for almost all of the expenses of the cofradía. Don Apolonio's father is deceased. Don Apolonio has remained unmarried and is devoted to his mother, who manages the household, organizes the women who cook the food for the cofradía festival, and walks in a leading position in the processions. Apolonio owns and operates two businesses, a shop that sells relatively high-end women's traditional skirts and blouses and a transportation service, using his Toyota microbus. The family is wealthy by local standards, having accumulated capital while don Apolonio's father was alive through operating a beverage distribution business. While the family is no longer in this business, much of the money from the business was invested in local land acquisitions, and don Apolonio reports that he is now selling off his share of the land for about Q 15,000 each year in order to cover the expenses of the cofradía.

Don Apolonio is somewhat vague and a bit evasive about his training in Costumbre. He accepted the vara at age twelve, which is a little young for this major step but not unique, making him a diviner with a responsibility to make offerings on each 8 Batz. He has been an aj mesa since age twenty-five, a status that requires far more extensive offerings at specified, more powerful mesa altars and that usually implies a serious commitment to divination and representation of private clients before the local supernatural powers. He acknowledges a now-deceased and unnamed master, an elder from the aldea Xequemeya, who taught him how to make offerings and read dreams and signs. He has subsequently acquired knowledge from his dreams and from signs and revelations that have come during ceremonies at many of the most powerful altars in Guatemala.

In 2007 and again in 2008 a young woman dressed in the traditional clothing of Quetzaltenango was seated at the shrine and accompanied don Apolonio in the procession and also at the vigil at the hermandad chapel. In 2007 they danced with each other and, as a pair, they danced with the image of Santiago. We learned later that the young woman was not don Apolonio's wife but his fiancée. During a conversation in 2009 when he was asked about her absence from the festival at the cofradía house he reported that they had broken off their relationship. He offered two reasons. His betrothed wanted them to go undocumented to the United States, and don Apolonio was not willing to engage in such a risky venture. But he also reported that his religious duties, serving as alcalde of the cofradía and as chuchkajaw for the hermandad de bandas and for the candles brought from Antigua during Holy Week, forced him to abstain from sex for lengthy periods and this would have made for a difficult marriage.

While don Apolonio's choice to accept so many demanding cargos was not compelled by local authorities nor by tradition, which in fact would not have allowed an unmarried man to serve in a cofradía, let alone serve as alcalde, the issue of prolonged sexual abstinence is a problem that has yet to be effectively confronted by the new cargo system, which makes such demands on those who serve year after year without replacement. A system that forces those most committed to cultural reproduction to accept draconian strictures on sexual relations while selling off their inheritance is not likely to be successful in the long run.

At the same time, though, both don Mauricio and don Eligio, as described above, are comfortable with moving women into active public roles within the cult of Santiago. This has not yet begun to happen in the dances but is now well established within the more embattled and more radically transformed cofradía/festival/procession system. This appears to have its origins in Maya cultural activism and in the prominent role that specific women and an indigenous women's movement have played in the political awakening of the Maya.

Don Apolonio's motivations, and those of other similarly committed leaders of the current Costumbrista complex related to Santiago and the feria, are sometimes clear and explicit. They have all been called to this service by a combination of social pressure and their dreams. Don Apolonio and his deputy don Anselmo, who also serves as chuchkajaw of the Monkeys, provide the traditionally appropriate testimonials to their initial reluctance to serve and their efforts to discharge their calling in less expensive and less demanding undertakings, like serving in the group of rocketeers or serving as ritualist for the hermandad de bandas. In this they stand apart a bit from other leaders described above, don Eligio and don Mauricio, who seem to be overtly seeking opportunities to serve. It is, of course, not possible to read minds nor to gauge the extent to which the more-traditional resistance to the call is simply a stylistic feature serving to legitimize the quest for a leadership position among those with more traditional community values. It is true that we have encountered gossip about and suspicion of those who actively seek leadership and recognition in the cult and have not encountered similar critiques of don Apolonio and don Anselmo.

All of these positions in the cult cost money and seem to represent the willingness to convert money into social recognition and prestige and to pay for the opportunity to be a leader, with active and lively engagement with others in the pursuit of common goals. This became especially apparent in 2009 when the struggle with the mayor over his effort to shut down the festival led to many meetings, trips to the capital, the hiring of lawyers, and meetings with national-level government officials. The participants were energized in the process and were victorious, and they had the sense that they had achieved a victory for the community. They were, in fact, rather heroic in their quest for vindication for the community and for its traditions, and in leaving the familiar local world for the world of state-level powers and processes they secured political allies and returned with a boon for the community. This secular parallel for the activity of the *aj vara* or aj mesa serving as an advocate for his clients before the supernatural authorities is not a coincidence. The same willingness to risk contact with potentially dangerous greater powers and the same need to be an eloquent representative and to make a compelling case is involved in both.

AGENCY AND TRADITION IN THE CONTEMPORARY CULT OF SANTIAGO

In addition to the apparent desire for recognition from within the Costumbrista community and the related desire for a stimulating, interesting, and socially engaged career that can be played out in the local setting, the current leaders of Santiago's cult also share a religious calling that involves a personal quest for supernatural patronage and empowerment. This empowerment may be limited to protection against witches, envy, and evil spirits and to the straightening of one's road, as in the case of the dancers. But note that in the Monkeys Dance at least the empowerment is also experienced directly, as fearlessness in high places and as possession by animal spirits, and so is proved.

The quest involves prolonged contact with powerful, often jealous and vindictive supernaturals and is perilous. For all the participants—dancers, autors, chuchkajaws and cofrades—the undertaking of service during the feria is an exact embodiment of the hero myth as depicted by Joseph Campbell. The initiand leaves the world of work, avoids sexual contact in the material world, and travels for days in the dream world in the company of spirits. The protective power of the altars appears to men in their dreams as a lovely young woman who is offended by their earthly material wives and demands sexual abstinence during the period of service. In the successful quest there is atonement with the ancestors and with the demanding and patriarchal nawal of Santiago, followed by the boon of material success in the following year and protection for the larger community. This journey is a dangerous passage. Santiago will kill the child of a servant who is ambivalent about the service or of a pilgrim who begins to resent the demands of the journey.

There are no guarantees of success, though, and even apparently faithful servants may suffer terrible fates. Don Pedro had been warned by dreams and was deeply engaged in apparently successful service to Santiago when he was murdered in October 2007. Don Mauricio had just accepted the autorship of the dance, legitimized by divination, when he fell and broke his tibia and fibula during a dance pole erection. Don Eligio's wife and baby were nearly killed in an accident and suffered from prolonged and expensive medical problems during the second year of his novena for Santiago and only two months after gifting the image with new boots.

Within the fatalistic world view of traditional Maya religion there are limits to what can be accomplished by the deities, and all must ultimately accept their destinies. However, since destiny cannot be known in detail in advance the protection conferred by correctly performed invocations and offerings and by personal fealty to a protective spirit makes it possible to take risks and to live the kind of engaged and stimulating public life that attracts envy and makes enemies. Thus, while there is no forestalling of destiny or eliminating the influences of the day of one's birth, there are ways to secure the blessings of ancestors and of the nawales at their altars and, by visiting and serving them through obeisance to their holy physical embodiments, to mitigate risks. During the period of service there is an intensification of signs and dreams and so an enhanced opportunity to assess one's acceptance by the powers and one's prospects. This cultural logic provides a culture-specific framework within which the psychologies and personal motivations of the agents of cultural production and reproduction operate, whether they are traditionalists or entrepreneurs, to produce and reproduce the core rituals of indigenous religious expression.

Tradition endures in Momostenango, though often with significant attrition to reduce the costs or adapt to changes in social and economic infrastructure. Sometimes the social organization replicates itself faithfully, as in the Monkeys Dance. Other times ritual symbols retain continuity with the past but the social organization is completely revamped, as in the cofradías. Local community also endures, though pluralism has in reality largely replaced community with communities, and some communities are increasingly realized only periodically, during rituals of return and nostalgia. The processes of reconstitution and revitalization of indigenous religion and of related indigenous models for community amid changing circumstances that we observe in contemporary Momostenango offer insight into unfolding processes of potential regional significance. We summarize key findings and present some implications of our investigations for tracking and understanding the unfolding future of indigenous religion in the highlands in the conclusion.

Conclusion

The Future of Village-Level Indigenous Religion

The authors began this project in 2005 with a desire to return to Momostenango to assess how the religious expressive culture was adapting to the post-peasant situation and to twenty-first-century globalization. Cook had an explicit intention of critiquing the late twentieth-/early twenty-first-century movement toward constructivism and the related replacement of the traditional Mayanist focus on villages and their cultures with a focus on ethnicity, identity, and national cultural and political contention. Ethnicity and identity are worthwhile subjects of inquiry and interpretation, but should we redesign Mayanist ethnography to completely supplant the village study and the study of locality-based cultural dynamics? What we seek here is the commonsense reconciliation of ideologically opposed models for practice and interpretation and the redemption of locality-based Mayanist ethnography. Critiquing ideological and radical constructivism is now beating a dead horse. Still, some positive models for the study of local cultural dynamics as a way to understand the evolution of distinctively Maya local cultural tradition or traditions is useful as a corrective to some of the excesses of radical constructivism, the replacement of or confusion of culture with identity, and the recent dominance in publications of a focus on Maya activism and the nation-state.

Such corrective models are illustrated in this volume in the Cook and Offit research on the Monkeys Dance and the cofradía of Santiago and in the Taube contribution on the disfraces dance. This conclusion seeks to review the findings of this research as they apply to issues and questions raised in the introduction.

Local adaptations to transnationalized post-peasant village culture in the institutions that produce public performances of indigenous religion during community festivals need to meet the emotional needs of performers and of audiences experiencing this new kind of culture; they will do so utilizing available economic, social, and cultural capital. We followed the ground-breaking work of Jennifer Burrel on the transnational festival in Todos Santos to provide a detailed case study that localizes twenty-first-century processes of cultural adaptation to globalization and the impacts of economically motivated emigration, remittances, and expectations of return. In chapter 2 we offered a description within a historical context of the evolution of a new stage in the organization and meaning of the patron saint's festival.

STAGES IN THE EVOLUTION OF THE FESTIVAL

While earlier festivals were the grounds for ethnic contestation and for contestation between religious communities (Catholic vs. Costumbrista), the current festival operates in a pluralistic and hybridized culture and no longer is dominated by expression of these earlier forms of antagonism. There was a politicized struggle over control of the festival in 2009. The Evangelical mayor, presumably supported by his faction of coreligionists, sought to use the danger of the swine flu epidemic to shut down the festival. He canceled the big parade of the schools, creating a public uproar in town, and was opposed by many Catholic and Costumbrista performing groups and vendors, and some Protestant vendors as well. They managed to gain the upper hand by enlisting the support of federal authorities and the departmental governor, who rescinded the order and provided police and soldiers to supplement the local municipal force controlled by the mayor's office in keeping order. The rest of the festival went on as usual, though, and within the symbolism presented in, or read out of, the expressive culture and spatial organization of activities in the town center, the earlier forms of dualistic contestation were absent.

In spite of the social and religious pluralism within the indigenous population, though, there is a relatively new and problematic duality in meanings and purposes that informs our analysis of the expressive culture in the festival.

Indigenous Momostecans today represent themselves as concurrently traditional and modern, local and cosmopolitan, and they are in fact both of these at once, both collectively and within their individual psyches. As the older forms of contestation have been largely superseded by the evolution of the post-peasant transnational village and its growing pluralism, this opposition has emerged with growing force. The challenge for reproduction and construction of local culture in the new era, and for the coherent identities that derive from and use it, is to find ways to mediate this opposition. The emphasis in chapters 2 and 3 on the Monkeys Dance and the cofradía is on strategies for reproducing Momostecan religious tradition under changing circumstances, while chapter 5 presents a strategy for constructing and representing Maya/Momostecan modernity, a process that is there seen as involving a local and indigenous cultural logic in combination with a shift to some modernist thematic concerns. These three chapters together investigate how the agents producing the local expressive culture are experimenting with mediation of the tradition/modernity opposition while adapting the expressive culture to the larger and more inclusive pluralistic, transnational village culture.

MODES OF ADAPTATION OF EXPRESSIVE CULTURE
TO THIS STAGE IN THE EVOLUTION OF LOCAL CULTURE

The Monkeys Dance, described in chapter 3, preserves a century-long connection with the originating community and families and continues to have the explicit purpose of pleasing the ancestors and the patron saint. It has the form of an indigenous medicine society led by a ritualist/diviner, a nineteenth-century system of funding via authorship—that is, a primary sponsor/producer—and the very Maya goals for the performers of initiation via ordeal and the bestowing and confirming of supernatural protection and power. The adaptations have involved accepting attrition in the Deer Dance story attached to the Monkeys Dance proper and accepting the possibility that the traditional marimba music, which cannot be heard during public performances on the plaza anyway, could be lost with the death of the marimbista. This dance, then, has adopted both the truncated and appended strategies defined by Waldemar Smith (1977:6) but as yet has avoided the administered strategy. This dance is perhaps the paramount symbol of tradition, about which we have encountered the most positive sentiment, and though it is supported and produced by a very localized and committed cadre of Costumbristas, it plays a major role in preserving a Momostenango to which various postcommunities seek to return.

It also embodies the traditional model for initiation. Dancers perform many offerings on difficult pilgrimages and risk their lives performing aerial tricks above the plaza. They must observe sexual abstinence for forty days, during which they are sojourners in the world of spirits, protected by the shaman leader in a quest for supernatural power—power legitimized by signs given during ceremonies, by their contacts with spirit spouses and the patron saint in their dreams, and by fearlessness when they don the magical animal masks and, possessed by animal spirits, perform death-defying stunts.

The cofradía described and analyzed in chapter 2 preserves traditional purposes of pleasing the saint and the primeros who founded the customs and preserves the offering cycles and vigils of Momostecan tradition, but with a new social organization. The cofradía has had to adapt to the loss of compulsory service and membership and loss of municipal oversight and control in the neoliberal Guatemala and local pluralistic society. It has adjusted, for now, by creating a new council of elders who are the heads of an hermandad del bandas, replacing the official principales of twentieth-century tradition, and with a new strategy for funding. The alcalde, now recruited, not appointed, by the elders, does not rotate out of office annually and produces the festival with some supplementary funding from subscriptions through the hermandad del bandas. In terms of Waldemar Smith's (1977) funding strategies, it has so far avoided truncation or simplification of its rituals, and with the collapse of the appointment of cofrades with specific financial and labor responsibilities it no longer takes advantage of the cost-spreading appended strategy with multiple annual sponsors. The primary funding models are now a combination of the administered strategy, copied after Ladino hermandades, with permanent fund-raising via the hermandad del bandas selling hundreds of small subscriptions, and a new and possibly doomed strategy of a voluntary principal sponsor who has vowed a novena to serve as alcalde. A replacement is not currently evident, and the costs of this service have forced the incumbent to sell both his inheritance of land and his women's clothing store in order to cover costs. He has sought to develop a shrine to San Simon in the cofradía house in an effort to capitalize on his service as alcalde and to provide some additional funds for the ceremonies, traditional vigils, and parties.

While attendance at vigils and visits during processions follows tradition, there are some problems with transporting the images during lesser processions, since the loss of cofrades has resulted in the loss of a dependable number of bearers. The result is that men and women recruited by the alcalde and lacking any formal public recognition are involved in carrying the images; on two occasions Garrett Cook and several Baylor University undergraduates of both sexes have been involved in carrying the images from the cofradía cha-pel to the church. If community support of the cult does not increase it seems likely that the alcalde might begin to question his faith as the larger commu-nity demonstrates tangible doubt about the power of the patron saint.

The adaptation of a sixty-year-old Ladino dance form, the convite, to local indigenous culture has produced the disfraces in Momostenango. The dance team may be composed of either males or females, unlike the traditional all-male dances, and the dance celebrates modernist values like competition, egoism, and novelty, which are contrary to traditional Maya values. It also lacks a storyline and represents characters from television and movies rather than local spirits, culture heroes, ancestors, or ethnic groups. It allows local indigenous performers and audiences to display their knowledge of modern media and so to contend with Ladino claims to authoritative or hegemonic representations of modernity. It is of great relevance to this analysis, because while the form and major thematic concerns are borrowed from Ladinos and reflect post-peasant modernist values, the dance is supported by typical offer-ings at Maya altars. At the same time, it may be understood as a depiction of the denizens of a quasi-supernatural otherworld, the Gringolandia of Momostecan collective imagination as mediated by movies and television. In Taube's analysis this is a new Tollan visited by the new Maya hero, a sojourner in El Norte rather in the world of local spirits and powers, whose quest brings the tangible boons of remittances and new social and cultural capital to the community rather than the blessings of local supernatural powers. In this analysis, then, the disfraces represent an indigenous take on globalism, media, and modernization and a claim for an indigenous modernity that is not exactly Ladinoization.

WHAT THE FUTURE HOLDS: PLURALIZED
EXPRESSIVE CULTURE AND COMPETING
COTRADITIONS IN INDIGENOUS RELIGION

Our research has documented that in the production of the village festival, traditionalism (i.e., Costumbre, a syncretized world order with locally rooted symbolism), concretized as ritual expressing the motivating ideol-ogy for some actors, confronts an indigenous constructivism (i.e., cultural activism, antisyncretic religion with more universalizing symbolism) that is intentionally changing expressive culture, though at least in part guided by an indigenous cultural logic. Below we address issues of localized cultural dialectics and the potential for claims of authenticity on both sides and argue for the constructive role of a shared cultural logic in providing for some integration of the two traditions. Yet we wish to be clear here that the notion of a continuing tradition of Maya religious thought and practice as put forward in Hart (2008) and Molesky-Poz (2006) is more problematic—at the very least, much more complicated—than their conceptual frameworks suggest. In fact, what seems to have developed over the past two decades is two coexisting syncretized traditions lacking common roots, with Costumbre here understood as a very local syncretizing of Spanish Catholic and indigenous religion with colonial period roots and Maya Spirituality as a late-twentieth-century regional or national (and "Maya" rather than Momostecan) syncretizing of Protestant and indigenous forms of worship, with a hybridization of indigenous traditions, readings of the *Popol Wuj*, and new age cosmology.[1]

Our investigation, documented in the chapters above, has sought to explicate the cult of the patron saint in Momostenango today as an adapting embodiment of Maya tradition, producing a twenty-first-century, village-level version of what Nancy Farris (1984) has called reconstituted Indian culture, at least within the sector of expressive culture. In pursuing this research we have discerned some emerging patterns in the relationships between the two cotraditions as they interact at the local level.

The existence of these two cotraditions in the first decade of the twenty-first century suggests several logical alternatives for how indigenous religion might evolve: (1) persistence of the status quo, with the coexistence of two traditions with minimal interaction, each maintaining its own communalistic cult institutions; (2) contention between increasingly well-defined factions exhibiting these two tendencies, with some struggles for control of public spaces and sacra, similar to the twentieth-century struggles between Costumbrista and Catholic Action; (3) gradual replacement of aging Costumbristas by younger carriers of the new religion (as suggested by Deuss 2007); and (4) dialogic processes that create a synthesis, producing localized communalistic and shamanic cult institutions that participate in a wider highland Maya religious movement with universalizing tendencies, blending the ritual symbols and cosmologies, and revitalizing a distinctively Momostecan Costumbre. Our research suggests that the first alternative has been dominant so far but that there has been little evidence of the second, the emergence of contention. While the third alternative remains plausible and is consistent with some current trends, our work supports the increasing salience of the fourth alternative.

ACCOMMODATIONS WITHIN A SHARED CULTURAL LOGIC

In the context of existing ideological and practical differences between the two cotraditions, arguments about authenticity could lead to increasing polarization. In actual practice, though, neither a Costumbrista appeal to an ongoing local tradition and to the primeros to legitimize their practices and beliefs nor a Maya Spirituality appeal to the *Popol Wuj* and the need to purge "foreign" (Spanish and Christian) elements from religious practice seem to be creating any deeper or more contentious division. The nawales, after all, might have developed a taste for candles and Catholic incense as well as pom (copal), and the primeros who founded Costumbre are now nawales in their own right, and for Costumbristas there is no problem with invoking Tojil, Tepeu, and Gucumatz along with saints and angels and volcanoes and days. The more patrons and powers that a ritualist can call on, the more power the ritual has, after all.

The mediation of the opposition between syncretized local tradition and antisyncretic, purified nativistic religion is made possible by these psychological/logical considerations but is not at all made inevitable. The social and cultural process of developing a synthesis is best understood in terms of the rewards for individuals who in one way or another facilitate the process. Our research suggests that to the extent that this is happening, and that extent is not measurable based on our qualitative research and development of illustrative case studies, it is best characterized as relocalization of Maya Spirituality.

RELOCALIZATION OF MAYA SPIRITUALITY

The problem faced by religious entrepreneurs working within the antisyncretic and universalistic Maya Spirituality movement is that they need to attract followers who will support the groups they found or who will become their clients for supernatural services, as in apprenticeships, curing, or counseling. These goals are most effectively met by marketing of some kind, and those who can perform in public roles in which they are highly visible would have an advantage in enhanced contact with possible followers or clients, while also developing reputations for supernatural power legitimized by their close association with community sacra such as venerated images of Jesus or saints or their leading roles in processions, vigils, and the like.

The main form of public performance of the Maya Spirituality movement involves congregational services performed in the round at important altars on special days of the Maya calendar. These are generally attended by existing members of a local group of spiritual guides (aj q'ijab) who are already active in the cult and their students and may be witnessed by traditional Costumbristas celebrating the same day at the same altar complex, but not by large audiences. They are therefore not fertile occasions for advertising the group or for enhancing the reputations of group leaders in a wider setting.

The alternative venues for public performance are within the annual festivals for Santiago and Jesu Cristo, with processions and vigils that are observed or attended by hundreds, but these are problematic given the official position of antisyncretism of early twenty-first-century Maya Spirituality and given the existing control of these cults by Costumbristas. There is, therefore, an interesting internal conflict faced by the entrepreneurial, locally based participant in Maya Spirituality. Remaining committed to core antisyncretic principles restricts access to major venues of traditional indigenous religious performance and to opportunities for leadership in a much wider local world, while also restricting access to supernatural patrons. In fact, rigid adherence to antisyncretic ideology, while it might be desirable as part of the building of a national indigenous political movement, has more in common with the orthodoxies of the imported Christian religions than with the flexible and pragmatic religion of village Maya.

Thus it happens that the cult of the patron saint appears to be fertile ground for the early stages of a blending of the two cotraditions as guias espirituales of the new movement seek to learn and master the invocations and offerings of the Costumbristas and to participate in their public cults, while the Costumbristas, lacking the financial resources and the cadres of conscripts that used to staff the cofradías, may be a bit suspicious of the motives and practices of the previously antisyncretic and congregationally oriented new partners but may also be willing to consider collaborations. As collaborations deepen and ideologies become more pragmatic the two groups will lose their identities, and a revitalized and universalized Maya religiosity will find expression in syncretized local cults.

RELIGIOUS AGENCY: PATTERNS OF RELIGIOUS LEADERSHIP AND ENTREPRENEURIALISM

As illustrated in detail in chapters 4 and 5, leadership within the dance teams has always involved a combination of two factors, charisma and wealth. Personal charisma is needed on the part of both producers (autors) and ritualists (chuchkajaws), making it possible to recruit dancers and to retain them over the course of their novenas. For dance producers there has also been the need for sufficient wealth to underwrite substantial expenses. The relevant cultural logic that shapes leadership and decision making begins with the importance of being called to leadership by ancestral spirits and the patron saint, though with initial resistance to the call and with legitimation by divination. Just as the members of a cofradía were once appointed by the principales, a retired board of elders to whom the cofrade was ultimately responsible, the host of local ancestral spirits, especially the primeros, the spirits of the deceased dancers going back to the start of the dance, are the only ones with the authority to appoint individuals to positions of leadership in the dances. Legitimation of leadership continues during the period of service through signs and dreams and through directing successful performances.

When novel circumstances arise that require decisions, they are reached collectively in accordance with tradition via divination, a process that is able to reduce the development of factionalism while seeking consensus and ultimately reaching a confirmed decision that reduces anxiety in the group and instills the group with a sense of common purpose. The leadership of traditional dance teams is not entrepreneurial in the full sense, since it does not involve goals of novelty or growth and is committed to social and cultural reproduction rather than construction. Yet it has provided an acceptable social role for individuals with extroverted personalities or a need for social recognition, and in a post-peasant context the challenges of reproducing a culture designed for and by peasant villagers in the past are myriad and in fact require regular social and cultural engineering. As indicated in two of the case studies in chapter 5, individuals, whether guias espirituales or Costumbristas, who are also openly seeking leadership roles in the cult of the patron saint, are viewed with suspicion.

Two examples of openly entrepreneurial religious behavior were presented in chapter 5. In one case the alcalde of Santiago's new kind of cofradía, described in detail in chapter 2, is seeking to use that position and the temporary control of community sacra that come with it to enhance the prospects of a private shrine in his house and the consulting practice that accompanies it. In another case a leader of one of the groups of guias espirituales that exist in Momostenango is working to become one of the leaders of the cult of Santiago through sponsoring and improving a neglected traditional vigil during the festival. In both cases the individuals have so far spent a great deal of money, little of which has been recovered through any enhanced business as religious specialists, and in both cases the guiding psychological motivation seems to be about finding ways to enhance their supernatural power and reputations for having power, for community service, and in connection with both of those goals, to engineer and receive credit for the maintenance, recovery, and enhancement of local tradition.

Momostenango has a long tradition of village-level entrepreneurs, the merchants, or *commerciantes*, who designed new woolen products in accordance with changing tastes, found new and expanding markets for locally produced products, or more recently, found buyers within Momostenango for consumer goods from the international market. The Momostecan entrepreneur might develop a new product but more commonly was a risk-taking mediator who developed some relatively new and effective way to connect producers and consumers. The role of the religious entrepreneur within the sector of early twenty-first-century indigenous religion in Momostenango, if it is to be effective, will be to develop and implement new models to profit from mediating between postcommunities that have identity needs and nostalgia that can be met through paying for performances and services conveying "authentic" encounters with tradition within the sacred physical and calendrical infrastructure. The role of the traditional agent of cultural reproduction will be to seek to keep the local traditions going. Neither type of agency will succeed without the other.

THE CONSTRUCTION OF CONTINUITY

The key to understanding continuity within a local Maya tradition seems to be the realization that an institutional structure whose organization adjusts to economic and political and demographic realities but is still based on Maya principles of social organization and Maya understandings of the supernatural, fate, and history is in place and is directing the process of culture change within a local and very meaningful physical infrastructure. The post-peasant version of Costumbre will then be different from its classic expressions in the early to middle twentieth century, but even though sacramental corn farming may be on its way out and the expressive culture is no longer controlled by a landed patriarchal gerontocracy, the Costumbre of Santiago continues and continues to be negotiated by creative agents engaged in expensive and sometimes perilous multigenerational undertakings in the same places and with the same purposes, though with variable contents, as was the case forty years ago.

Notes

INTRODUCTION

1. The social history of Momostenango from conquest up to the 1970s has been published (Carmack 1995) and the specifics of Momostenango history directly relevant to the cult of the saints and the annual festival are also available in Cook 2000. The recent history of Momostenango has not been documented and will not be presented here, except in some very limited areas related to specific dances and the cofradías.

2. Ortner's (1997) conception of postcommunity seems relevant to the new Maya world and is discussed in detail in connection with the post-peasant model below.

3. An excellent discussion of the functionalist model in Mesoamerican studies and an excellent example of a critical political economy and ecological reaction against it are in Waldemar Smith's (1977:24–43) discussion of ways to think about the Maya cargo system and Zinacantán.

4. Vogt (1964) wrote of "genetic empiricism" and proposed the agenda of reconstructing a Maya protoculture via methods analogous to those of historical linguistics. Mendelson (1967) found puzzle pieces scattered in various Mayan communities that could be reassembled into an original, the fragmented mother culture of the Maya. Vogt's students Gary Gossen (especially in Gossen 1986) and Freidel (especially through his part in Freidel, Schele, and Parker 1993) sought to operationalize the genetic empiricist approach by identifying

recurring patterns in a variety of local ethnographic cultures, in Freidel's case by linking these to archaeological and epigraphic evidence.

5. Kearney's (1996) thesis that this focus on peasants was a psychological and in some sense ideological/political prerequisite within an essentializing West's strategy of creating and containing a polarized "other" is opposed to the traditional anthropological model of science as a theorizing and generalizing activity based on constructing and comparing types. In the traditional perspective peasants were discovered in nature, not created by the observer, and the current recognition of a need for a critical reevaluation of the typology derives from historical changes in nature and from science's internal self-correcting processes, rather than from a critical deconstruction of Western ideology. The authors of the current work have somewhat different, generationally based takes on postmodernism in general and on Kearney-style deconstruction in particular, and thus cannot agree completely on a resolution of this controversy; however, it seems that its resolution is not critical to the analysis pursued here.

6. A recent synthetic overview of the study of peasants, Schüren 2003, traces this critique back to Wolf 1955; Mintz 1956; Wolf 1957; and Wolf and Mintz 1957.

7. Kearney also introduces the term *polybian*, derived from *amphibian* but replacing the implicit dualism of *amphi-* with the prefix *poly-* to refer to his conception of the extremely fluid and internally differentiated identities of the post-peasants as over and against the fixed and homogenous identity of the peasant that preceded it (1996:141), a term designed to emphasize the fluidity of the economic strategies and multiplicity of concurrent identities that arise within the cohort of post-peasants.

8. Conrad Kottak (see, e.g., Kottak 1987:550–55) has argued that for Americans Disneyland would represent such a localized symbolic place of origins and hence has become a secular alternative to the religious pilgrimage. It is a shame that this cogent analysis was removed from his introductory texts years ago.

9. This position became popular among cultural anthropologists developing dependency theory, who, in the 1970s and 1980s, perceived a break in tradition between the preconquest Mesoamerican indigenous traditions and the village cultures of the twentieth century, which for them were not primarily the cultures of traditional societies but rather were the cultures of peripheral societies of a rural working class who maintained subsistence farming within an exploitative economy designed to subsidize the cost of their labor for their employers and whose cultures were conceived theoretically as adaptations made over five centuries to regional plantation capitalism, rather than as Mesoamerican traditions (see Carlsen and Prechtel 1991:23–24; Wilk 1991:21–23). During this same period, within Guatemalan national life, ethnicity and the reality of Maya culture were rejected by the left as false consciousness and by the right as antinationalist (Watanabe 1995:33; Fischer 2001:95–96).

10. Watanabe (1990:131–32, 146) identified a "primordialist" perspective that finds "essential" Mayanness in contemporary syncretized culture, while an opposed "historicist" position sees "the Indian" as a creation of colonial repression rather than a survivor carrying an indigenous tradition with significant continuity. As

we will discuss, Watanabe later (1995) suggested the terms *romantic* and *tragic* as orientations for the same distinction, while Watanabe and Fischer (2004) use the terms *essentialist* and *constructivist*. In general we reject the "essentialist" label for bona fide empirical research that documents indigenous Maya themes in twentieth-century village cultures and tend to prefer the less weighted, freighted, and negatively connoted terms *continuity* and *discontinuity models* (Carlsen and Prechtel 1991:23–24). In its most extreme form, postcolonial constructivism opposes what it calls essentialism as a "neocolonial strategy of social containment that makes 'simplistic or universalistic assumptions about domination and uncritically assumes the possibilities or impossibilities of resistance based on a particular form of collective identity.' . . . Constructivism (antiessentialism) seeks to break down neat categorizations and the political dominance they reify. . . . From a strong constructivist stance the concept of culture itself becomes suspect as an essentializing category" (Fischer 1999:473).

11. Some Mayan writers have attempted this (e.g., Pedro Gonzalez 1995; Montejo 2005), and this is, of course, the job for Mayan cultural activists. It is not part of the agenda here.

12. Here syncretism is considered in its value-neutral social scientific mode as a process rather than in its theological/political mode as error. That is, in its "objectivist," not its "subjectivist," mode (Droogers and Greenfield 2001:31).

13. As in the following: "In Latin America, 'where traditions have not yet disappeared and modernity has not completely arrived,' Néstor García Canclini employs the concept of hybridity to describe culturally and historically situated strategies for entering and leaving modernity. This is a particular Latin American style of hybridity which Amia Loomba reads as a postcolonial cultural weapon inherited from the colonial era; indeed, 'anti-colonial movements and individuals often drew upon Western ideas and vocabularies to challenge colonial rule'"(Kitiarsa 2005:468).

14. Droogers and Greenfield (2001:33) suggest that cognitive models deriving from preexisting local traditions (e.g. as in D'Andrades *schemas* and Bordieu's *habitus*) are used to model both reproduction and new production of structure, an approach that is illustrated in Droogers 2001 in analyzing the construction of an individual worldview using schemas from several traditions and elsewhere is used to analyze Cakchiquel cultural dynamics via a model of cultural logic (Fischer 1999, 2001). In a similar vein Zehner discusses the cognitive dimension of "transitional hybridities" functioning in the conversion from Buddhism to Christianity in Thailand:

> These words and concepts are hooked into separate realms of understanding yet are sufficiently similar that they provide segues into conversion. It could be said that these are cases of "frame overlap," drawing on Erving Goffman's (1974) notion of the "frame" as a cognitive-behavioral set entailing particular understandings of and prescriptions for behavior. . . . [Frame overlap] might also be applied to a situation that arises internally within a single individual in the course

of conversion. This situation involves an internal cognitive overlap, a kind of confusion or unbidden creativity within the mind, in which at certain points competing frames become congruent. At these points of congruence, symbols become so multivalent—due to having roughly the same meanings and resonances in both frames—that they can facilitate cognitive movement from one frame to the other. (2005:605)

This conceptualization is the cognitive corollary to Greenfield's (2001) explanation of preexisting parallels in folk Catholicism and African religion that facilitated syncretic constructions in Brazilian Condomble.

15. Numerous examples of studies that accomplished this goal in relation to Maya tradition encountered in the field in the twentieth century include LaFarge and Byers 1931; LaFarge 1947; Oakes 1951; Bunzel 1952; Mendelson 1959; Holland 1964; Mendelson 1965; Carmack 1966; Vogt 1969; Gossen 1974; Hunt 1977; Bricker 1981; B. Tedlock 1982; Gossen 1986; Hill and Monaghan 1987; Carlsen and Prechtel 1991; McAnany 1995; Freidel et al. 1993; Cook 2000.

CHAPTER ONE

1. Levitt (2001:14) defines transnationalism as a specific form of globalization in which a dyadic social field is created through migration. Transnational villages are local communities that send a significant number of migrants to another nation and in which the sending community is transformed by migrants to such an extent that even nonmigrants are involved in relationships spanning both settings. Social remittances—that is, ideas, behavior, and social capital from outside—shape their values and strategies. Generally she finds that generational and class differences increase and inequality is heightened as a community is transnationalized (Levitt 2001:11–12).

2. Carmack (1995:164) cites Franz Termer's 1957 observation that a shift from ritual to the earth to saint-focused ritual took place in Momostenango in the early twentieth century. An agrarian peasant village that focused on crops and the magic of ensuring a harvest, as well as the politics of local patrilineage- or patriclan-controlled landholdings that were still largely adequate to its population, was transformed in the early twentieth century to a village that focused much more on issues of competition for land and resources with neighboring villages (San Carlos Sija and San Francisco el Alto in particular) and on a cult of collective and individual safety, since many men served in the caudillo's militia. Carmack (1995:421–22) estimates about 120,000 man-days were devoted to military drills in the late liberal period and 98,000 man-days devoted to active military service, including three border disputes with Mexico, a war with El Salvador, and several responses to coups and the quelling of several uprisings, while only about 16,000 man-hours were devoted to local service to the municipality. Under these circumstances increasing devotion to the patron saint makes eminent sense as a psychological response.

Similarly, a decline is such support would be likely in a world with less dangerous collective and individual endeavors and different forms of on-the-ground patronage in a less personalistic political economy.

3. As one recorded example, Carmack (1995:197) reports an incident in which an indigenous militia colonel who was a close confidant of the general was murdered in a fit of jealousy by one of the general's sons. Clearly a fine line had to be walked in a very dangerous world by the upwardly mobile indigenous leaders who sought to advance themselves through Cifuentes's patronage or by mediating between their people and the caudillo. As we will show, service in dance teams and cofradías by devotees of Santiago is very dangerous.

4. Carmack (1995:163) finds that in 1894 more than 90 percent of the population was composed of peasants, including a substantial category he refers to as "commercialized peasants" who did some weaving and selling of crafts in addition to farming. In 1900 only 5–10 percent of Momostecans worked in seasonal migrant plantation labor. As a result of increasing population and of the effects of the liberal agenda described above, about 25 percent of the population was engaged in plantation labor by the 1930s. Nevertheless, writing in the 1990s and citing Carol Smith (1978) Carmack argues that at least as late as the middle 1970s "Momostenango's commercialism is said to underwrite a persisting peasant condition as well as a strong capacity to maintain the institutions of Indian identity" (995:xviii).

5. During the colonial period both church-affiliated and private cults were organized to adore church and private images, respectively. A privately owned image with a private cult was referred to as wachibal (*guachibál* in colonial orthography, i.e., images or statues) as opposed to cofradías. See Hill 1992:93–95 for this pattern among the related Cakchiquel speakers). In Momostenango in the 1970s there were still privately owned images of the crucified Christ and various saints with local reputations for power, local visitation, and local fiestas. They were called wachibals. However, in 1976 the cofradía system, though it had begun contracting as some distant aldeas withdrew from the system set up by Teodoro Cifuentes, was still largely intact and the cofradía of Santiago was an official cofradía recognized by the church.

6. A shortened version of this video, accompanied by an English-language report authored by Cook and Offit that includes program notes, is available on the Foundation for the Advancement of Mesoamerican Studies (FAMSI) website under research reports for 2007, http://www.famsi.org/reports/07075/index.html.

7. Except that some cacique families, like the Herreras of Pueblo Viejo, and the Vicentes of San Vicente Buenabaj, seem to have rebuilt their decentralized power bloc through Catholic Action in the 1970s (see Fox and Cook 1996; Cook 2001a, 2001b, 2007).

8. A useful summary of the historical development of Maya spirituality and its link to cultural activism is provided in Molesky-Poz 2006:29–32.

9. During our work in Momostenango between 2005 and 2008 we found that Rhonda Taube, sometimes accompanied by her husband, Karl, as well as Maury

Hutcheson, Matt Krystal, and Marvin Cohodas were also involved in studying expressive culture at the fiesta, and we ran into several unaffiliated young international travelers who were studying the calendar or divination with teachers in Momostenango. Our main contact within the cultural activist faction has dozens of photos of international visitors for whom he has conducted ceremonies or served as a mentor over the past several years.

CHAPTER TWO

1. It is not clear how old the oldest clothing of the Patrón may be. In 1976 a retired diputado reported that some years earlier when he entered the cofradía, probably in the late 1950s, Santiago had only one set of clothes (Cook 2000:88–89), and as indicated in chapter 1, most of the current fiesta patronal, and so an unknown portion of the Santiago cult, derives from changes in the early twentieth century.

2. In his description of the altars, he has omitted the one on top of Paclom hill. *Pila* (well or tank), *uja'l* (his water), or *sacramento* (as in the baptismal font in church) are all terms used interchangeably for a burning place next to a small tank of water that collects from a seep at the western base of Paclom hill. The hilltop (ujuyubal) and stream or springside (uja'l) altar complex is a typical arrangement in traditional religious practice. The account also mentions the sacred mountains of the four directions and the altars located above Chiantla, where rock crystals used in divining bundles are found.

CHAPTER THREE

1. At the time of this writing our English-language ethnography of the dance, accompanied by a video, is on the FAMSI website under research reports for 2007, http://www.famsi.org/reports/07075/index.html.

2. As in the Sun Dance of the most famous Plains Indian medicine society, the central undertaking is the cutting and raising of an *axis mundi*. While the Crow would count coup on the fallen tree before raising it again as a lodge pole (Lowie 1959:198), the Momostecans run around the fallen tree in rank-order file, thrashing it with their whips. And the medicine bundles that figure prominently in North American societies are duplicated by the bundled costumes of the dancers, each surmounted with its sacred mask, being blessed in the smoke of the fires at the six mundos within Momostenango the day before the final two practice sessions lead into the festival itself.

3. The Deer Dance of highland Guatemala has been described in the literature. See, e.g., Paret-Limardo 1963; Mace 1970; Cook 2000:110–12; Hutcheson 2003:366–498. The Momostecan connection between a team of acrobatic and death-defying performers costumed as tigres, leónes, and monkeys and the Deer Dance is unique, though Monkeys Dance teams are still found in a few other places and the origins of this association have not become evident as a result of fieldwork to this point.

4. The giving of flowers is associated in Momostecan culture with the cofradías. Until recently, when a new cofrade was asked to serve a representative group of

the principales who had nominated him brought flowers to his house. He was told it was his duty to serve and that he could be relieved of that duty only if he brought the flowers to someone else who then accepted the duty in his place (see Cook 2000:40–43). While the flowers in this case are being presented by social subordinates to their superiors, they still may carry some of the meaning of a call to service, that is, that the town is hereby asked to fulfill its obligation in service to Patrón Santiago, who is represented in the transaction by his dance team.

5. Campbell's (1949) monomyth is his theoretical construct of an archetypal transformative journey undertaken as a quest by an initially reluctant hero, who departs to an unfamiliar place and encounters and overcomes obstacles and adversaries there, including an encounter with the goddess/female generative principal and atonement with the father. The quest leads to apotheosis for the hero and his return with new powers or with boons for the sending community. It is given expression repeatedly in world mythology and enacts in narrative form the general pattern of a rite of passage or initiation. Variations on this theme exist in the literature, including, for example, Propp's (1968) seminal and earlier morphology of the folk/fairy tale, which configures the encounter with the goddess as marriage and ends the account without the atonement function, or the more recent Leeming (1998) model, which reenvisions the hero's quest as an entire life rather than a transformative episode. Following Segal, it could be argued that the Proppian account is a hero tale for the first half of life, ending with "a job and a mate" (Segal 1990:43), while the Campbell/Leeming monomyth is more complete and focuses on the second half of life. Unlike Campbell, Leeming specifies that the hero must be a scapegoat who conquers death, but he nevertheless incorporates Campbell's monomyth in the recurring actions within the adult sequence (parts 3–8). Campbell's monomyth has been critiqued for its male bias (Weigle 1998) and for using a methodology of selecting illustrations rather than empirically testing the model (Dundes 1984). These critiques, however, are not relevant to its application here, since the dancers within the Maya tradition under analysis would perforce be male and since the claim of universality, whether sustainable or not, is not at issue in identifying and exploring a single application. The encounter with the goddess in Campbell's monomyth corresponds to the spirit bride (Eliade 1964), or the less sexist spirit spouse (Vitebsky 2001), associated with shamanic initiation, and the presence of this element in the Momostecan model for initiation demonstrates its roots in Maya shamanism.

6. A similar argument is made by Montejo (2005:235), who calls attention to the parallels between a pilgrimage and the journey to El Norte by Jacaltec migrants. A pilgrimage is an initiatory event, and as in other initiations it enacts the archetypal structure of the hero myth.

CHAPTER FOUR

I would like to thank a number of people who offered comments, critiques, and helpful advice in the writing of this paper. I am grateful to Garrett Cook and Tom Offit, Maury

Hutcheson, Dennis Tedlock, Cecelia Klein, Marvin Cohodas, Andrew Weeks, Robin Blotnick, Linda A. Brown, Kata Faust, Diana Rose, Alan Christenson, Edwin Román, Marcelo Zamora, Grant Kester, Roberto Tejada, Lesley Stern, Eric Van Young, Steve Fagin, Jessica Craig, Astrid Runggaldier, and Karl Taube.

1. Although brief, an astute mention of the disfraces appears in Matthew Hutcheson's (2003) doctoral dissertation; this is not the norm. After I presented an early version of my research, one anthropologist who works in the highlands stated very clearly that what I studied was decidedly not Maya and I may as well just study New Orleans Mardi Gras.

2. Ladino costume designer Pedro Roberto Rodas (pers. comm., August 8, 2006), described the convites as a "reflection" of indigenous Maya dance, one that borrows the basic format of expressive, public religious worship but also emphasizes a different social meaning.

3. Although, as Diane M. Nelson (1996:300) notes, as soon as most Maya in Guatemala achieve the same level of education, socioeconomic status, and health as Ladinos they are appropriated by the Ladino class. Robert Carmack (1995:264–68) discussed how mid-twentieth-century acculturated Maya who achieved a certain degree of upward mobility separated themselves in a new social class, "*gente civilizado.*"

4. Ladino citizens living in Momostenango and Chichicastenango also celebrate this same type of Ladino convite at Christmastime.

5. In addition, Zamora (2003:56) suggests that in San Miguel Totonicapán the community views the dancers as having attained an international status, as they have had the opportunity to travel to Mexico to dance in the Carnavál de Veracruz on three separate occasions.

6. Countries that contributed military observers: Argentina, Australia, Austria, Brazil, Canada, Ecuador, Germany, Norway, Russian Federation, Singapore, Spain, Sweden, Ukraine, United States, Uruguay, and Venezuela.

7. Although the mission has officially ended, I often saw MINUGUA vehicles in Guatemala as recently as August 2006.

8. The Arbenz government that was toppled by the civil war and U.S. involvement was in favor of agrarian reform, regulating foreign monopolies, raising wages for workers and peasants, and establishing organizations to support equality, justice, and equity.

9. Although Ladino communities attempt to connect themselves to the global community, in reality it is the elites that are the true transnationals, linked to world markets; the peace accord was a victory for the hegemony of their power (Jonas 2000:223).

10. From 1981 to 1983, 440 Maya villages were entirely wiped off the map, 150,000 civilians were "disappeared," and over 1 million persons were displaced through the deliberate destruction of large areas of the highlands (Jonas 2000:24). Rios Montt's aim was to eliminate the guerillas' support base within indigenous communities and destroy the Maya culture, identity, and communal structure.

11. My host, Eligio, did not participate in the last set or the removal of the masks. Although he is proud of participating, he was concerned that revealing his identity might infringe on his business (pers. comm., August 1, 2006).

12. On the surface, however, the Ladino community insists the years of prejudice are long gone. As Charles Hale (1999:302) notes, in adopting antiracist language the Ladinos shut off any true multicultural discourse.

13. According to the International Organization for Migration (IOM), Guatemala (2003b, 2004), it is difficult to determine the exact number of individuals who have migrated from Guatemala to the United States, as approximately one-third are undocumented. In addition, it is next to impossible to tease out ethnic affiliation for this group. At least 1 to 1.5 million Guatemalans, 10 percent of the population, now live in the United States. The IOM (2005) notes that the total dollar value of foreign remittances to Guatemala topped $3 billion for the first time in 2005, with 97.6 percent sent from the United States alone. This is a significant contribution to Guatemala's economy and is the second-largest source of foreign exchange after coffee exports (Jonas 2000:225).

14. For a contrasting opinion on the subject, see Diane M. Nelson's (1996) work on Maya "hackers" and the pan-Maya movement's use of the Internet as a means of networking.

CHAPTER FIVE

1. It seems likely that this culturally distinctive model for local community has also found expression and been revitalized in the rise of little Pentecostal churches (Cook 2001b; Cook and Offit 2008) and in some of the rural, aldea-based organization of Catholic Action (Cook 2001a, 2007).

2. Andrés Xiloj who was the síndico segundo—that is, the head of the auxiliary municipal government of aldea officials—in 1975 became the spiritual master of anthropologists Dennis and Barbara Tedlock, inducting them into Costumbre and providing a native exegesis of the *Popol Wuj* for Dennis's translation. Vicente De Leon, who followed don Andres as síndico was the source of a very important myth text on the origins of Costumbre (Cook 1981:654–77, 1986:143, 145; B. Tedlock 1986). The hermandad chapel was supported by the leaders of the Costumbrista community and was a very important element in Costumbrista efforts to retain local power and reproduce Momostecan tradition.

3. Research in the 1970s (B. Tedlock 1982:37; Cook 2000:39) documented that the expected "civil-religious hierarchy" (Tax 1952; Cancian 1967) with alternating service in the municipal government and the cofradías for the saints did not then exist in Momostenango, and perhaps never had. Rather, in Momostenango the principales were the retired alcaldes of aldeas and barrios and they oversaw and controlled the cofradías, but the alcaldes of the cofradías did not become principales, and it was very rare for an individual to serve in both hierarchies. As a result, the collapse of the cofradías was not really a threat to the traditional indigenous authority system.

4. Belejeb Batz is a day name associated with midwives in the K'iche' Maya divining calendar.

5. In the middle twentieth century the cofrades would take Santiago to visit private houses for festivals and could keep the money that was offered. The cofradía of Niño San Antonio owned and managed a flock of sheep and ran a concession stand when they brought the image to visit aldeas or private houses. By the 1970s the priest and the municipal authorities had assumed greater control of the images and the money-making ventures had been closed down. Then in the 1980s the priest instituted a policy of keeping all the alms collected and not providing subsidies to help cover the costs of the cofradía festival and offerings.

6. The most important ethnographic descriptions of the complex are in Mendelson 1958, 1959, 1965; Cook 2000; Carlsen 2001; Stanzione 2003; and Mackenzie 2005.

7. The nawal mesa holds midnight séances at a table in which the four yearbearers or other powerful spirits are called and, ordinarily in the darkness, are asked questions on behalf of the client. Early descriptions of these practices appear in the work of Benson Saler (1960, 1964). Momostecan informants report that there is a rushing sound like the flight of pigeons when the spirits arrive in the rafters and then one hears thumps as they drop down to land on the table. While there may be some influence of Kardecian spiritualism in the séance format, the nawal mesa calls on powerful spirits associated with sacred mountains rather than on the spirits of the dead.

CONCLUSION

1. Though we wish we were the first to publish on this division of culturally Maya religionists into these two camps, Mackenzie (1999, 2005) and Deuss (2007) were there ahead of us, as discussed in our first chapter. Also see the discussion in a review of Hart's book (Cook 2010).

References

ANNIS, SHELDON
1987 *God and Production in a Guatemalan Town.* Austin: University of Texas Press.

APPADURAI, ARJUN
1996 *Modernity at Large.* Minneapolis: University of Minnesota Press.
2001 Grassroots Globalization and the Research Imagination. In *Globalization,* ed. A. Appadurai, 1–21. Durham, NC: Duke University Press.

BARBERO, JESUS-MARTIN
1993 Latin American Cultures in the Communications Media. *Journal of Communication* 43(2):18–30.

BASTIAN, JEAN-PIERRE
2001 Pentecostalism, Market Logic and Religious Transnationalisation in Costa Rica. In *Between Babel and Pentecost: Transnational Pentecostalism in Africa and Latin America,* ed. Andre Corten and Ruth Marshall-Fratani, 163–80. Bloomington: Indiana University Press.

BAUDRILLARD, JEAN
2001 *Selected Writings.* 2nd ed. Ed. M. Poster. Stanford, CA: Stanford University Press.

BELLAH, ROBERT N.
1964 Religious Evolution. *American Sociological Review* 29:358–74.

BERGER, PETER L.
1967 *The Sacred Canopy: Elements of a Sociological Theory of Religion.* Garden City, NY: Doubleday.

BRICKER, VICTORIA

1973   *Ritual Humor in Highland Chiapas.* Austin: University of Texas Press.

1981   *The Indian Christ, the Indian King: The Historical Substrate of Maya Myth and Ritual.* Austin: University of Texas Press.

BRUNER, EDWARD M.

1999   Return to Sumatra. *American Ethnologist* 26(2): 461–77.

BUNZEL, RUTH

1952   *Chichicastenango: A Guatemalan Village.* Seattle: University of Washington Press.

BURREL, JENNIFER L.

2005   Migration and the Transnationalization of Fiesta Customs in Todos Santos Cuchumatan, Guatemala. *Latin American Perspectives* 32(5):12–32.

CAMPBELL, JOSEPH

1949 [1996]   *The Hero with a Thousand Faces.* New York: Bollingen Foundation; reprint, New York: MJF Books, facsimile edition, by arrangement with Princeton University Press.

CANCIAN, FRANK

1965   *Economics and Prestige in a Maya Community: The Religious Cargo System of Zinacantán.* Stanford, CA: Stanford University Press.

1967   Political and Religious Organizations. In *Handbook of Middle American Indians,* vol. 6, *Social Anthropology,* ed. Robert Wauchope and June Nash, 283–98. Austin: University of Texas Press.

CARLSEN, ROBERT S.

2001   Maximón. In *The Oxford Encyclopedia of Mesoamerican Cultures: The Civilizations of Mexico and Central America,* ed. Davíd Carrasco, 179–81. New York: Oxford University Press.

CARLSEN, ROBERT S., AND MARTIN PRECHTEL

1991   The Flowering of the Dead: An Interpretation of Highland Maya Culture. *Man,* n.s., 26:23–42.

CARMACK, ROBERT M.

1966   La perpetuación del clan patrilineal de Totonicapán. *Antropología e Historia de Guatemala* 18(2):43–60.

1973   *Quichean Civilization: The Ethnohistoric, Ethnographic, and Archaeological Sources.* Berkeley: University of California Press.

1979a   *Evolución del reino Quiché.* Guatemala: Editorial Piedra Santa.

1979b   *Historia social de los Quichés.* Guatemala: Seminario de Integración Social.

1992   *Harvest of Violence: The Maya Indians and the Guatemalan Crisis.* Norman: University of Oklahoma Press.

1995   *Rebels of Highland Guatemala.* Norman: University of Oklahoma Press.

CARRASCO, DAVÍD, LINDSAY JONES, AND SCOTT SESSIONS, EDS.

2000   *Mesoamerica's Classic Heritage: From Teotihuacan to the Aztecs.* Boulder: University Press of Colorado.

CARRASCO, PEDRO

1961   The Civil Religious Hierarchy in Meso-American Communities: Pre-Spanish Background and Colonial Development. *American Anthropologist* 63(4):483–97.

CHANCE, JOHN K., AND WILLIAM B. TAYLOR

1985   Cofradías and Cargos: An Historical Perspective on the Mesoamerican Civil-Religious Hierarchy. *American Ethnologist* 12:1–26.

CHIAPPARI, CHRISTOPHER L.

2002   Toward a Maya Theology of Liberation: The Reformulation of a "Traditional" Religion in the Global Context. *Journal for the Scientific Study of Religion* 41(1):47–67.

CHRISTENSON, ALLEN

2001   *Art and Society in a Highland Maya Community: The Altarpiece of Santiago Atitlan.* Austin: University of Texas Press.

COHEN, ABNER

1980   Drama and Politics in the Development of a London Carnival. *Man*, n.s., 15: 65–87.

1993   *Masquerade Politics: Exploration of the Structure of Urban Cultural Movements.* Berkeley: University of California Press.

COOK, GARRETT W.

1981   Supernaturalism, Cosmos and Cosmology in Quichean Expressive Culture. PhD diss., State University of New York at Albany.

1983   Mitos de Momostenango comparados con el *Popol Vuh*. In *Nuevas perspectivas sobre el "Popol Vuh,"* ed. Robert M. Carmack and Francisco Morales Santos, 135–54. Guatemala: Editorial Piedras Santos.

1986   Quichean Folk Theology and Southern Maya Supernaturalism. In *Symbol and Meaning beyond the Closed Community: Essays in Mesoamerican Ideas*, ed. Gary Gossen, 139–53. Albany: Institute for Mesoamerican Studies, State University of New York at Albany.

2000   *Renewing the Maya World: Expressive Culture in a Highland Town.* Austin: University of Texas Press.

2001a   Charter Myths in Santiago Momostenango, Guatemala. In *The Past and Present Maya: Essays in Honor of Robert M. Carmack*, ed. John M. Weeks, 107–24. Lancaster, CA: Labyrinthos.

2001b   The Maya Pentecost. In *Holy Saints and Fiery Preachers: The Anthropology of Protestantism in Mexico and Central America*, ed. James W. Dow and Alan R. Sandstrom, 147–68. Westport, CT: Praeger.

2007   Heterarchy and Homoarchy in Maya Village Politics. In *Hierarchy and Power in the History of Civilizations: Selected Papers, Third International Conference*, ed. Dmitri M. Bondarenko and Alexandre A. Nemirovskiy, 67–78. Moscow: Center for Civilizational and Regional Studies of the Russian Academy of Sciences.

2010   Mayan Spirituality and the Resurgence of Mayan Activism. *Latin American & Caribbean Ethnic Studies* 5(1): 93–95.

COOK, GARRETT, AND THOMAS OFFIT

2009   Renewing the Maya World in a Time of Change: Pluralism and Transculturation in Indigenous Maya Religion. *Ethnology* 47(1):45–59.

DAVENPORT, GUY

1997   *The Geography of the Imagination.* Boston: Nonpareil Books.

DEBERNARDI, JEAN

1999   Spiritual Warfare and Territorial Spirits: The Globalization and Localisation of a "Practical Theology." *Religious Studies and Theology* 18(2):66–96.

DE JANVRY, ALAIN

1981   *The Agrarian Question and Reformism in Latin America.* Baltimore: Johns Hopkins University Press.

DEUSS, KRYSTYNA

2007   *Shamans, Witches and Maya Priests: Native Religion and Ritual in Highland Guatemala.* London: Guatemalan Maya Centre.

DROOGERS, ANDRÉ

2001   Joana's Story: Syncretism at the Actor's Level. In *Reinventing Religions: Syncretism and Transformation in Africa and the Americas,* ed. S. Greenfield and A. F. Droogers, 145–61. Lanham, MD: Rowman and Littlefield.

DROOGERS, ANDRÉ, AND SIDNEY M. GREENFIELD

2001   Recovering and Reconstructing Syncretism. In *Reinventing Religions: Syncretism and Transformation in Africa and the Americas,* ed. S. Greenfield and A. F. Droogers, 21–42. Lanham, MD: Rowman and Littlefield.

DUNDES, ALAN

1984   *Sacred Narrative: Readings in the Theory of Myth.* Berkeley: University of California Press.

ELIADE, MIRCEA

1964   *Shamanism: Archaic Techniques of Ecstasy.* Princeton, NJ: Princeton University Press.

ERVIN, ALEXANDER M.

1980   A Review of the Acculturation Approach in Anthropology with Special Reference to Recent Change in Native Alaska. *Journal of Anthropological Research* 36(1):49–70.

ESPINOZA, SELVIN

2006   Baile de 60 año: Tradicion convite: Ángel Pérez Quiroa alegró el 25 de diciembre. *Prensa Libre* (Guatemala), December 27.

FALLA, RICARDO

1993   *Massacres in the Jungle: Ixcan, Guatemala, 1975–1982.* Boulder, CO: Westview Press.

FARRIS, NANCY

1984   *Maya Society Under Colonial Rule: The Collective Enterprise of Survival.* Princeton, NJ: Princeton University Press.

FISCHER, EDWARD F.

1993   The West in the Future: Cultural Hegemony and the Politics of Identity. *American Anthropologist* 94(4):1000–1002.

1999 Cultural Logic and Maya Identity: Rethinking Constructivism and Essentialism. *Current Anthropology* 40(4):473–99.

2001 *Cultural Logics and Global Economies: Maya Identity in Thought and Practice.* Austin: University of Texas Press.

FISCHER, EDWARD F., AND R. MCKENNA BROWN, EDS.

1996 *Maya Cultural Activism in Guatemala.* Austin: University of Texas Press.

FOSTER, GEORGE M.

1960 *Culture and Conquest: America's Spanish Heritage.* Viking Fund Publications in Anthropology, no. 27. New York: Wenner-Gren Foundation for Anthropological Research.

FOX, JOHN W., AND GARRETT W. COOK

1996 Constructing Maya Communities: Ethnography for Archaeology. *Current Anthropology* 37(5):811–21.

FREIDEL, DAVID, LINDA SCHELE, AND JOY PARKER

1993 *Maya Cosmos: Three Thousand Years on the Shaman's Path.* New York: William Morrow.

FROESE, PAUL

2008 *The Plot to Kill God: Findings from the Soviet Experiment in Secularization.* Berkeley: University of California Press.

GARCÍA CANCLINI, NÉSTOR

1995 *Hybrid Cultures: Strategies for Entering and Leaving Modernity.* Minneapolis: University of Minnesota Press.

GARRARD-BURNETT, VIRGINIA

1998 *Protestantism in Guatemala: Living in the New Jerusalem.* Austin: University of Texas Press.

GEERTZ, CLIFFORD

1961 Studies in Peasant Life: Community and Society. *Biennial Review of Anthropology* 2:1–41.

GOFFMAN, ERVING

1974 *Frame Analysis.* Cambridge, MA: Harvard University Press.

GOLDIN, LILIANA R.

2001 Maquila Age Maya: Changing Households and Communities of the Central Highlands of Guatemala. *Journal of Latin American Anthropology* 6(1):30–57.

2008 *Global Maya: Work and Ideology in Rural Guatemala.* Tucson: University of Arizona Press.

GOLDIN, LILIANA R., AND BRENT METZ

1991 An Expression of Cultural Change: Invisible Converts to Protestantism Among Highland Guatemala Mayas. *Ethnology* 30(4):325–39.

GOSSEN, GARY

1974 *Chamulas in the World of the Sun: Time and Space in a Maya Oral Tradition.* Cambridge, MA: Harvard University Press.

1986 (ed.) *Symbol and Meaning beyond the Closed Community: Essays in Mesoamerican Ideas.* Albany, NY: Institute for Mesoamerican Studies.

GRANDIN, GREG

2000 *The Blood of Guatemala: A History of Race and Nation.* Durham, NC: Duke University Press.

GREEN, LINDA

2003 Notes on Mayan Youth and Rural Industrialization in Guatemala. *Critique of Anthropology* 23(1):51–73.

GREENFIELD, SIDNEY

2001 The Reinterpretation of Africa: Convergence and Syncretism in Brazilian Candomblé. In *Reinventing Religions: Syncretism and Transformation in Africa and the Americas,* ed. S. Greenfield and A. F. Droogers, 113–29. Lanham, MD: Rowman and Littlefield.

GUSS, DAVID M.

2000 *The Festive State: Race, Ethnicity, and Cultural Performance.* Berkeley: University of California Press.

HALE, CHARLES R.

1996 Mestizaje, Hybridity, and the Cultural Politics of Difference in Post-revolutionary Central America. *Journal of Latin American Anthropology* 2:34–61.

1999 Travel Warning: Elite Appropriations of Hybridity, Mestizaje, Antiracism, Equality, and Other Progressive-Sounding Discourses in Highland Guatemala. *Journal of American Folklore* 112(445, Theorizing the Hybrid):197–315.

HALL, STUART

1997 The Local and the Global: Globalization and Ethnicity. In *Culture, Globalization and the World System: Contemporary Conditions for the Representation of Identity,* ed. A. King, 19–40. Minneapolis: University of Minnesota Press.

HART, THOMAS

2008 *The Ancient Spirituality of the Modern Maya.* Albuquerque: University of New Mexico Press.

HAWKINS, JOHN

1984 *Inverse Images: The Meaning of Culture, Ethnicity, and Family in Postcolonial Guatemala.* Albuquerque: University of New Mexico Press.

HILL, ROBERT M., II

1992 Colonial Cakchiqueles: Highland Maya Adaptations to Spanish Rule, 1600–1700. Orlando, FL: Harcourt Brace Jovanovich.

HILL, ROBERT M., II, AND JAMES MONAGHAN

1987 *Continuities in Highland Maya Social Organization: Ethnohistory in Sacapulas, Guatemala.* Philadelphia: University of Pennsylvania Press.

HOLLAND, WILLIAM R.

1964 Contemporary Tzotzil Cosmological Concepts as a Basis for Interpreting Prehistoric Maya Civilization. *American Antiquity* 29(3):301–6.

HOUK, JAMES

1996 Anthropological Theory and the Breakdown of Eclectic Folk Religions. *Journal for the Scientific Study of Religion* 35(4): 442–47.

HOWES, DAVID

1996   Introduction: Commodities and Cultural Borders. In *Cross-Cultural Consumption: Global Markets, Local Realities*, ed. D. Howes, 1–18. London: Routledge.

HUNT, EVA

1977   *Transformation of the Hummingbird: Cultural Roots of a Zinacantecan Mythical Poem*. Ithaca, NY: Cornell University Press.

HUTCHESON, MATTHEW F. M.

2003   Cultural Memory and the Dance-Dramas of Guatemala: History, Performance, and Identity Among the Achi Maya of Rabinal. PhD diss., Department of Anthropology, SUNY Buffalo.

HUXLEY, ALDOUS

1939   *Beyond the Mexique Bay*. London: Phoenix Library Press.

IOM (INTERNATIONAL ORGANIZATION FOR MIGRATION)

2005   *World Migration 2005: Costs and Benefits of International Migration*. IOM World Migration Report, vol. 3. Geneva: IOM.

IOM GUATEMALA

2003a   *Encuesta nacional sobre emigración internacional de Guatemaltecos*. Cuadernos de Trabajo sobre Migración, no. 15. May. Guatemala: Ministerio de Relaciones Exteriores, IOM.

2003b   *Encuesta nacional sobre remesas familiares*. Cuadernos de Trabajo sobre Migración, no. 17. August. Guatemala: Ministerio de Relaciones Exteriores, IOM.

2004   *Encuesta nacional sobre el impacto de remesas familiares en los hogares Guatemaltecos*. Cuadernos de Trabajo sobre Migración, no. 19. September. Guatemala: Ministerio de Relaciones Exteriores, IOM.

JANSSENS, BERT, AND RUUD VAN AKKEREN

2003   *Xajooj Keej: El baile del venado de Rabinal*. Rabinal, Guatemala: Museo Communitario Rabinal Achi.

JONAS, SUSANNE

2000   *Of Centaurs and Doves: Guatemala's Peace Process*. Boulder, CO: Westview Press.

KEARNEY, MICHAEL

1996   *Reconceptualizing the Peasantry*. Boulder, CO: Westview Press.

KITIARSA, PATTANA

2005   Beyond Syncretism: Hybridization of Popular Religion in Contemporary Thailand. *Journal of Southeast Asian Studies* 36(3):461–87.

KOTTAK, CONRAD PHILLIP

1987   *Anthropology: The Exploration of Human Diversity*. 4th ed. New York: Random House.

KRAIDY, MARWAN M.

2005   *Hybridity, or the Cultural Logic of Globalization*. Philadelphia: Temple University Press.

KRYSTAL, MATTHEW B.

2001   Resistance of Meaning: Masking in the "Dance of the Conquest" of Guatemala. PhD diss., Department of Anthropology, Tulane University.

LA BARRE, WESTON

1970   *The Ghost Dance: The Origins of Religion*. New York: Dell.

LA FARGE, OLIVER

1940   Maya Ethnology: The Sequence of Cultures. In *The Maya and Their Neighbors*, ed. C. L. Hay et al., 281–91. New York: D. Appleton-Century.

1947   *Santa Eulalia: The Religion of a Cuchumatan Indian Town*. Chicago: University of Chicago Press.

1962   Maya Ethnology: The Sequence of Cultures. In *The Maya and Their Neighbors*, ed. Alfred M. Tozzer, 281–91. New York: D. Appleton-Century.

LAFARGE, OLIVER, AND DOUGLAS BYERS

1931   *The Year Bearer's People*. Middle American Research Institute publication, no. 3. New Orleans: MARI, Tulane University.

LEEMING, DAVID ADAMS

1998   *Mythology: The Voyage of the Hero*. 3rd ed. New York: Oxford University Press.

LEVITT, PEGGY

2001   *The Transnational Villagers*. Berkeley: University of California Press.

LITTLE, WALTER E.

2005   Introduction: Globalization and Guatemala's Maya Workers. *Latin American Perspectives*, 32(5):3–11.

LITTLE-SIEBOLD, CHRISTA

2001   Beyond the Indian-Ladino Dichotomy: Contested Identities in an Eastern Guatemalan Town. *Journal of Latin American Anthropology* 6(2):176–97.

LOWIE, ROBERT

1959   *Indians of the Plains*. New York: McGraw Hill.

MACE, CARROL

1970   *Two Spanish-Quiché Dance Dramas of Rabinal*. New Orleans: Tulane University Press.

MACKENZIE, C. JAMES

1999   The Priest, the Shaman, and Grandfather Judas: Syncretism and Anti-syncretism in Guatemala. *Religious Studies and Theology* 18(2):33–65.

2005   Maya Bodies and Minds: Religion and Modernity in a K'iche' Town. PhD diss., Department of Anthropology, SUNY Albany.

MACLEOD, MURDO J.

1973   *Spanish Central America: A Socioeconomic History, 1520–1720*. Berkeley: University of California Press.

MALINOWSKI, BRONISLAW

1944   *A Scientific Theory of Culture and Other Essays*. Chapel Hill: University of North Carolina Press.

MARCUS, GEORGE E.

1995   Ethnography in/of the World System: The Emergence of Multi-sited Ethnography. *Annual Review of Anthropology* 24:95–117.

MCANANY, PATRICIA A.

1995   *Living with the Ancestors: Kinship and Kingship in Ancient Maya Society.* Austin: University of Texas Press.

MCARTHUR , HARRY S.

1972   Los bailes de Aguacatan y el culto de los muertos. *America Indígena* 32(2):491–513.

MCCRACKEN, GRANT

1988   *Culture and Consumption: New Approaches to the Symbolic Character of Consumer Goods and Activities.* Bloomington: Indiana University Press.

MENCHÚ, RIGOBERTA

1983   *I, Rigoberta Menchú: An Indian Woman in Guatemala.* London: Verso.

MENDELSON, E. MICHAEL

1958   The King, the Traitor, and the Cross. *Diogenes* 21:1–10.

1959   Maximón, an Iconographical Introduction. *Man* 59(87):57–60.

1965   *Los escándalos de Maximón.* Guatemala: Seminario de Integración Social Guatemalteca, Ministerio de Educación.

1967   Ritual and Mythology. In *Handbook of Middle American Indians*, ed. Robert Wauchope, 6:392–415. Austin: University of Texas Press.

MINTZ, SIDNEY

1956   The Role of Middlemen in the Internal Distribution System of the Caribbean Peasant Economy. *Human Organization* 15(2):13–18.

MOLESKY-POZ, JEAN

2006   *Contemporary Maya Spirituality: The Ancient Ways Are Not Lost.* Austin: University of Texas Press.

MONTEJO, VICTOR D.

1987   *Testimony: Death of a Guatemalan Village.* Willimantic, CT: Curbstone Press.

2005   *Maya Intellectual Renaissance: Identity, Representation and Leadership.* Austin: University of Texas Press.

MOTTA, ROBERTO

2001   Ethnicity, Purity, the Market, and Syncretism in Afro Brazilian Cults. In *Reinventing Religions: Syncretism and Transformation in Africa and the Americas*, ed. S. Greenfield and A. F. Droogers, 71–86. Lanham, MD: Rowman and Littlefield.

NASH, JUNE

1967   Death as a Way of Life: The Increasing Resort to Homicide in a Maya Indian Community. *American Anthropologist* 69(5): 455–70.

NAVARRETE PELLICER, SERGIO

2005   *Maya Achi Marimba Music in Guatemala.* Philadelphia: Temple University Press.

NELSON, DIANE M.

1996   Maya Hackers and the Cyberspatialized Nation-State: Modernity, Ethnostalgia, and a Lizard Queen in Guatemala. *Cultural Anthropology* 11(3):287–308.

1999   *A Finger in the Wound: Body Politics in Quincentennial Guatemala.* Berkeley: University of California Press.

OAKES, MAUD

1951 *Two Crosses of Todos Santos: Survivals of Maya Religious Ritual.* Bollingen series, no. 27. Princeton, NJ: Princeton University Press.

OFFIT, THOMAS

2008 *Conquistadores de la Calle: Child Street Labor in Guatemala City.* Austin: University of Texas Press.

2011 *Cacique* for a Neoliberal Age: Neoliberalism, Entrepreneurship, and the Highland Maya in Guatemala City. In *Securing the City: Neoliberalism, Space, and Insecurity in Postwar Guatemala,* ed. Kevin L. O'Neill and Kedron Thomas, 66–83. Durham, NC: Duke University Press.

OFFIT, THOMAS, AND GARRETT COOK

2010 The Death of Don Pedro: Insecurity and Cultural Continuity in Peacetime Guatemala. *Journal of Latin American and Caribbean Anthropology* 15(1):42–66.

ORTNER, SHERRY B.

1997 Fieldwork in the Postcommunity. *Anthropology and Humanism* 22(1):61–80.

PARET-LIMARDO, LISE

1963 *La danza del venado en Guatemala.* Guatemala: Centro Editorial Jose de Pinada Ibarra, Ministerio de Educación Pública.

PEDRO GONZALEZ, GASPAR

1995 *A Mayan Life.* Trans. Elaine Elliot. Rancho Palos Verdes, CA: Yax Te' Press.

PROPP, VLADIMIR

1968[1928] *Morphology of the Folktale.* Trans. Laurence Scott. Austin: University of Texas Press.

RADIN, PAUL

1926 *Crashing Thunder: The Autobiography of an American Indian.* New York: D. Appleton.

REDFIELD, ROBERT

1955 *The Little Community: Viewpoints for the Study of a Human Whole.* Chicago: University of Chicago Press.

1956 *Peasant Society and Culture: An Anthropological Approach to Civilization.* Chicago: University of Chicago Press.

REDFIELD, ROBERT; RALPH LINTON, AND MELVILLE J. HERSKOVITS

1936 Memorandum for the Study of Acculturation. *American Anthropologist,* n.s., 38(1): 149–52.

REED, NELSON A.

2001 *The Caste War of Yucatán.* Stanford, CA: Stanford University Press.

REINA, REUBEN E.

1966 *The Law of the Saints: A Pokomam Pueblo and Its Community Culture.* New York: Bobbs-Merrill.

ROBYNS, CLEM

1994 Translation and Discursive Identity. *Poetics Today* 15(3):405–28.

ROJAS LIMA, FLAVIO

1988 *La cofradía: Reducto cultural indígena.* Guatemala: Litografía Moderna.

ROMBERG, RAQUEL

1998   Whose Spirits Are They? The Political Economy of Syncretism and Authenticity. *Journal of Folklore Research* 35(1): 69–82.

SALER, BENSON

1960   The Road from El Palmar: Change, Continuity, and Conservatism in a Quiché Community. PhD diss., Department of Anthropology, University of Pennsylvania.

1964   Nagual, Witch and Sorcerer in a Quiché village. *Ethnology* 3: 305–28.

SCHÜREN, UTE

2003   Reconceptualizing the Post-peasantry: Household Strategies in Mexican Ejidos. *Revista Europea de Estudios Latinoamericanos y del Caribe* 75:47–63.

SEGAL, ROBERT A.

1990   *Joseph Campbell: An Introduction.* New York: Meridian.

SHARON, DOUGLAS

1974   *Wizard of the Four Winds: A Shaman's Story.* New York: Free Press.

SHERMAN, AMY

1997   *The Soul of Development: Biblical Christianity and Economic Transformation in Guatemala.* Oxford: Oxford University Press.

SIEGEL, MORRIS

1941   Religions in Western Guatemala: A Product of Acculturation. *American Anthropologist* 43:63–76.

SMITH, CAROL

1978   Beyond Dependency Theory: National and Regional Patterns of Underdevelopment in Guatemala. *American Ethnologist* 5:574–615.

1995   Race-Class-Gender Ideology in Guatemala: Modern and Anti-modern Forms. *Comparative Studies in Society and History* 37(4):723–49.

SMITH, TIMOTHY, AND THOMAS OFFIT

2010   Confronting Violence in Postwar Guatemala: An Introduction. *Journal of Latin American and Caribbean Anthropology* 15(1):1–16.

SMITH, WALDEMAR

1977   *The Fiesta System and Economic Change.* New York: Columbia University Press.

STANZIONE, VINCENT

2003   *Rituals of Sacrifice: Walking the Face of the Earth on the Sacred Path of the Sun: A Journey Through the Tz'utujil Maya World of Santiago Atitlán.* Albuquerque: University of New Mexico Press.

STEWART, CHARLES

1995   Relocating Syncretism in Social Science Discourse. In *Syncretism and the Commerce of Symbols*, ed. Göran Aijmer, 13–37. Göteborg, Sweden: Institute for Advanced Studies in Social Anthropology.

STEWART, CHARLES, AND ROSALIND SHAW, EDS.

1994   *Syncretism/Anti-syncretism: The Politics of Religious Synthesis.* New York: Routledge.

STOLL, DAVID

1990   *Is Latin America Turning Protestant?* Berkeley: University of California Press.

1993 *Between Two Armies in the Ixil Towns of Guatemala.* New York: Columbia University Press.

SWATOS, WILLIAM H., AND DANIEL V. A. OLSON

2000 *The Secularization Debate.* Lanham, MD: Rowman and Littlefield.

TAUBE, KARL A.

1989 Ritual Humor in Classic Maya Religion. In *Word and Image in Maya Culture,* ed. W. A. Hanks and D. S. Rice, 351–82. Salt Lake City: University of Utah Press.

TAUBE, RHONDA

2006 Foreign Characters: Visualizing Identity in the 21st-Century Guatemalan Highlands. Unpublished manuscript version of a paper given at the Annual Meeting of the American Anthropological Association, San Jose, November.

TAX, SOL

1937 The Municipios of the Midwestern Highlands of Guatemala. *American Anthropologist* 39:423–44.

1952 *Heritage of Conquest: The Ethnology of Middle America.* Glencoe, IL: Free Press.

TEDLOCK, BARBARA

1982 *Time and the Highland Maya.* Albuquerque: University of New Mexico Press.

1986 On a Mountain in the Dark: Encounters with the K'iche' Maya Culture Hero. In *Symbol and Meaning Beyond the Closed Community: Essays in Mesoamerican Ideas,* ed. Gary Gossen, 125–38. Albany: Institute for Mesoamerican Studies, State University of New York at Albany.

2002 Review of *Art and Society in a Highland Maya Community: The Altarpiece of Santiago Atitlan,* by Allen J. Christenson. *Journal of Anthropological Research* 58(4):606–7.

TEDLOCK, DENNIS

1993 *Breath on the Mirror: Mythic Voices and Visions of the Living Maya.* San Francisco: Harper.

2003 *Rabinal Achi: A Mayan Drama of War and Sacrifice.* Oxford: Oxford University Press.

THOMAS, NICHOLAS

1991 *Entangled Objects: Exchange, Material Culture, and Colonialism in the Pacific.* Cambridge, MA: Harvard University Press.

TOFFLER, ALVIN.

1970 *Future Shock.* New York: Random House.

TURNER, VICTOR

1977 Symbols in African Ritual. In *Symbolic Anthropology,* ed. Janet L. Dolgin, David S. Kemnitzer and David M. Schneider, 183–94. New York: Columbia University Press.

VITEBSKY, PIERS

2001 *Shamanism.* Norman: University of Oklahoma Press.

VOGT, EVON Z.

1964 Genetic Model and Maya Cultural Development. In *Desarollo cultural se los Mayas,* ed. Evon Vogt and Alberto Ruiz L., 9–48. Mexico City: Universidad Nacional Autónoma de México.

1969   *Zinacantán.* Cambridge, MA: Harvard University Press.

WALLACE, ANTHONY F. C.

1956   Revitalization Movements. *American Anthropologist* 55(3):264–81.

1966   *Religion: An Anthropological View.* New York: Random House.

1969   *The Death and Rebirth of the Seneca.* With the assistance of Sheila C. Stern. New York: Vintage Books.

WALLERSTEIN, IMMANUEL M.

1979   *The Capitalist World-Economy.* London: Cambridge University Press.

WARREN, KAY B.

1998   *Indigenous Movements and Their Critics: Pan-Maya Activism in Guatemala.* Princeton, NJ: Princeton University Press.

WATANABE, JOHN M.

1990   From Saints to Shibboleths: Image, Structure, and Identity in Maya Religious Syncretism. *American Ethnologist* 17(1):129–48.

1992   *Maya Saints and Souls in a Changing World.* Austin: University of Texas Press.

1995   Unimagining the Maya: Anthropologists, Others, and the Inescapable Hubris of Authorship. *Bulletin of Latin American Research* 14(1):25–45.

WATANABE, JOHN M., AND EDWARD F. FISCHER, EDS.

2004   *Pluralizing Ethnography: Comparison and Representation in Maya Cultures, Histories, and Identities.* School of American Research Advanced Seminar Series. Santa Fe, NM: School of American Research Press, 2004.

WEBER, MAX

1963   *The Sociology of Religion.* Trans. Ephraim Fischoff. Boston: Beacon Press.

WEIGLE, MARTA

1998   Women's Expressive Forms. In *Teaching Oral Traditions*, ed. John Miles Foley, 298–307. New York: Modern Language Association.

WILK, RICHARD R.

1991   *Household Ecology: Economic Change and Domestic Life Among the Kekchi Maya in Belize.* Tucson: University of Arizona Press.

WILSON, RICHARD

1995   *Maya Resurgence in Guatemala: Q'eqchi Experiences.* Norman: University of Oklahoma Press.

WOLF, ERIC R.

1955   Types of Latin American Peasantry: A Preliminary Discussion. *American Anthropologist* 57:452–71.

1957   Closed Corporate Peasant Communities in Mesoamerica and Central Java. *Southwestern Journal of Anthropology* 13(1):1–18.

1959   *Sons of the Shaking Earth* Chicago: University of Chicago Press, 1959.

1966   *Peasants.* Englewood Cliffs, NJ: Prentice-Hall.

WOLF, ERIC, AND SIDNEY MINTZ

1957   Haciendas and Plantations in Middle America and the Antilles. *Social and Economic Studies* 6:386–412.

YUDICE, GEORGE

1992 Postmodernity and Transnational Capitalism in Latin America. In *On Edge: The Crisis of Contemporary Latin American Culture*, ed. George Yudice, Jean Franco, and Juan Flores, 1–28. Minneapolis: University of Minnesota Press.

ZAMORA MEJÍA, FABIÁN MARCELO

2003 *Ser "moderno" en San Miguel Totonicapán: El baile del convite y la globalización cultural.* Guatemala City: Editorial de Ciencias Sociales, FLACSO.

ZÁRATE, FLAVIO PÉREZ

2006 A manera de opinion sobre el convite del 8 y 12 de Diciembre. *Qab' Antajik, Nuestra Identidad* 4(9):4–5.

ZEHNER, EDWIN

2005 Orthodox Hybridities: Anti-syncretism and Localization in the Evangelical Christianity of Thailand. *Anthropological Quarterly* 78(3): 585–617.

Index

Note: Photographs found throughout the text are indicated by *f* following the page number.

pan-Maya movement, xxviii, xxxv–xxxvi, 173n13

parcialidades, 2

Pa'Sabal altar, 109f, 109

Pa Sanyep' altar, 62; circle run, 67f, 67–68; offerings, 65f

Pascual Abaj, 145

patron saint cult: blending of cotraditions, 161; changes and viability, xv; instituted by Cifuentes, 11; protector functions, 8; as reconstituted Maya tradition, xviii, 153; shift to, 168n2

Patzun, xxxiii, xxxiv, xxxvii, 54

Pa Xetun altar, 62

Pa Xoral Mundo, 46, 47

peace process, 104, 116, 172n9

peasant communities: folk religions in, xxii; intermediate forms, xxiii; postmodern analysis, xxii–xxiv; scholarly understanding of, xxi–xxii; vis-à-vis indigenous communities, xxvi

peasants: classic type, xxii; commercialized, 169n4; land shortage impact, 13; as "other" for the West, 166n5

Pedro, don, murder of, 120

Pentecostalism, xvii, 53, 173n1

Pérez Quira, Ángel, 102

Pérez Rivera, Miguel, 102

Pérez Zárate, Flavio, 115–16

performance, nature of, xxvii

perpetuation under transformation, xxxi

Peru, xxxiii

Pipil Abaj, 145

Pipil altar, 91

plantation agriculture, xxii, 9, 169n4

Pollo Campero, 18

Pologua, 30

polybian, 166n7

Popol Wuj, xiii, xvii

popular culture, 117

population, xvi; growth, 9; pressure, xxiii

porobal, 34, 35

postcolonial constructivism, 167n10

postcolonialist critiques of culture, xxviii

postcommunitarians, xix; religious institutions, xxi–xxvii

postcommunities, xxv; four kinds, xxvi

postmodernism, xxviii

post-peasants: coining term, xxii; context for Monkeys Dance, 95; in "disarticulated" economy, xxiii; global, xxiii; Momostenango shift, xxxvii–xxxix; as multifaceted persona, 25; nostalgic and idealized villages, xxvi; as polybian, 166n7; postmodern analysis, xxii–xxiv; religious institutions, xxi–xxvii; terms used, xxiii; version of Costumbre, 163

power relations, identity construction and, 100

practice pole: author participation, 55, 57; consecration, 70; crisis resolution with, 125–30; erecting, 60; fork at top, 71–72

Predator character, 96, 97f, 111

primeros, 14–15, 160, 162

primordialist perspective, 166n10

principales, 9, 10, 51, 153, 173n3

privatization of land, 9

processions: adaptations in transporting images, 157–58; arrival at hermandad, 42f, 42; changes overview, 22; children in, 50–51; described, 30, 105–8; festival processions described, 16–17; important changes, 50–51; music and dance in, 39; readying image for, 41; saints described, 105; starting off, 41f, 41–42; women's role, 51

Propp, V., 171n5

Protestantism: among acculturated indigenous families, 140; among indigenous bourgeoisie, 12; conversion impact, 21; growth of, xxviii, 24; increasing pluralism, 49

protoculture, Maya, 165–66n4

pseudonym use, xxxix

Pueblo Viejo, 7, 10, 17, 31, 35, 36; costumbre at, 46, 47; main altar for Santiago, 47, 48

Puerto Joyam altar, 62, 65, 66

Puja'l Santiago, or Sacramento, 48, 60

Quetzaltenango, 150

radical constructivism, xxvi–xxvii, xxxiv, 154

Radin, P., xxxi

rain and/or wind ceremonies, 6, 28

reality defining agencies, xxxii